THE SHANKILL BUTCHERS

Martin Dillon is a native of Belfast although educated in England. He lived in France for a time and
returned to Northern Ireland to work as a journalist
with the *Irish News* before joining the *Belfast Telegraph*. He has also worked as a freelance journalist
for several national newspapers and American per-
iodicals. In 1973 he wrote *Political Murder in Northern Ireland* (with Denis Lehane) which is regarded
as the definitive study of political assassination in
Northern Ireland. His second book, *Rogue Warrior
of the SAS* (with Roy Bradford), is a biography of
the Second World War hero, Lt. Col. Robert Blair
Mayne, and is published by Arrow.

Martin Dillon has written plays for BBC radio
and television and has been Editor in Northern
Ireland of many of the BBC's programmes in the
area of current affairs. *The Shankill Butchers* is the
first in a trilogy of books about Northern and Sou-
thern Ireland.

Also in Arrow by Martin Dillon

Rogue Warrior of the SAS (with Roy Bradford)

THE
SHANKILL BUTCHERS

A Case Study of Mass Murder

Martin Dillon

ARROW BOOKS

Arrow Books Limited
20 Vauxhall Bridge Road, London SW1V 2SA

An imprint of Random Century Group

London Melbourne Sydney Auckland Johannesburg
and agencies throughout the world

First published in Great Britain by Hutchinson 1989

Arrow edition 1990

© Martin Dillon 1989

Printed and Bound in Great Britain by
Courier International Ltd, Tiptree Essex

Phototypeset by Input Typesetting Ltd, London

ISBN 0 09 973810 4

To all victims of violence
in Northern Ireland

Contents

Murder is negative creation.
Every murderer is the rebel
who claims the right to be omnipotent.
His pathos is his refusal to suffer.

W. H. Auden, 'The Dyer's Hand'

List of Illustrations

Acknowledgements

Many people provided help and assistance to me while I was writing this book. Foremost among them was Stephen Dillon who helped with some aspects of the research and possessed a genuine appreciation of the story. Bill McGookin of the Royal Ulster Constabulary Press Office made it possible for me from the outset to gain access to police files and to those men in the Force who were frontline detectives and relevant to the story. I must pay tribute to all the policemen who spoke with me. They all demonstrated integrity. The person within the RUC to whom I owe the greatest debt is Superintendent Jimmy Nesbitt who was unceasing in his efforts to unearth material I required, who constantly sought out detectives who were central to the story and who at all times was honest and frank with me. There were also detectives such as Jim Fitzsimmons, Cecil Chambers, John Scott and Roy Turner who provided me with invaluable insights.

One man who encouraged my writing of this book was Jim Campbell, northern editor of the *Sunday World* newspaper who survived an attempt on his life while he was trying to expose this story in the early eighties.

Others who deserve to be mentioned are: Chris Ryder of the *Daily Telegraph*, David McKittrick of the *Independent*, Jim Cusack of the *Irish Times*, David Ross, a senior producer at the BBC, and freelance journalist, Ivan McMichael.

I also owe much to my wife, Kathy, who lived with the evidence of the horror of this story.

The former Nationalist politician, Paddy Devlin, who is

now a writer and broadcaster, provided me with interesting perspectives of the Northern Ireland conflict as did the writer and broadcaster, Andrew Body, who encouraged me to examine the important writing of Father McGriel SJ.

Unfortunately there are those whom I would not name because in doing so I would place their lives in jeopardy. They are members of the legal profession, policemen who work undercover and former members of paramilitary associations. To all those I owe a debt of gratitude for their trust and the revealing manner in which they responded to my questions.

Pacemaker Press in Belfast assisted with my photographic requirements and the *Belfast Telegraph* kindly provided relevant photographs from its archives.

Finally, I must thank the criminologist, John Bach, for assisting me in an understanding of the criminal law in Northern Ireland and the BBC librarian, Adele Gilding, for seeking out historical works relevant to my study.

Foreword

The particular atrocities which are horrifyingly documented by Martin Dillon in this book were legitimized in the name of 'God and Ulster'. Other atrocities are legitimized in the name of 'God and Ireland' (or simply 'Ireland', with 'God' vaguely present). Both kinds of atrocities continue in 1989 in a sinister pattern of sectarian and political 'tit for tat'.

That is the general picture, but it needs more qualification. The Shankill Butchers remain unique in the sadistic ferocity of their *modus operandi*. The Provisional IRA – by far the most important of the various murderous organizations of Northern Ireland – never unleashed on society anyone quite like Lennie Murphy, the chief of the Shankill Butchers.

At the time of these ghastly random murders of innocent Catholics by Protestant sadists, Catholics found a crumb of comfort in the thought of their own moral superiority. 'Our own' murderers might murder more people in the course of time, but at least they didn't do such horrible things to them before they died, and while they were dying. Catholics were confirmed in their traditional belief that Protestants have a dose of Original Sin.

I don't find the theological explanation convincing, but I remain puzzled both by the phenomenon of the Butchers, and the absence of an exact parallel among the Catholic murderers. Lack of centralized authority on the Protestant side and the relatively tight hierarchical structure of the Irish Republican Army may partly account for the difference. The rest of the difference may be accounted for by the fact that the IRA is much more interested in its public 'image' than the Protestant paramilitaries have been in theirs. The IRA has had its quota of psychopaths, but it has been on its guard against them, most of the time, if only because of the 'image' problem; and it has been better able to control them, because of its tighter discipline. In any case, anyone who may imagine that there is no 'Butchers' *potential* on the Catholic side should reflect on the stripping and lynching of those British soldiers by those Republican mourners at that IRA funeral last year.

Martin Dillon speaks of 'the subculture of a paramilitary world', and his book gives startling insight into that subculture. Lennie Murphy belonged to a Protestant family which had the misfortune of having a 'Catholic' surname. The family suffered a good deal of ostracism on that score, as Martin Dillon shows, and this family situation may have been among the factors which turned him into a hunter and killer of Catholics. I suspect, however, that Lennie was primarily a sadist and only secondarily a hater of Catholics. He longed to hurt and kill *people* and, according to the values of his particular subculture, Catholics were the people who might legitimately be treated in this way.

Contemplating such horrors, we are apt to say that a person like Lennie Murphy has to be 'mad'. Maybe. But he was certainly crafty. He cut people's throats for the pleasure of doing so, but he was also capable of calculation on the subject of throat-cutting. As Martin Dillon tells it, Lennie Murphy – within a week of his confinement in the Maze Prison (not for murder but for a firearms offence) – received a visit from his accomplice 'Mr A.' (who is still at large). Murphy told 'Mr A.' that the cut-throat murders were to continue in order to throw the police off his track and allay any suspicions they might have about his associates.

These calculations proved to be correct. In accordance with Murphy's instructions, the cut-throat murders continued while he was in jail. (Those who hold that it is necessarily a humane policy to allow persons convicted of terrorist-associated crimes to have their quota of visitors should reflect a little on the bloody consequences of 'Mr A.'s' visit. The murders continued, the authorities were duly fooled, Murphy was set free and went on to cut more throats.

Murphy's *modus operandi* was such as to convince even 'normal' murderers, on both sides of the political-sectarian divide, that he had to be eliminated. In the end, he seems to have been set up by Protestant paramilitaries, in order to be murdered by the Provisional IRA. So in a way he died a curiously ecumenical death; nothing in his life became him like the leaving it.

There were those who mourned the Butcher, as Martin Dillon records. Eighty-seven death notices in the *Belfast Telegraph* (a very respectable newspaper, as also is the Belfast Catholic *Irish News*, which used to carry death notices of IRA volunteers 'killed on active service'. Business is business). Messages from old friends in the Maze Prison, men with names like 'Basher', and 'Hacksaw'. And there was Lennie's Aunt Agnes who wrote . . . 'To us you were very special and God must have thought so too.'

I suppose He must. It is a chilling thought. And Martin Dillon has written a chilling book. Chilling, but fascinating. Martin Dillon knows Northern Ireland extremely well, and knows both sides of it, without lending himself to the propaganda of either. The *Shankill Butchers* is the first book of a trilogy, covering both sides of that divide. When the trilogy is completed and published, we shall know a lot more about Northern Ireland than we do now. And not only those of us who are outsiders; Northern Ireland itself will know more. At present, Northern Ireland hardly knows more about itself than the outside world does, since both sides of the divided population feed themselves on their own inherited myths about the other side. But people on both sides – some of them – are likely to read Martin Dillon, and to learn from him.

DR CONOR CRUISE O'BRIEN
May 1989

Introduction

When I began to write this book I was determined not to apportion blame to either of the two communities in the Northern Ireland conflict, because both Catholics and Protestants must share equally the guilt for what has happened over the past twenty years. This was exceedingly difficult to achieve and I leave it to the reader to decide if I remain true to my intention. The central story in this book deals with a group of men who became known infamously as the 'Shankill Butchers', not simply for their crimes but because they were based in a Protestant district of West Belfast known as the Shankill. The book is also about those people who have been lost to memory: the victims. The story of how innocent people met their deaths will, I hope, illustrate the futility of violence.

The long war in Northern Ireland is littered with tragedy but the 'Butcher' murders remain fixed in my mind long after they happened. This is firstly because of the macabre way in which young and old were tortured and killed, secondly because of the ability of the killers to evade capture for so long, and thirdly because of my interest in the factors which created the potential for mass murder. I felt that definitions were required to explain the central theme of the conflict but I detected other factors within the 'Butcher' murders which bore similarities to American serial murders. Much has been written about the manner in which terrorists operate but little has centred on the elements within the psychological make-up of the terrorists which, when placed against the prejudice in the society, coalesce to produce mass murderers. It was never my intention to produce a political thesis or to imply support for any of the protagonists. Northern Ireland has its share of heroes and villains and often they are inseparable. If I sought to evidence anything from my research, it was to show that the prejudice which is endemic in Northern Ireland inevitably leads to extermination. At the outset I talked to people who had studied similar cases of mass murder, whether it was the serial murder phenomenon in the United States, or the killings by the Yorkshire Ripper and the Moors Murderers. Most of those I spoke to had never heard of the Shankill Butchers, even though they killed more people than any other mass murderers in British criminal history. The realization of that lack of knowledge persuaded me that this book should be written. I was not to know at the time of the difficulties I would face, nor that I would uncover thirteen other murders for which the leader of the Butcher gang was never charged, or that at least seventeen people who were implicated in some of the killings were never brought before the courts. I discovered that investigating this kind of dimension to the Northern Ireland conflict has its risks, and further, I found myself faced with myths which were difficult to dispel without thorough investigation. The Royal Ulster Constabulary was unstinting in its efforts to provide me with all its files and notes connected with the case.

The Head of the RUC Press Office was generous with his time and help, and the officer who tracked the Butchers, Superintendent Jimmy Nesbitt, provided me with hours of analysis and access to the members of his team, who studied and eventually trapped most of the Shankill Butchers.

It was by working closely with the police, studying their methods, their successes, their failings and failures, that I also discovered the immense problems they faced while dealing with this case. There were detractors of the police when the Butcher killings were happening and even after they ceased. The role of the police was denigrated for political reasons and through ignorance. A squad of eleven detectives hunted the Butchers, whereas in the Yorkshire Ripper enquiry there were 304, and yet the trial of the Butchers was the biggest in British criminal history, with forty-two life sentences handed down at one sitting. How many more would have been handed down had all those responsible for the crimes committed been brought to justice, and not just those who committed the nineteen murders dealt with by the Northern Ireland judiciary? This book deals with the reasons why it took so long to bring the Butchers to justice, why some of the guilty are still walking the streets of Northern Ireland, what is fundamentally wrong with the procedures for dealing with terrorists and where the blame for such failings should lie. These are the central issues which unfold with this story.

For the benefit of the reader I will seek to outline some of the background which is central to an understanding of the organization to which the Shankill Butchers belonged. They were members of the Ulster Volunteer Force (UVF) which has its roots in the years before the 1914–18 War. The UVF was formed by Lord Edward Carson to defend Ulster against Home Rule. However, events took the UVF in a different direction and onto the battlefields of France in the Great War.

UVF members fought bravely with the 36th Ulster Division and provided a heroic legacy, which was not necessarily mirrored in the manner in which it was later to address itself to the conflict within its own society. Within the ranks of the UVF was a junior wing known as the Young Citizen Volunteers, who formed a battalion within the 36th Ulster Division. In many respects this structure was to mirror that of the IRA, which had within its ranks young men who were members of *Na Fianna Éireann* (The Youth of Ireland). Two years after the War many of those men who had swelled the ranks of the UVF in 1912 behind the rallying cries of Carson were back in civilian life, tired and weary of fighting, but there were others who chose to remain in the organization to defend the Protestant population. This time the action took place not on the battlefields of the Somme but in the back streets of Belfast, where a historic struggle was about to manifest itself as it had done in the nineteenth century. Between 1920–22, in what is known as the 'Belfast Pogroms', the UVF became involved in communal violence and sectarian assassination.

Much has been written about that period by commentators on each side of the religious divide. As with much of the history of Northern Ireland, each of the protagonists has a hidden agenda. The death toll for the two years tells its own story: 267 Catholics, 185 Protestants. The violence of the period recalls events of the past twenty years. The Pogroms unleashed prejudice which created its own barbarity. Sectarian assassination became a daily way of life and young and old, male and female, became its victims . . . the innocent suffered. After 1922 the UVF was rarely active and by the Second World War it had almost faded into folk memory.

The advent of civil rights protests in the early sixties, and the fact that Catholics were beginning to agitate for political and social reforms, persuaded influential elements within Ulster Unionism that the UVF should be reactivated. That is the simplistic analysis, but it was in fact more serious and sinister than that. The early sixties saw the release of the last of the IRA detainees who had watched the failure of the IRA Border Campaign of the 1950s and the change in political emphasis within the ranks of the Republican Movement towards a more socialist policy. This revaluation of IRA strategy led to Republican involvement in civil rights issues and a belief that nothing was to be achieved from armed insurrection. There were also young men, not Republicans, within the Catholic community who had benefited from the 1947 Education Act and who were determined to mimic the tactics of civil rights protesters in the United States.

As a result of this change in attitude within the Catholic Nationalist community the IRA sold its arsenal of weapons to the Welsh Nationalists. The prospect of a rebellious and truculent Catholic minority making demands was anathema to hardline Unionists who felt that the only way to deal with organized non-violent rebellion was to use force to eradicate it. However, Unionism was also changing. In 1965 the Prime Minister in charge of Northern Ireland, which at that time had its own parliament, was Captain Terence O'Neill, who felt that it was a time for change, whether in recognition of trades unions or appeasement of Nationalist demands. Terence O'Neill is remembered by many people to this day as the first Unionist politician who was determined to break the mould of sectarian politics in Northern Ireland, and to introduce an awareness of a need for change within his own party. Like many of the leading Unionists before him, he possessed the demeanour and voice of an aristocrat with a bearing which signified his English public-school training and his career in the British Army. His ancestry can be traced back to one of the O'Neills who was King of Ireland and to a Chichester who was prominent among English Planters in the seventeenth century in Ulster. His father was MP for Mid-Antrim at Westminster and was the first member of Parliament to be killed in the 1914–18 War. Terence was educated at Eton and later served as a captain in the Irish Guards in the Second World War, during which his two brothers were killed in action. In 1946 he embarked on a political career and was elected the Westminster MP for the County Antrim constituency of Bannside. In 1956 he was appointed by the Northern Ireland Prime Minister, Lord Brookeborough, to the post of Minister for Home Affairs. He proved to be a competent cabinet minister and a short time later he was made Minister for Finance, which he remained until he succeeded Lord Brookeborough as Prime Minister in 1963. At that time, Captain O'Neill, as he preferred to be called, was regarded by some of the new breed of Unionists, such as Faulkner, as benefiting from his Anglo-Irishness. In fact, although O'Neill may have had a renowned ancestry he was not part of the Unionist landowning class such as Brookeborough. When he became Prime Minister he exhibited a willingness to learn about and associate with Catholics and demonstrated what some of his colleagues saw as an ecumenical attitude and a dangerous trait. O'Neill was willing to meet with Catholic clerics and to pursue a course of reconciliation which, at that time, was anathema to Unionism and to the Brookeborough tradition. O'Neill was not simply a Unionist but part of the liberal Anglo-Irish tradition. That did not suit the hardliners in O'Neill's Cabinet; men such as Brian Faulkner, who felt he should have had O'Neill's job and who did in fact later become Prime Minister. There were others, most notable amongst whom was the Minister for Home Affairs, William Craig. They were convinced that O'Neill was not the man to deal with the gut realities of Ulster politics and, as a consequence, there were plots and counter-plots to oust him. These plots were hatched in private, with Faulkner as the leading conspirator, but they failed.

This was also the period when a fiery orator, Ian Kyle Paisley, was convincing many working-class Protestants that their Catholic neighbours were preparing to rise up and drive them into a United Ireland.

Paisley was also bitterly anti-O'Neill. Like many others, he knew that O'Neill had been appointed by the elite ruling class within Unionism because he was part of that elite, but that he lacked the hard, uncompromising character of his predecessor, Lord Brookeborough. The former cabinet minister, William Craig, has confirmed for me that no one in the Cabinet was informed of O'Neill's appointment as Prime Minister on 5 March 1963, until after he was given the job. The UVF was quickly re-established and one man was chosen to lead the organization in Belfast. He was Augustus ('Gusty') Spence, an ex-soldier whose father had fought with the UVF in the 36th Ulster Division. Spence was an ideal choice. He was born and still lived in the Shankill area of Belfast, which was the touchstone of hardline Protestantism and Unionism, its history mirrored in sectarian conflict with the Catholic Falls area which ran parallel to Spence's birthplace. Spence, as he now readily admits, was a bigot, and therefore suitable raw material for the sectarian conflict of Northern Ireland. He was sworn into the UVF, not in Belfast but well away from prying eyes in Pomeroy in County Tyrone. He says now he didn't know what he was entering into or who was pulling the strings. He claims that it was only years later when he was being interviewed by Special Branch detectives that he began to realize he was being questioned about a conspiracy when at that time he had seen himself as nothing but a mere foot soldier carrying out his duty. Spence says: 'When I was interviewed by Special Branch they were not interested in shootings but rather conspiracies. I was puzzled. They knew what I didn't know. It was then I realized that we should have turned our guns on those who were manipulating us, and not the Catholics.'

But that was retrospective analysis. In 1966 Spence did what was required of him in a manner which was to have echoes many years later when the 'Troubles' began in earnest.

In 1966 tension was high. The UVF bombed reservoirs and the State immediately blamed the IRA, but it was essentially the callousness with which the Shankill UVF, headed by Spence, behaved towards innocent Catholics which is of particular significance to this book. Spence admits he was born with the prejudices that afflict many people in Northern Ireland. He hated and feared Catholics and says he was uneducated and unable to think politically for himself. There is little doubt that he was willing to see himself as a soldier fighting for 'God and Ulster'. We can see this from a statement issued by him and his associates on 21 May 1966: 'From this day we declare war on the IRA and its splinter groups. Known IRA men will be executed mercilessly and without hesitation. Less extreme measures will be taken against anyone sheltering them or helping them, but if they persist in giving them aid then more extreme measures will be adopted. Property will not be exempted in any measure taken. We will not tolerate interference from any source and we solemnly warn the authorities to make no more speeches of appeasement. We are heavily armed Protestants dedicated to this cause.' What this statement omitted to mention was that two weeks earlier, while the UVF was attempting to firebomb a Catholic-owned pub, a seventy-seven-year-old Protestant widow who lived beside the premises was severely burned and subsequently died.

The UVF statement took on a more ominous character in the weeks following its publication. On 26 May 1966 Spence held a meeting of his unit in a room in the Standard Bar on the Shankill Road. A bar was chosen as a meeting place because it was familiar territory, though there may also have been an anaesthetic quality in the sense that drink was available. This was later to be a feature of many of the Butcher killings. However, on that evening in 1966 alcohol was not the primary reason for the meeting; the killing of a Republican was. Spence outlined that the target was a prominent man who was an IRA intelligence officer. The hit was timed for the following night at the IRA officer's home in the neighbouring district of the Falls Road, across the sectarian divide. Four men were selected to carry out the killing. When one of the four was asked to steal a car for 'the job' he replied that he was a soldier and not a common criminal. Eventually it was decided that the UVF's 'official' car should be used for the task. Spence provided the name of the intended victim: Leo Martin. The plan was simple. The four would drive around the Catholic Falls area in search of Martin and then to Baden-Powell Street where he lived. Leo Martin was not at home on the evening in question, nor was he seen walking around the Falls Road, but the UVF men were not to be outdone. They took the decision to kill someone else, anyone, as long as the victim was a Catholic. As they were leaving the Clonard area of Falls they saw a man walking along the pavement in an obvious state of drunkenness. That man was twenty-eight-year-old Patrick Scullion who had no connection with the IRA. Scullion was shot there and then and died three weeks later in hospital. His killing is significant because it symbolizes a mentality which is only too prevalent in both parts of the sectarian divide to this day. Spence expresses it with terrible clarity: 'At that time the attitude was that if you couldn't get an IRA man you should shoot a *Taig*** [Catholic], he's your last resort.' This statement implies that within the Protestant paramilitary mind there was a crudely held belief that Catholicism, Nationalism and Republicanism were in some way inseparable.

The shooting of Scullion did not have as much impact on the public as the events which took place in Malvern Street off the Shankill Road on the night of 25 June 1966. That evening Spence held a meeting of his unit to consider once again the killing of Leo Martin. Again, Martin was

---

*The word '*Taig*' appears frequently in this book and it is worth briefly seeking to clarify it. According to the Oxford English Dictionary the word *Teague* (*teg, tig*) reaches back to 1661. The dictionary classifies the word as colloquial and defines it as the anglicized spelling of the Irish name *Tadhg*, which is variously pronounced *teg, tig,* or *taig*, and is a nickname for an Irishman. The date 1661 would suggest that the nickname was brought into English usage by the Ulster Planters or by soldiers of the English armies returning home. It is unlikely that the word *Teague* was used in Ireland by English speakers before 1661. *Teague* was in common usage in the eighteenth century and was known to Samuel Johnson. In Northern Ireland it was spelt *Taig* and used pejoratively rather like 'nigger' or 'Commie' in the United States.

not at home and, after searching unsuccessfully for him in the neighbouring streets, the UVF set fire to his house. They returned to the Shankill, not to the Standard Bar but to the Malvern Arms, and joined Spence and some others for a drink. Spence and his men were despondent at not having succeeded in killing Martin. The events which unfolded in the Malvern Arms in the hours which followed were described in a statement later made by a member of Spence's unit: 'When we were in the Malvern Arms for about an hour four lads came in and went for a drink to the counter. The conversation came up about the religion of these fellows. Spence asked the company if they could be Catholics and then joined the four lads to buy a drink. When he returned to our table he said, "I have been listening to their conversation and they are four IRA men." We had some more drinks and then Spence turned to us and said, "These are IRA men and they'll have to go." '

The four young men standing at the bar were indeed Catholics but they were not members of the IRA and there was nothing to suggest that they were in any way connected with it. The Malvern Arms was familiar to them because it was possible to drink there after closing time and one among the four, eighteen-year-old Peter Ward, was a barman who knew which pubs in Belfast ignored licensing hours. Ward had been in the Malvern Arms on previous occasions. On 25 June, however, he was in the wrong place at the wrong time. Peter Ward's naivety was to cost him dearly.

After midnight Spence and three of his men left the pub and prepared an ambush in the street outside. When Ward and his companions left the Malvern Arms at 1.45 A.M. Ward was shot and fatally wounded. One of his friends, Liam Doyle, saw Spence in action: 'I saw this man running after me. I saw flashes coming from him and he started to shoot into me. I was hit six times. I asked him why he was shooting at us as we were doing nothing.

I pleaded with him not to shoot at me and shouted, "Please don't." He made no reply and kept shooting.'

At the trial of Spence and his unit, Spence was also credited with shooting Peter Ward, though he may not have personally fired the fatal shots. He did shoot Doyle. There was general revulsion in the Protestant community at what had happened in Malvern Street, and the life sentence given to Spence was greeted with relief. Spence was not then regarded as a hero but that view would soon change. He had set the tone, if not established the equation: 'If you can't get an IRA man get a *Taig*, he's your last resort.'

Three years later Spence masterminded the growth of the UVF from his prison cell in response to serious civil unrest and sectarian warfare. The bigoted attitude which was so aptly symbolized by his actions found expression once again in both communities. It lay at the root of a politically and religiously divided community, waiting for events to trigger it, and in the late summer and autumn of 1969 killings and destruction enveloped Belfast in sectarian warfare. Painful folk memories were evoked in both communities and the IRA and UVF emerged as the defenders of their respective tribes. Young men were drawn immediately into a conflict which their mothers and fathers knew only too well would have inevitably tragic results. Romantic nationalism and romantic loyalism were given a new lease of life and many young men, some of them still in school uniforms, swelled the ranks of the paramilitaries. On the Nationalist side the IRA was unprepared and Citizen Defence Committees were established which were later to become the Provisional IRA. Likewise, on the Unionist side, the UVF was not at full strength and as a result it too set up Defence Committees. These Protestant Defence Committees would provide the genesis for the Ulster Defence Association which was later to become a sister organization of the UVF. Into the ranks of the junior wing of the UVF in 1970 (Young Citizen

Volunteers) went a young man, Hugh Leonard Thompson Murphy, known to his friends as 'Lenny', who would express a power and an evil hitherto unrivalled in the UVF.

1

The Making of a Killer

This story begins in the late 1940s in Sailor Town in the docks area of Belfast. At that time the docks area represented Belfast in miniature because it mirrored all the political and religious divisions which were central to a sectarian city. The area, now redeveloped and consigned to folk memory, was then equally divided between Catholic and Protestant families, living in close proximity and often as next-door neighbours. The labour force from the docks was also divided and sons followed fathers into the part of the docks reserved for their particular tribe. Sailor Town was known to be a tightly knit district where outsiders were regarded with suspicion. The name Murphy was common to the area, though most of the families bearing the name were Catholics. An exception to the rule was the Murphy family – William Murphy, his wife Mary and their son William – who lived at 8 Fleet Street and were staunchly Protestant, making no secret of their religion or politics to their Catholic neighbours. William junior was a quiet, unassuming young man who had followed his father's example and was working as a dock labourer. The young William spent much of his time at home and was not given to drinking or standing on street corners talking to other young men. His father would have preferred him to be more assertive but was pleased that his son was working and helping to support the family financially. William was aware that his surname often led to him being regarded as a Catholic and he would have preferred his mother's maiden name, Carson. Taking everything into account, he kept a low profile and did not come to the attention of many of the people around him.

In 1948, at the age of twenty-one, William found himself attracted by a young girl who visited relatives in a neighbouring street. The girl was Joyce Thompson and was five years younger than him. The prospect of William having a girlfriend five years his junior did not please his parents and their worries were soon realized when he told them at the beginning of 1949 that seventeen-year-old Joyce was pregnant. It was decided that they should get married before the child was born, but that they would not live in Fleet Street, where gossip was rife. This suited Joyce who decided they should live in her home at 28 Percy Street in the west of the city. They were married in the Belfast Registrar's Office on 2 August 1949. Joyce's father, Alexander, consented to them living in his home, which was situated between the two roads in Belfast where the two communities have fought each other from the middle of the nineteenth century; the Falls and Shankill.

Joyce was far more assertive than her husband and, though five years younger than William, she was the more dominant of the two. She had no love for Catholics and the tradition of the Shankill area where she lived was hardline Unionism. From her house she was able to view the other side of the sectarian divide. Unlike the docks, the issues in West Belfast were always more intense. In essence, two warring factions lived opposite each other, each side riddled with suspicion, fear and prejudice. It was in this atmosphere and within one month of her marriage that she gave birth to her first child, a boy, in the Jubilee Wing of the Royal Maternity Hospital in Belfast. He was called William after his father but he was given no middle names. Life in the Thompson household was not what Joyce wished for her family, and within one year and with the arrival of a second child imminent they moved to 15 Penrith Street in the heart of the Shankill. Her husband continued to work as a dock labourer and, as always, was diligent, kept a low profile, and returned straight home after work, remaining there until he was required to leave again for work. On 26 August 1950 Joyce Murphy gave birth to her second son but this time the choice of name for the child was slightly more complex. It was decided to call him John but in recognition of her father and her family his full name was John Alexander Thompson Murphy. Within twelve months the Murphy family was on the move again, this time to the docks area, though not to Sailor Town. The street chosen by Joyce was North Thomas Street, several hundred yards from William Murphy's parents, with whom the young couple retained little contact. On 2 March 1952 Joyce Murphy gave birth to her third and final child, Hugh Leonard Thompson. At this point it is worth examining why the Murphys moved house so frequently within a short space of time. I was told by people who had known the family that Joyce and William were very sensitive about people questioning them on account of their name and asking whether they were related to the Murphy families in the docks, meaning the Catholic Murphys. Each time such questions surfaced, Joyce Murphy would make a decision to move on. I discovered there was a further problem with which she and her husband had to contend at that time and which has remained with them as a family to this day. The perceived wisdom in the Shankill was that they were Catholics and were merely hiding the fact. Their neighbours believed that Joyce was certainly Protestant but that her husband was a Catholic and for this reason didn't associate with neighbours and rarely left his home. While researching this book I was informed by two people who knew the Murphy family that William Murphy was in fact from the Lower Falls area of Belfast. My informants, themselves born on the Shankill Road, told me that William Murphy was from Sevastapol Street in the Clonard district of the Falls Road. I set out to investigate this claim and was astonished by the coincidence I uncovered. In the

3

1940s and 1950s there was indeed a Catholic family called Murphy in that street and the names of the four sons in the family were William, Alexander, John and Patrick. Three of those names were chosen by Joyce and William Murphy for their two elder sons, and the name William fitted the story perfectly. However, the claim was false but the coincidence was in itself significant in that Joyce's childhood home in Protestant Percy Street was only 200 yards from Sevastapol Street. The similarities in the names combined with the reticent behaviour of William Murphy were sufficient to create a myth which would generate great resentment and bitterness within the minds of Joyce Murphy and her family and remain common currency in Protestant minds to this day. In such a small community the belief that William Murphy was a '*Taig*' would always have created difficulties. Joyce Murphy knew the finger was being pointed at her family, if only in a surreptitious manner. Though veiled, such attitudes were menacing and made the family behave like gypsies, continually on the move. By 1957 they had moved again, this time back to the Shankill area, and some of the residents who had forgotten what the mild and introverted William Murphy looked like came to believe that another Mr Murphy, in other words someone using the same name, had moved in with Joyce. This erroneous belief was strengthened by the fact that William Murphy was becoming increasingly reticent and retiring in his ways.

This latest house move brought the Murphys close to Argyll Primary School, where in 1957 Hugh Leonard Thompson Murphy joined his two older brothers in pursuit of an education. Those who remember those days recall that in his first few years of primary school Hugh Leonard, who preferred to call himself Lenny, was given a nickname by his classmates, 'Murphy the Mick'. This was a derogatory way of indicating their belief that he was a Catholic since the word 'Mick', though applied affectionately to the Irish Guards, was used in Belfast in the same pejorative manner as the word '*Taig*'. Whether or not it was in reaction to this branding, Lenny Murphy was a belligerent child and by the time he was ten years old he was threatening other children and removing their pocket money from them at knifepoint. Unlike his brothers, he was small in stature and rarely impressed others with any physical prowess. Instead, he assembled his own gang and when confronted with overwhelming numbers would threaten his adversaries with his older brothers. He is remembered by a classmate as follows: 'We all called him Mick because we believed that he was a "*Taig*". With a name like Hugh Murphy there was little doubt. He never called himself "Hughie" as most kids would have done because Hughie Murphy would have certainly made him a Catholic. But most people in the district believed his father was "one of the other sort". My parents certainly did. He was a tough wee nut and his brothers were known to be hard men. He would always have threatened you with his brothers if you confronted him on his own. He wasn't particularly bright. Another thing that struck me was that he never talked about his father or, like other kids, threatened you with his father if you hit him. He was devious. I remember him taking my lunch money off me on the way into school one day. I gave it to him because he had a penknife. You just knew not to mess with him.'

The accuracy of these observations can only be assessed in the light of Lenny Murphy's later development, but there is little doubt that he was a troublesome child. The comment about him not being 'bright' probably refers to his lack of application to school work, but those who remember him would add that he was cunning. It is possible that there was considerable instability in his life created by the way in which he was viewed by schoolmates, and the constant upheaval caused by house-moves together with a young mother over-compensating for her husband's lack of dynamism. Joyce Murphy was proud of her sons and was tough with them, encouraging them to behave properly at home and in front of the neighbours. She is not known to have taught them to hate Catholics, though there is little doubt that her three sons grew up with a bitterness towards the other community and a resentment of authority, particularly the police.

Lenny Murphy first came to the attention of the police at the age of twelve when he was found guilty of shop-breaking and larceny. He was given two years' probation and ordered to pay eight shillings in compensation. By this time he was at secondary school, where he displayed all the traits of a petty criminal. He is remembered for showing a lack of interest in his studies and more interest in running his own little rackets. One such racket was very similar to the one he ran when at primary school and involved threatening other pupils, stealing their meal tickets and then selling them to other boys at a reduced rate. His attitude to authority in the classroom was such that teachers preferred to leave him to his own devices. In the metalwork room he is known to have exercised his authority by brandishing a metal poker which he had made and on one occasion hitting another pupil over the head with it.

One of his classmates remembers vividly how Murphy dominated the class to the extent that other boys preferred to avoid his company and did not confront him when he treated them roughly. Still relatively small in stature, he continued to use the threat of his two older brothers when he found himself facing overwhelming odds or a fellow pupil who was willing to confront his belligerence. Unlike his early days when fellow pupils chided him for being a *Taig*, there was no question of anyone daring to do that at the Model Secondary School. He called himself Lenny and that was the manner in which he was referred to by teachers and pupils alike.

It was at secondary school that an example of his cunning emerged which illustrated the mind of a developing criminal. A classmate tells the story. 'Lenny was always extorting money from us all but none of us dared to challenge him. There was always the threat of him calling on the support of his brothers lurking in the background if anyone decided to take him on. He wasn't big physically but you all knew that he was capable of having you sorted out. One day in the classroom he stole another boy's wallet and flung it out of the window onto the roof of a porta-kabin. The teacher was too busy writing on the blackboard to notice the incident and the boy in question did not notice Lenny removing the wallet, but some of us watched how it was expertly removed from a jacket pocket. During the lunchtime break Lenny retrieved the wallet and removed the money from it, taking only the pound notes. Someone in the class told the boy who had lost his wallet about the guilty party and in turn the teacher was informed. No one was willing to give evidence against Murphy, and he knew it. That afternoon the teacher asked everyone to turn out their pockets and the contents were closely scrutinized. Lenny went free. He boasted afterwards that he had rolled the pound notes between fingers and fed them through a hole in his tie which he wore in class with the money carefully concealed.'

Lenny Murphy knew the right people to target in the school and he chose the boys whose fathers owned news-agent, confectionery or butcher shops; the type of pupils who, unlike himself, were likely to have a plentiful supply of pocket money. In 1968 he left school and was soon in trouble with the law again for theft. He was placed once more on probation for two years, and on this occasion the compensation which he was ordered to pay was £4 10s. In the same year he took a job as a lorry driver's helper and within a few months was prosecuted for a driving offence. The year 1968 was one of considerable change in Northern Ireland and, though Lenny was not aware of the complexity of the political events which were taking place, he was beginning to associate with people who had a vested interest in what was happening.

The civil rights movement was developing a policy of street confrontation with the police, and within the Protestant community there were fears that it would all lead to communal violence. Eminent Unionist politicians were talking of the civil rights movement as a front for the IRA which was preparing to overthrow the State. The IRA was certainly present with a new agenda and long-term objectives and, though the guns had not come out on either side, hatred, suspicion and prejudice were about to surface in a virulent way.

Lenny Murphy was beginning to behave as an adult rather than a teenager, keeping company with men in the Shankill district. He did, however, retain contact with his own age group by attending a disco near his home. A man who also attended the disco at that time recalls that Lenny would take over the running of it as if he owned it, and it was he who decided who should be allowed entry. It was, says this informant, just another example of the means by which he exercised his control over others. Some of the teenagers who went to the disco were pupils from the Model Secondary School and they noticed changes in Lenny's appearance and temperament. He now dressed trendily and was fond of demonstrating how much he could drink. One Friday night in the spring of 1969 his demeanour at the disco left no one in any doubt that he had drunk too much. Half-way through the evening Joyce Murphy arrived and, after fighting her way through the dancers, she sought out her son and dragged him by the hair from the premises. When Lenny returned to the disco the following week no one dared to mention the incident for fear it might arouse his anger. It was a demonstration of the way in which Joyce Murphy handled her son, even publicly, but it was something she would never be allowed to do again.

Not long after this, Lenny was regularly seen frequenting two bars on the Shankill Road, the Gluepot and the Bayardo, the latter being a haunt for men connected with

8

the UVF. It was at this time, as events in Northern Ireland were beginning to make headlines, that he joined the junior wing of the UVF. He was observed associating more openly with prominent figures in the community, unlike his brother, William, who was regarded as a loner, and his other brother, John, who had a small circle of friends but did not visit bars where trouble was easily found.

An example of the way Murphy behaved when he was under the influence of drink occurred in the Bayardo Bar and was witnessed by a former pupil of the Model Secondary School: 'Lenny was standing at the bar drinking when a chap called Ritchie accidentally knocked against him, making him spill his drink. Lenny rounded on Ritchie and began threatening him and suggesting that he would take him outside and sort him out. A guy we knew to be a member of the UVF approached Lenny and told him that there were several people in the bar who were likely to give Ritchie support. Lenny immediately backed off. I heard a few weeks later that Lenny and a few of his mates waited outside the Bayardo until closing time and when Ritchie came out they beat him badly.'

That same witness is of the view that Murphy was developing as a thug, and the more his reputation for being a 'hard man' spread around the Shankill area, the more he sought to illustrate his potential for violence. Society around Lenny at this time was starting to get out of control and, added to this, there was a new dimension to his life. His mother was no longer able to control him, his brothers seemed indifferent to his activities and his father did not feature in the equation. The fact that there were fewer restrictions on the world around him and at home was a recipe for disaster.

In August 1969 Protestant mobs invaded Catholic streets on the nearby Falls Road and hundreds of homes were burned. The same happened in other parts of Belfast with thousands of Catholic families fleeing the city in what amounted to the greatest population displacement since the Second World War. Most of the violence occurred in what was the historic battleground for the two communities, West Belfast, and particularly that area between the Shankill and Falls Roads. Some of the Protestant mobs moved down Percy Street and onto the Falls Road. In the midst of the violence was Lenny Murphy. An associate of his at that time, who has now moved away from Belfast, says that he remembers Lenny being elated with the opportunity to be in the middle of it all. Murphy was not a prime mover in those events but they allowed him to vent some of the hatred which he felt for Catholics. This was the first occasion that it was manifested, though he often talked overtly while drinking in the Bayardo bar of his hatred of all Catholics because they were 'scum and animals'! This may have been Murphy's way of distancing himself from his own history and those school days when he was viewed as a Catholic. He was beginning to develop into what one UVF man later called a 'super Prod', which was shorthand for saying that Murphy was more anti-Catholic, anti-Nationalist and anti-Republican than even the most bitter man on the Shankill Road.

The violence of the summer and autumn of 1969 changed the situation in Northern Ireland utterly and, as the poet, Yeats might have said, on both sides 'a terrible beauty was born'. The Army arrived on the streets of Belfast and Derry in August 1969 following attacks on Catholics' homes in both those cities. Their arrival followed demands from the Dublin Government and Nationalist politicians in Northern Ireland for a peace-keeping force. Although the soldiers were welcomed by the Catholic population this did not prevent the erection of barricades in both communities where the hatred of the other side had reached an unparalleled intensity. The Army did not attempt to remove the barricades, on the basis that it was an understandable reaction by two communities who had fought and hated each other and were terrified that the conflict could start again at any moment.

Behind the barricades other groupings began to flourish, particularly vigilante organizations who set themselves up as protectors of their respective communities. None of the paramilitary groups in the two communities was well prepared for the communal violence on the streets of Northern Ireland in August 1969 and the vigilantes were able to thrive though they would later be sucked into paramilitarism. In many respects the barricades provided the closed atmosphere in which Republican and Loyalist paramilitary organizations could begin to reform and restructure. Initially, the vigilantes or defence organizations, as they were commonly known, were in a primacy role though this was to be short-lived. The Army in those early days saw its role as keeping the two communities apart in those areas where they lived in close proximity. The ghetto system was reinforced. On the Catholic side of the divide there was disillusionment at the failure of the IRA to defend its own districts, and vigilante groups were set up and organized into Citizen Defence Committees. These provided the genesis of the Provisional IRA which was formed in January 1970.

Similarly, in the Shankill area and other Loyalist strongholds of Belfast the UVF was found wanting. It did not have the arms or the manpower to patrol its own neighbourhoods, and vigilante groups took to the streets. These groups later developed into another paramilitary force, the Ulster Defence Association. The vigilantes established what were called 'no-go' areas which in effect meant that they controlled the streets, though in most Catholic districts the British Army held the balance of power. Tension remained high in 1970 but, with the emergence of the Provisionals, romantic nationalism took to the stage and it was not long before the Provisionals turned back the historical clock and engaged in a struggle with the old Republican enemy, the British. But even this did not detract from the fact that the geography of Belfast was being carved up by the vigilantes in a way which was to ensure

11

the permanence of old sectarian divisions and the creation
of new ones. There were now areas where Catholics and
Protestants could not afford to travel for fear of being
apprehended and questioned. Many observers of the situation have failed to understand the significance of the
vigilantes and how, on both sides, they determined the
manner in which the city would be divided, with the result
that sectarian gangs were able to identify the religion of
their victims simply by the streets on which they happened
to be walking or working. There were subtleties which
were recognized only by killers; for example, outside the
ghettoes there were public routes but the direction in
which a person was travelling on one of those routes
would indicate whether he or she was heading towards
a Protestant or a Catholic housing estate. This type of
information sealed the fate of hundreds of people and was
later the basis on which the Shankill Butchers operated
and selected their victims.

The years 1970 and 1971 were crucial in the development of Lenny Murphy. He was in the UVF and was
surrounding himself with a group of people loosely known
as the 'Murphy gang'. Among them were two young men,
Robert Bates and Samuel McAllister, two nonentities
ideally suited to be Murphy's cohorts, and who were to figure
prominently and infamously in Murphy's later life. Bates,
who was nicknamed 'Basher', was a man with a short fuse
who ran his own gang but abandoned it in favour of being
an associate of Murphy. Bates was four years older than
Lenny but was nonetheless willing to become a subordi-
nate. He also had a criminal record which dated back to
1966, with seven separate charges of assault and disorderly
behaviour. He lived in the Shankill area close to Murphy's
home and had a reputation for having beaten people with
beer glasses or bottles in pub fights.

McAllister was a classic example of a petty criminal
from an early age and, like Murphy, was remembered for
having extorted money from other boys at school. He was

12

born in Argyll Street in 1955 and by the age of eleven was the subject of probation orders for shopbreaking, theft and malicious damage. Two years later he faced similar charges, including one of breaking into his own school and stealing office equipment. His criminal record from childhood until he met Murphy in 1971 is a disturbing litany of petty crime and he was well known on the Shankill Road as a tough individual. He towered over other boys, being over six feet in height and heavily built. He used his size to full advantage when it came to intimidating others. 'Basher' Bates and 'Big Sam' both attended Ballygomartin Secondary School in West Belfast and were two of the most violent and unruly pupils at the school. McAllister ran a protection racket and those who refused to pay were summarily punished by a beating in the school toilets. When a pupil persistently refused to pay up it was not unknown for McAllister to bash his head against a wash basin.

Murphy encouraged Bates and McAllister to join the UVF, though this took little persuasion. The UVF at that time was not in a position to vet recruits and, like the IRA, it was only too glad to have as many members as would join its ranks. It was also competing with the vigilante groups, which were beginning to assert their independence and form themselves into a properly structured paramilitary organization. From his prison cell Gusty Spence was trying to mastermind a reorganization of the UVF and it was his belief that the organization should, as soon as possible, try to incorporate members of the vigilante organizations. His plan did not come to fruition because those running the vigilante groups were unwilling to relinquish the power they exercised in many Protestant districts. In 1971–2 the UVF and UDA operated alongside each other to protect Protestant areas and jointly carry out acts of violence. Lenny Murphy exploited this dimension to the situation because it afforded him an opportunity to engage in violence whenever the opportunity arose. In essence

13

this dual membership enabled Murphy to undertake operations with whichever grouping was engaging in violence at a particular time which coincided with Murphy's availability. Murphy was therefore able to exploit his own potential for violence by taking full advantage of whatever opportunities were provided by both organizations.

March 1972 saw the major change that the Nationalists and Republicans had been demanding: the abolition of the Stormont Parliament. Unionists watched their edifice crumbling without resistance and saw Provisional IRA leaders being flown to London for talks with the British Prime Minister, Edward Heath. In the Protestant community there was not just despondency but a feeling of political impotence and an increasing suspicion that, with Stormont gone, they were about to be driven into a United Ireland. The fall of Stormont created a trauma in the Protestant community which has never been properly evaluated in relation to the subsequent development of Loyalist paramilitary thinking. The Provisionals achieved something which the Loyalists had believed could never happen: the destruction of so-called Protestant supremacy. The Protestants were immersed in feelings of frustration and despair. They could not attack the British Army or the police because they saw them as their security forces; instead they reverted to terror against the other community. They had no ideological struggle to wage so they used the strategy which Gusty Spence had initiated in 1966: 'If you can't get an IRA man, get a *Taig*.' One political scientist has suggested that the Loyalist paramilitaries recognized the impact of the Provisionals' terrorist campaign and felt they could never emulate its success or tactics. The British Government appeared to be conceding to a guerrilla movement which was capable of acquiring new weaponry, making sophisticated bombs and waging an urban guerrilla campaign against a formidable army, namely the British Army. The Protestant population received a bad press after August 1969 and subsequently compounded the problem by behaving aggressively towards journalists who were interested in reflecting the story in both communities. As a result, Loyalists generally recognized they had no friends internationally and likewise Loyalist paramilitaries knew that, unlike the Provisionals, they could not seek to raise money internationally to buy weapons or to ask for weapons from left-wing regimes who in any event viewed Ulster Protestants as oppressors. As a result, the UVF and UDA recognized that they could not acquire the weapons or perhaps the expertise to fight 'the enemy'. So they decided it was better to engage in a 'dirty war' of indiscriminate terror which would prove that the IRA was incapable of defending its own people. Such a view is simplistic, though there is little doubt that by the summer of 1972 a decision had been made by the UDA/UVF to conduct a sectarian assassination campaign. Spence, who would not have agreed with this tactic, was interned in prison at the time, together with the entire UVF leadership. With the introduction of internment without trial in 1971 the conditions had been created for new, younger recruits on both sides to devise different tactics for the paramilitaries. Initially, all internees were Republicans, and the Loyalists could not accept that such legislation could ever be used against them, but it was. By the summer of 1972 the UVF, with its leaders interned, was being led by younger men who saw themselves as terrorists and not as soldiers. The old guard of the organization, men like Spence, preferred to describe themselves as soldiers but their incarceration precluded their orders from being obeyed.

The absence of the older men paved the way for Lenny Murphy, 'Basher' Bates, 'Big Sam' McAllister and many others like them to develop their own type of warfare in alliance with the omnipresent UDA, which was prepared to flex its muscles to establish credibility as a paramilitary force.

2
A Killer is Blooded

In the opening weeks of 1972 two killings were carried out by the IRA which clearly illustrated to Loyalists the sheer ruthlessness of their adversaries. The first was the shooting of a twenty-eight-year-old Catholic publican who, when his killers burst in and shot him, was at home counting a night's takings from his pub. The IRA escaped with the money but it was widely believed that the act was not simply robbery but was meant to serve as a warning to other publicans to pay protection money when demanded. Several weeks later another IRA squad arrived on the doorstep of a forty-six-year-old Protestant bus driver, Sidney Agnew, and shot him dead in front of his family. His 'crime', as the IRA saw it, was that he had given an affidavit identifying three young IRA men who had hijacked his bus. It was callous treatment and a warning to others not to cooperate with the police, although the IRA knew that his evidence could be posthumously presented at trial, which it was and the three hijackers were convicted. The killing of Sidney Agnew horrified and incensed the Protestant population, who were convinced that the IRA could assassinate civilians, and particularly Loyalists, with impunity. Both murders came at a time when Protestants were beginning to believe that history was betraying them, that the British Government cared little for their plight, and that they were about to be sold into a United Ireland. An indication of the intensity of feeling in working-class areas of the Protestant community can be seen in a letter to a Loyalist paramilitary news sheet of the period:

I want to remind Protestants that these animals are crawl-
ing into Ulster, hitting vital points like RUC stations etc.
The ugly thing is that the bastards are getting away with
it. Then the question arises, what the hell are the UVF
doing about it? You've got to fight fire with fire. I don't
think they've enough fire to make the animals sweat. I am
not against the UVF but I would like to see a new UVF
fighting for the cause and willing to give their lives for
what others gave their lives for.

The rhetoric in this letter was not new and had been
expressed during earlier troubles, but its nature was a
factor in dehumanizing the enemy before the battle.
Another phrase which frequently found its way into Loyalist news sheets and bulletins was 'the Provos and their
passive sympathizers'. A lack of any proper definition of
the enemy encouraged many Loyalists to believe that all
Catholics were IRA sympathizers, if not actual supporters.

On 30 January 1972 members of the 1st Parachute
Regiment shot dead thirteen innocent civilians in Londonderry on what was to become known to the world as
'Bloody Sunday'. The reaction to this event within the
Catholic community and within the Irish Republic placed
increasing pressure on the Unionist Government at Stormont. The Prime Minister, Brian Faulkner, told his Cabinet that it was a grave moment in the history of Northern
Ireland. The former Cabinet minister, William Craig, who
had been sacked by Captain Terence O'Neill in 1969,
also recognized that events were running away from the
Unionists and announced that he had an answer which
would arrest that trend. He told a rally held outside Belfast
that the time had come for Protestants to preserve their
British traditions and way of life. His speech carried a
more sinister message in the words: 'God help those who
get in our way'. If there was any semblance of doubt
about the import of the threat, the meaning was certainly
understood by the Loyalist paramilitaries with whom Craig
maintained continuing dialogue. Craig's words carried

authority because he had held the post of Minister of Home Affairs during the crucial days of 1968. He was remembered by nationalists as the man who ordered police onto the streets of Londonderry on 5 October 1968 to deal with a civil rights march. The result was that many of the marchers were batoned by police and film of the event was beamed by television into homes throughout the world. 5 October produced an event which the SDLP leader, John Hume, later described as 'the spark that lit the bonfire'. Loyalists saw Craig as a man who was staunchly anti-Republican and who was sacked by Terence O'Neill because he was prepared to deal firmly and decisively with truculent Nationalists.

Rumours were rife in early 1972 that Stormont was about to be abolished, and a public assertion to this effect came from the lips of the Reverend Ian Paisley, who was regarded by many Protestants as being not only astute but also possessed of prophetic powers. Edward Heath was indeed planning to get rid of Stormont and, as often with British political manoeuvring, a decision was taken to use a shred of leaked information to test reaction and to prepare people for the inevitable. The British perception of Paisley was that he would be listened to by hardline Unionists and it was this section of the population that Edward Heath and his advisers were interested in studying. Paisley was to be used in a similar way in the late seventies when the British Government wished it to be known retrospectively that the IRA had made calls to 10 Downing Street to bargain for the release of the Price sisters in return for the freedom of the kidnapped German industrialist, Herr Neidermeyer.

In 1972 there were those who were convinced that Ian Paisley was speaking the truth but the Ulster Prime Minister, Brian Faulkner, was obliged publicly to deny the claim. Faulkner did, however, privately suspect that Paisley was being used as a loudspeaker and, as a result, went to see Heath who reassured him that no such thing was happening. Within one month of Faulkner's visit to 10 Downing Street the Stormont Parliament was abolished. The shock to the Protestant psyche was damaging and it took some time before it was accepted and before reaction was manifested. William Craig repeated his earlier ominous warning that the time for talking was over and Loyalists must commit themselves to action. There were talks between the UDA and UVF and joint operations were discussed as well as the policing of Protestant communities by bands of vigilantes. It was agreed that vigilantes should ensure that there were no IRA incursions, that the identity of strangers should be thoroughly checked, and that suspicious persons should be held for interrogation. William Craig made it clear in an interview for the Irish Republic's broadcasting service, RTE, that Loyalists might have to resort to killing. He kept more threatening words for a massive rally in Belfast in which he warned that if politicians failed to protect the Protestant heritage it would be for Ulster Loyalists to 'liquidate the enemy'.

At that rally, which came within days of direct rule being imposed on Ulster, Craig talked of dossiers being compiled on 'known IRA sympathizers'. It was dangerous talk but it was exactly the kind which many people wished to hear. Within three months of direct rule the British Government negotiated a truce with the IRA and a prelude to this truce was the release from internment of Gerry Adams, who was at one time the Army's 'most wanted' Provisional in Belfast and would later become the President of Sinn Fein. He was placed in the custody of the SDLP Chief Whip, Paddy Devlin, who was given a Military Intelligence Order guaranteeing immunity for Adams should he be stopped at Army roadblocks. An IRA negotiating team was flown to London but not before the IRA leader in Londonderry, Martin McGuinness, had received a guarantee from the British Government and Army authorities that he would return safely. Two Army Intelligence men were handed over to the IRA in Londonderry and were held under guard until McGuinness returned home from the London talks.

In the months between direct rule and the IRA truce the UDA increased in size, as did the UVF, but both organizations were unable to vet those who joined the swelling ranks. There were many in both organizations who were from criminal backgrounds and were intent on using both the UDA and UVF for criminal purposes. The fact that joint membership was not ruled out by either body also led to a lack of control over the activities of certain individuals. The joint membership, however, was used particularly by members of the UVF who saw advantage in using the UDA's weight of numbers in street confrontations. Between March and June there were signs that Craig's threat was being realized. The killing of Catholics had begun and in Protestant neighbourhoods large numbers of men in combat jackets were seen patrolling the streets. At the beginning of May the first ritualistic killing occurred and the victim, Victor Andrew, was the first IRA man to be killed by Loyalist paramilitaries. He was a member of the Official IRA and the nature of his death indicated the lengths to which Loyalist assassins would go when they encountered an enemy. Andrew was stabbed to death and his body dumped in an alleyway. This killing signalled the beginning of a sustained campaign of sectarian assassination which began in earnest after the meeting between the IRA and members of the British Government.

In the first six months of 1972 Lenny Murphy was preparing for his terrorist career in a most unusual fashion by attending many of the murder trials being held in Belfast's Crumlin Road courthouse. He not only appeared in the public gallery at the trials of those UVF members whom he knew but also at trials involving members of the IRA. Murphy was learning about the law, the nature of witness and forensic evidence, and when such evidence was ruled admissible or inadmissible. He sat and listened intently to the most complex legal arguments. A detective who remembers seeing him regularly in the courthouse says that Murphy would attend every sitting of a trial and was not perturbed by the fact that his presence was obvious to the security forces. The detective believes that Murphy had a second reason for attending IRA trials: to identify IRA supporters in the public gallery who could later be targeted for assassination. Murphy's dress sense was such that he was always clearly identifiable from a distance. He wore an expensive leather jacket and a scarf which he casually draped over his left shoulder. One other feature of his dress provides a bizarre insight into the man. He carried in his jacket a pair of leather driving-gloves which he wore on special occasions. A policeman who met him several times at the courthouse remembers him this way: 'Lenny loved his notoriety and the fact that we knew who he was. He enjoyed watching the reaction of his friends when he talked to me or my colleagues. It was as if he was saying to his friends, "Look, I can talk to these jerks and they don't know what the hell I'm up to and even if they suspect me there is nothing they can do about it." One thing which always stuck in my memory about those brief encounters with Lenny was that when he walked over to me he always put on his driving-gloves before he shook my hand. It was as though he was saying to himself, "I will shake hands with this cop, but not in an intimate way." It was his way of suggesting that I was diseased. The one thing about him I never could forget was his eyes . . . those blue eyes that pierced you. I could almost detect a look which suggested that if he had half a chance he would have blown me away. He was like the smiling assassin. When I saw him in the scarf and the leather jacket he reminded me of those First World War pilots who were going off in glory to battle and were loved by the women. He was like that. He always had young girls around him even in the courthouse. There was a Jack-the-Lad quality about him as well. I'm not a homosexual, you understand, but I have to say he was good-looking. I think in retrospect that he saw himself as a film star.'

Lenny Murphy was a womanizer and enjoyed being seen around the Loyalist clubs of the Shankill, chatting to whichever woman looked available. He was also a loner and was careful not to be seen publicly with known members of the UVF or UDA, unlike many of his associates who stood on street corners exchanging gossip. On those occasions when he was seen on the street it was invariably when he was travelling from his home to a meeting. This was a curious side to his nature when one considers that he was willing to be seen attending murder trials. It was indicative of the fact that when Murphy was active with the UVF he was careful about his security.

His first direct involvement in killing was on Friday 21 July 1972. That day a thirty-four-year-old Catholic, Francis Arthurs, from Fallswater Street off the Falls Road, was travelling in a taxi from the predominantly Nationalist Ardoyne area in North Belfast. The taxi was stopped on the Crumlin Road, which runs parallel to the Shankill Road. The mistake made by Arthurs was a classic one, in that the enclave from which the taxi emerged signalled to those watching the area that the occupant of the vehicle was a Catholic. Arthurs was drunk and was unaware that the previous night a young Catholic couple, also travelling in a taxi, had been apprehended and murdered. When Arthur's taxi was stopped he was bundled out of the vehicle unceremoniously and was hit over the head with a metal object. He was then taken to the Lawnbrook Social Club, a Loyalist club off the Shankill Road. In the club that night were Lenny Murphy and other members of Loyalist paramilitary organizations, drinking and making merry. Arthurs was now in a place which later would be given the name 'a romper room'.*

*When this term was first used by myself and a co-author of a Penguin Special entitled *Political Murder* no one was willing to believe that such a term existed or that Loyalist paramilitaries talked of 'rompering' victims.

The word 'romper' was derived from an Ulster Television series which involved children talking and playing with a television presenter. How the word 'rompering' came to be associated with killing can be better understood in the context of the manner in which killers disposed of their victims. Francis Arthurs, when he was dragged from the taxi, was taken to be 'rompered', which involved torturing him in front of an audience, in this case in the Lawnbrook Club. The involvement of large numbers of people guaranteed silence in much the same way as the Mafia

---

While I was working as a journalist investigating sectarian killings, I put it to the editor of the *Belfast Telegraph*, Eugene Wasson, that 'rompering' introduced a new dimension to the conflict but Wasson disbelieved the story. On another occasion I filed a story about a 'rompering', in which a mentally retarded Catholic boy named Benstead was branded with a hot poker. Again the story was treated with suspicion. On this occasion I had actually seen Benstead's body lying in an alleyway because the police at the scene mistook me for a member of their forensic Scenes of Crime team. At that time intimate details of the grisly aspects of some murders were not being released to the media. I was told later that this decision was taken both to spare the public the horror and to avoid giving publicity to the killer gangs. On the morning I saw Benstead's body I filed my story only to learn that the RUC Press Office had stated that the victim had not been tortured. I reacted angrily and informed my News Editor that I had personally viewed the body and had seen the burn marks on the boy's hands and feet and the cross which had been etched into his back with a number beside it indicating that he was the fourth victim of a particular murder squad which operated in east Belfast. The murder gang was run by an infamous homosexual paramilitary leader called John McKeague. The gang called the 'Red Hand Commandoes', was made up mostly of young men. McKeague was a sadist who initiated his followers by 'rompering' victims. This involved bringing a victim to a club, lock-up garage or a disused house, where a group of Red Hand Volunteers participated in the torture and murder of the victim. McKeague, who was shot dead by the INLA in the early 1980s, was believed by Military Intelligence to have been responsible for the murder of a young Protestant boy in Belfast in the mid-seventies. The boy's body was dismembered, burned over an open fire and dumped in the Lagan River which runs through Belfast. McKeague in some respects pioneered the 'rompering' process but it had a more bizarre application in the Shankill area.

code of *omerta*, and it also blooded potential recruits. On the night of 21 July Arthurs was held at the rear of the club until those drinkers with no paramilitary connections left for home. He was then paraded before the remaining drinkers and beaten severely by all of them. One man was seen to demonstrate that he could cause the victim the most pain by hitting him harder than anyone else. That man was Lenny Murphy. Joe Bennett, who later became one of the major UVF supergrasses, once told a friend that Murphy stood out from the others that night as the most barbarous gang member present. Arthurs was not just beaten until he was unrecognizable, he was stabbed repeatedly in different parts of the body with a knife wielded by Murphy. At 4.00A.M. the following morning, after he had been interrogated and tortured, Arthurs was shot on the premises, his body taken outside and bundled into a car, then dumped in a street less than a mile away.

A detective revealed to me details of Murphy's involvement in another murder which occurred around this period. I could not, however, trace the victim because of the number of unsolved crimes in June and July of 1972. The detective's source, which I cannot reveal here, could be described in journalistic terms as impeccable. This informant described how Murphy beat and tortured a Catholic man in a lock-up garage in a street running from the Shankill Road to the Catholic Springfield Road. The informant confirmed one detail about Murphy in these words: 'Lenny hit the guy harder than the rest of the people there that night. It was as if he was out to prove that he hated the *Taigs* more than the rest of us. He wanted to show that he was more violent and more capable than anyone else there. He was the one who used the knife before we shot the guy.'

The use of a knife was to be Lenny Murphy's trademark. Until now no one has known of Lenny Murphy's involvement in several murders in the summer of 1972, even though there was suspicion in the minds of detectives when Murphy eventually became infamous. It is incredible to think that Murphy was in fact a murderer at the age of twenty. There were many people at the time who would not have believed it. After all, he looked like most young men of his age, and his appearance did not suggest anything sinister about his character or his intentions. The only apparent thing was his pathological hatred of Catholics which he constantly stressed in all his conversations. He seemed a hardworking shop assistant, though his criminal activities paid for his flamboyant lifestyle of heavy drinking and womanizing. Indeed, many of his companions derived an income from Unemployment Benefit supplemented with proceeds from robberies or extortion. He was five feet six and a half inches in height, of slim build, with a crop of curly dark brown hair, blue eyes and a sallow complexion. He had a long face with overly long ears, a small, turned-up nose and a rounded chin. There was a scar on the back of his left hand and several tattoos on both arms. The tattoos were of King William of Orange on a horse, the words 'Mum and Dad', the Red Hand of Ulster and 'Rem 1690'. The tattoos were fairly typical of many working-class men of his age though he often kept them hidden from view. It has been suggested that vanity caused him to do this since the tattoos were drawn in his teens but later conflicted with his 'man-about-town' image.

The killing of Arthurs was gruesome but it was only the beginning of this type of murder involving torture or 'rompering'. One month after the Arthurs killing an elderly Catholic was murdered in a way which bears a striking resemblance to the Arthurs crime. Though no one was ever brought to justice for these murders, it was thought that the manner of killing strongly indicated the same hand at work. The third murder was that of forty-eight-year-old Thomas Madden who worked in a mill on the Crumlin Road and who, due to the geography of Belfast, was obliged to travel each day through tough Protestant

enclaves to reach his place of work. Madden was a bach-
elor, an inoffensive man who enjoyed a drink and went to
Mass on Sundays. He lived in a boarding house in Clifton-
park Avenue in North Belfast and worked as a security
guard, which involved night shift duty. Three weeks before
his death he was stopped by vigilantes and taken to a club
on the Shankill where he was interrogated. There is little
doubt that it was the Lawnbrook Social Club, where
Arthurs was murdered. He was detained at gunpoint in
the rear of the club for almost twenty-four hours. His
captors removed his personal possessions, which included
a pair of rosary beads, a small amount of cash, cigarettes
and a lighter, then interrogated him about his background,
where he drank and whether he knew any IRA men in
the area where he lived. After twenty-four hours he was
released and all his possessions, with the exception of his
money, were returned to him. His release was unusual,
since people picked up in this fashion were immediately
marked for death on the basis of their religion. We will
probably never know why he was allowed to go free,
though we can speculate that his captors intended that he
should be kept under surveillance. Unfortunately, if this
was the tactic, Thomas Madden's drinking haunts would
have placed him at risk, in particular one pub which he
frequented often and which was bombed several times by
Loyalist paramilitaries because it was a meeting place for
Republicans. On the evening before he met his death he
was drinking in his favourite pub, The Meeting of the
Waters, and appeared reluctant to go to work that night.
He mentioned to his drinking companions that he feared
for his life but did not elaborate beyond this comment.
However, he returned after 9.00 P.M. to his lodgings and
repeated his fears to his landlady. It may have been due
to the alcohol he had consumed that day, or perhaps the
fear of losing his job, that made him set out for the
Crumlin Road. Somewhere between his lodgings and his
place of work he was apprehended by his killers, most

likely in the vicinity of the Crumlin Road. He was taken
to a lock-up garage in Louisa Street off the Oldpark Road.
Between the hours of 10.00 P.M. and 4.00 A.M. he was
tortured. He was suspended by a rope from a wooden
beam and stripped of his clothing. A knife was used on
his body much in the manner a sculptor would chip away
at a piece of wood or stone. Long cuts were made down
his back and thighs and in all there were 147 stab wounds
on his body. This was the work of a sadist, and the pathologist's report indicates that it was the work of one man.
Not one of the wounds would have been likely to cause
death but Thomas Madden must have lost consciousness
frequently and been revived. Unlike Arthurs, his death
did not occur from a bullet wound but from gradual
strangulation from a slowly tightening noose. A woman in
the vicinity of Louisa Street later revealed that at 4.00A.M.
she heard a man screaming, 'Kill me, kill me.'

The body was dragged one hundred yards by the killers,
lifted to a height of six feet and thrown over a metal gate
into a shop doorway. The manner of Madden's demise
was similar to that of Arthurs and the wounds suggested
the use in each killing of a nine-inch double-bladed knife.
There was undoubtedly a lot of blood spilled in both
instances, and this was to become a feature of killings by
the Shankill Butchers, and particularly by Lenny Murphy.
It begs the question whether these two 'romperings' were
designed to extract information from the victim or simply
to provide sadistic pleasure for the murderers. There is
plenty of evidence to suggest that Lenny Murphy committed the crimes firstly for pleasure and secondly for information. The amount of time taken in torturing Madden
supports the thesis that his killing was for pleasure,
because he was stripped and almost every part of his body
was abused or cut with a knife. The nature of his wounds
and the obvious care taken to inflict them does not imply
a frenzied attack but, instead, a clinical act.

Four weeks after the death of Thomas Madden another

Catholic, fifty-year-old William Matthews, was found dead in the Glencairn Estate in a spot where Lenny Murphy was later to dump many of his victims. Matthews' body also bore the signs of torture and the use of a knife. Again, the character of the wounds indicated the hand which killed Arthurs and Madden.

Murphy's career in terror had certainly begun and it was soon to lead him into the hands of the police. On the evening of 28 September he set out on a murder mission with an accomplice, twenty-year-old Mervyn John Connor, who lived at Mayo Street not far from Murphy's home. They were travelling on a motorcycle with orders to kill a thirty-two-year-old Protestant, William Edward Pavis, who lived at Glenvarlock Street in the east of the city. Murphy was armed with a pistol and was under orders from the UVF leadership to carry out the hit personally. Pavis had been sent to prison a year earlier for illegally possessing firearms. It was not the offence which concerned the UVF but the fact that the person who appeared alongside him in court was a Roman Catholic priest, Father Eamon Corrigan. In court it was revealed that Pavis had taken a keen interest in firearms and was willing to handle them and sell them to anyone. He received a three-year sentence which was considered lenient because, though there was no evidence to connect him with paramilitary involvement, the guns he was willing to sell could have ended up in paramilitary hands. Father Corrigan, who had bought a shotgun from Pavis, was fined £20 for possessing an unlicensed weapon.

It was a strange case that unfolded in court, especially when one appreciates that Pavis, a flautist, not only played in an Orange band but also played in a Catholic hall, and went shooting with a Catholic priest. The unusual pact between the priest and Pavis had its origins in the 1960s and developed with their common interest in guns and game shooting. When it was revealed that Pavis had sold a shotgun to the priest, suspicions were aroused in the

UVF that perhaps he was also selling guns to the IRA. Unfortunately, after his trial, he was described in the press as an arms dealer, which he was not, but this description of him may well have sealed his fate. In prison, Pavis was threatened by UVF inmates, became depressed and was sent for treatment to Purdysburn Mental Institution on the outskirts of Belfast. There he was examined and treated with drugs. He was found to have an IQ of 150 but was said to be suffering from delusions that someone was going to kill him. The psychiatrist who treated him says that Pavis was not believed when he expressed this constant fear of assassination. Armed guards were eventually placed outside his private ward but this did not relieve his anxiety. Pavis knew what the psychiatrist did not know and the authorities did not suspect: that he should have been classified as a high-risk prisoner. In September 1972 he was released on parole and word was sent out immediately from Crumlin Road prison that he was on the outside. On the evening of 26 September, the day before Pavis was due to return to prison, Lenny Murphy arrived at his home and engaged his intended target in casual conversation during which he enquired whether Pavis had any guns for sale. Pavis assured Murphy that he did not and that he was returning to prison the following day. As the conversation drew to a close Murphy placed an arm round Pavis and accompanied him to the hallway of the house and finally to the doorstep. Murphy withdrew his arm and indicated that he was leaving but on good terms. As Pavis stood, hands by his side, Murphy pulled a pistol from inside his leather jacket and shot Pavis at close range before escaping with Connor on the motorcycle watched by several passers-by. They drove to the Glencairn housing estate, where they had stolen the bike earlier that day, and abandoned it.

Several months passed before the police picked up Murphy and his accomplice, during which time another motorcycle was stolen in the Glencairn estate and used in

the murder of a Catholic. While Murphy was content to
think he had escaped any connection with the Pavis killing,
detectives were busy encouraging the eye witnesses to
the shooting to cooperate in identifying Pavis's killers.
Eventually, both Murphy and Connor were arrested and
made available for an identification parade, where Murphy
demonstrated that his trips to Crumlin Road courthouse
did have a purpose. When the witnesses to the shooting
were asked to point out the killer, Murphy created a scene,
stepped out of the identification line-up and protested that
he had no wish to take part in the procedure. In effect,
he was preparing the groundwork for his defence by
attempting to make void the identification process. He
appreciated that any jury given the task of trying him would
be forced to consider whether the witnesses identified him
because they were sure he was the killer or because his
protest at the identification parade line-up made him the
most prominent person present. It was a clever ploy and
was recognized as such by a detective who was there and
who made the comment: 'We suddenly realized that we
had one cunning little bastard in our midst. I said to
myself, "We haven't seen the end of this guy." '

The police realized that in Murphy's case they would
have difficulty making the charge stick because he proved
impossible to break under interrogation. He refused to
answer questions put to him, would not make a statement
and simply told the police that they would have to prove
the charge. He added that it was unlikely to stick because
the witnesses had only pointed him out in the station
because of his behaviour. Mervyn Connor was a different
proposition and the police knew it. Initially, however, his
fear of Murphy prevented him telling the truth. While he
was in prison detectives decided it was worth presenting
Connor with a deal in return for his cooperation in convict-
ing Murphy since, of the two, Murphy was the one whose
cunning and cold method of killing indicated he was the
seasoned terrorist. Two detectives visited Connor in Jan-

uary 1973 in his prison cell with tight security provided
so that knowledge of their presence would not reach other
Loyalist paramilitary prisoners. But Crumlin Road Prison
was like a sieve and Murphy and other UVF men knew
about the police visit within twenty-four hours. Several
prison warders were under the control of the Loyalist
paramilitaries and whether they leaked information, due
to fear or blackmail, has to be a matter for speculation.
The police were aware of this problem but were unable
to counter it, short of removing Connor to a police station
for interview which would, in its own way, have had the
same effect. Connor agreed to give evidence against
Murphy in return for a lenient approach to his case by
the police but he also demanded that he be given special
attention to guarantee his security while he remained in
Crumlin Road Prison. The detectives spoke to the prison
governor and requested that Connor be treated as a high-
risk prisoner and that he be kept in a wing with ordinary
prisoners, well away from members of the UDA and UVF.
An assurance was given that two warders would guard
Connor round the clock, remaining outside his cell, and
that at meal times he would be closely scrutinized, but he
would have his meals with other prisoners. The rationale
for this decision was that if Connor did not eat with other
prisoners he would be virtually in solitary confinement
which could lead to a weakening of his resolve to testify
against Murphy.

At this time Crumlin Road Prison was a difficult place
in which to provide the kind of protection sometimes
necessary to keep a prisoner alive. An example of organizations going to amazing lengths to kill their enemies was
illustrated by the Provisionals in respect of a UVF man
named McKee, from the town of Larne in County Antrim.
A Provisional IRA prisoner ground a light bulb into
powder, put the substance in a bottle of orange juice and
replaced the cap perfectly. McKee was given the bottle of
juice, drank some and was rushed to the prison hospital

suffering from severe stomach cramps. He survived only because the powdered light bulb was a heavy substance which sank to the bottom of the bottle and thus McKee drank only a small quantity of ground glass. News of this attempt on McKee spread throughout the prison and one man who was impressed by the technique used by the Provos was Lenny Murphy.

He resolved to hatch a plan to kill his accomplice, Mervyn Connor, but he was faced not just with the security obstacle but also with the fact that even at mealtimes Connor was seated at a table surrounded by other prisoners. Murphy at this time was working in the prison hospital, well away from the wing which housed Connor. In the hospital Murphy had access to various medicines and, more disturbingly, substances such as cyanide. His first idea was that if he could only get to Connor during a meal break he could administer a dose of cyanide. The problem was getting close to him. Murphy's ruthlessness was soon displayed in a fashion which frightened even his own colleagues in the UVF: he decided that if he had to kill more than one person to get at Connor, he would do it. A course of action open to him was to poison some of the food served at the table where Connor always sat. This would result in the death of other prisoners at the table but this was of no concern to Murphy in his single-minded desire to murder Connor. During a lunchtime in the last week of March 1973 Murphy placed a large dose of cyanide in a pot of custard which was marked for serving at Connor's table. However, the poison changed the colour of the custard, which was then casually rejected by Connor and his fellow diners. The prison staff and the men at Connor's table were unaware of what had happened, and Murphy took great delight in telling this story after he left prison. However, this foiled plan did not dissuade him from his course of action and he set about developing another strategy.

On 24 April Murphy was given a pass by a member of

the prison staff at the hospital which allowed him to leave the hospital confines. He walked out of the wing in which he was housed and straight to the cell where Mervyn Connor was kept. In his pocket Murphy carried a quantity of cyanide, a pencil and a scrap of blank paper. The two warders whose job it was to guard Connor were some distance away watching television with other prisoners. Another prisoner witnessed Murphy with his hands tightly around Connor's throat while Connor was writing on a piece of paper. When Connor ceased writing, Murphy continued to hold him by the throat with his left hand and produced a phial from his pocket. He then poured a substance down Connor's throat and quickly left the cell. When the warders returned to the cell Connor was unconscious and was rushed to the prison hospital where attempts to revive him failed. He died the following morning.

Major Mullen, the prison's deputy governor, was incensed by the killing and decided that the seriousness of the matter warranted investigation by the police rather than by the prison authorities. Major Mullen was in no doubt as to who had committed the murder but he wanted some of his staff to be interviewed to establish whether there had been any collusion with Murphy. I can reveal that the police were contacted on three occasions and, to Major Mullen's surprise and consternation, made no effort to visit the prison. When they turned up eventually they conducted a cursory examination of Connor's cell and loosely interviewed one or two members of the prison staff. A report on the matter was produced which was forwarded to the prison authorities for scrutiny. When Major Mullen read it he was appalled by the lack of content and was convinced it was a blatant attempt to dismiss the issue by failing to reach any conclusions or suggest a course of action. Major Mullen, who died in 1986, was regarded by all who knew him as an honest and prudent man, someone who did not believe in obscuring the inadequacies of his own regime even if this produced an unfavourable public profile for the prison.

In this instance he decided to conduct his own enquiry to discover if members of his staff assisted Murphy in committing a murder. He interviewed the member of staff from the hospital who had given Murphy the pass and the two warders who should have been guarding Connor at the time of his death. He also spoke to Murphy, who dismissed as nonsense the contention that he was the only person with the motivation to kill Connor and the only prisoner with access to the cyanide which killed him. Major Mullen produced a report which he insisted be attached to the police file. The police file has disappeared and during the writing of this book I made repeated attempts to ask someone to clarify the reasons for the disappearance, since it would seem to any right-thinking person that an unsolved murder of this nature and the questions it raised should at least have been recorded somewhere. Those policemen who assisted with many of my enquiries for the writing of this book, in particular Superintendent Jimmy Nesbitt, made repeated attempts to trace some documentation of this episode, but without success. It also seems strange that a report by someone as senior as the late Major Mullen, and which I have been told was critical of the investigating officers assigned to the enquiry, should not be available for scrutiny. I know it exists but I was refused access to it despite several requests made to the prison authorities.

In the Connor enquiry serious questions required answers. How, in a prison that housed so many high-risk prisoners, was Murphy capable of strolling about freely? Why was he allowed to leave the prison hospital? Why were the two warders assigned to protect Connor watching television at the time of the murder? The prisoner who watched Murphy administering the cyanide dose spoke privately to Major Mullen but died later as a result of being battered against a cell wall. The fact that Connor's

murder was not satisfactorily resolved by the police led
Murphy to believe he was invincible. The episode also
increased his standing within the UVF and brought about
a situation in which people were terrified of him because
they knew that he would eliminate anyone willing to give
evidence against him and that, if he so wished, he could
take such steps even within the confines of a top-security
prison and get away with it. I believe that because this
enquiry was treated, in the opinion of Major Mullen, in
such an irresponsible manner, such laxity became a crucial
factor in the development of Murphy as the biggest mass
murderer in British criminal history. From the moment
he killed Connor, Murphy believed that he could act outside the law and that he had the resources to evade detection and, ultimately, prosecution.

The killing of Mervyn Connor was a salutary lesson for
others in the UVF who came to believe that Murphy was
always out of control and that for this reason, and his
potential for frightening retaliation, he was best left to his
own devices. An illustration of the fear he instilled in
others, and which relates directly to the fact that he would
have been willing to cause the death of eleven other men
to exact revenge on Connor, can be seen in the words of
one of Murphy's UVF leaders who told a detective:
'Murphy doesn't frighten me but it is what he could do
to my wife and kids if I crossed him and didn't dispose
of him quickly.'

An interesting dimension to the Pavis/Connor affair is
that before Murphy killed Connor he forced him to write
a confession exonerating Murphy of the murder of Pavis.
One can only speculate that when the police realized they
had lost their witness and that Murphy appeared to have
a more than even chance of beating the murder charge
they lost interest in the whole business. If such was the
case, then it was a serious error of judgment to allow
Murphy to go unchallenged and to fail to seek the necessary evidence to charge him with the unlawful killing of his

accomplice. A corollary to the missing file element is that one of the police officers placed in charge of conducting the enquiry in the prison was later connected with files which went missing in relation to the enquiry into the homosexual abuse of young boys at the Kincora Home in Belfast.

Aside from the killing, Murphy's time spent in prison was eventful in other respects: he was twice caught attempting to escape. Escapes were always being planned in the prison but mostly by Provisional IRA men who used cunning and inventiveness in producing imitation guns fashioned from bars of soap which were then coloured black with shoe polish. Murphy believed he could upstage these tactics by simply impersonating someone and walking free. It was a bold move considering the man's notoriety, and it almost succeeded.

At the beginning of the last week of January 1973 Murphy learned that a petty thief was completing his sentence and was due for release at 6.15P.M. on 30 January. In his inimitable style Murphy persuaded the man to accept that it was he, Murphy, who would be leaving in his place and that it would be advisable not to contest this. Murphy arranged to exchange clothes with the other prisoner half an hour before his release. With his usual eye for detail he spotted a range of tattoos on the man's arms which might well be used to identify him on leaving the front gate of the prison. The other prisoner was much the same size and build as Lenny Murphy, so if a distinguishing characteristic were to be sought by a guard it might well be a scar or a tattoo. Murphy arranged to meet the prisoner several days later to enable him to study the tattoos and have them copied onto his right arm with pen and ink on the day of the escape. At 6.15P.M. on 30 January Murphy, carrying the other prisoner's belongings and dressed in his clothes, walked through the prison and reached the front gate. An observant guard asked to check for a tattoo which was listed as being on the prisoner's arm. As Murphy rolled back his jacket and shirt sleeves the newly drawn 'tattoo' became smudged and Murphy was returned to his cell. Ten days later Prison Officer Desmond Ball saw Murphy climbing out of his cell window using a rope made of blankets. Ball challenged him and Murphy climbed back in. This escape attempt was not as ingenious as the first since, had Murphy reached the ground, he would have found himself in the prison yard, from where escape would have proved exceedingly difficult. A detective who interviewed Murphy in relation to this offence said that Murphy treated the matter as a joke. It was his impression that the escape attempt was made to enhance Lenny's reputation rather than because of any expectation of success.

On 18 June Murphy was marched through the underground tunnel which links the prison to Crumlin Road courthouse to stand trial for the murder of Pavis. Witnesses for the Crown told the jury that Murphy was the man they saw shoot Pavis. As this evidence was being given Murphy sat motionless in the dock, his face devoid of emotion. Murphy's defence was that he had never met Pavis and was somewhere else on the night of the murder, but the precise details of that 'somewhere' were lost to his memory. He suggested that he could possibly have been working on a car with a friend but could not say for sure that this was so. His lack of knowledge of his whereabouts on the night of the crime would in any other court, taking into account the eyewitness evidence against him, have convinced the jury of his guilt but the crucial factor for the jury in this case was the identification parade. As Murphy had shrewdly reckoned, this was described as central to the jury reaching a verdict. The trial was over within two days and Murphy was told he could walk free from the courthouse. Unknown to him, however, it had been decided that he should be re-arrested and held in detention under the Northern Ireland Special Powers Act. The arresting officers were waiting for him in the foyer of the courthouse and returned him immediately to Crumlin Road Prison. Murphy was returned to court on two subsequent occasions during the following six months to face charges of attempting to escape from lawful custody, and he received sentences totalling three years' imprisonment. The Crown Case against Murphy was weak. Connor was dead and the Crown did not seek to use a written statement made by him because Murphy would have been in a position to discredit it by referring to the note Connor wrote before he died. As a result the story of Connor's untimely death and his final confession remained a mystery.

In the second week of February 1974 he was moved from Crumlin Road Prison to what was then called Long Kesh and is now the Maze Prison outside Belfast. Long Kesh housed Republican and Loyalist internees who lived in compounds, separated from each other. The compounds were run on military lines by the leaders of the respective paramilitary organizations. Prisoners were obliged to undertake military drill every day, to salute their officers and to attend political and military lectures. The atmosphere was very much like that portrayed in movies about prisoner of war camps. The commander in charge of the UVF compound was Gusty Spence. He insisted on strict military discipline, personally drilled his men and did not tolerate breaches of the rules. At the time Murphy arrived in the camp so did many other young men and boys. Spence recalls a boy arriving still wearing his school blazer. He had been found guilty of shooting two people in the head.

Murphy disliked the atmosphere in the camp. Whereas Crumlin Road Prison had been relaxed and Murphy had had the adulation of other prisoners, Spence regarded him as another volunteer who should obey the rules. Spence has since remarked that many of the young men who were sent to his compound were gun fanatics who regarded themselves as terrorists and not soldiers, as Spence preferred to describe members of the UVF. He says: 'The job of the older ones like myself was to win them away from the gun, to make them think politically and positively. They just wanted to see themselves as terrorists and heroes yet those of us who had been in there for a long time didn't talk like that. In fact, if anybody boasted of what they had done it caused deep embarrassment.'

Murphy was not prepared for the rigorous routine in the camp: chores such as washing out the huts, cleaning the lavatories and the parade ground, or sitting on the roof of a hut to receive coded messages from other compounds. Such routines did not appeal to Murphy who preferred the relaxed lifestyle of Crumlin Road and the simple tasks in the prison hospital. More noticeably, Murphy soon showed that what he detested most of all was having to recognize the authority of others, and particularly those holding a higher rank than himself within the organization. The pattern of surrounding himself with a group of young admirers soon re-emerged. He would impress them with stories of his exploits in Crumlin Road Prison. Within the group was Robert 'the Basher' Bates, who was serving a sentence for a firearms offence. Within a short space of time Murphy found himself in serious conflict with authority following an incident in the UVF's Compound 12. The incident occurred when Murphy and Bates were asked by a UVF officer to undertake a task. They refused, and after a confrontation they gave the officer a severe beating. The penalty for such an offence was that a prisoner would be thrown out of the organization's compound and would have to seek accommodation in a compound run by another grouping. This punishment was considered by Spence and other leaders to be the equivalent of a court martial. Bates and Murphy were found guilty but the sentence was revoked due to the intervention of the Red Hand Commando leader, John McKeague.

A leading UVF man of the period has told me that his first impression of Murphy in Long Kesh was that he was a 'Billy the Kid' figure who was treacherous to the point that he was regarded as a 'back-shooter'.

In October 1974 Murphy was disciplined again for misbehaving after 'lights-out' in his hut. He was given additional chores for several days. He was also frequently reprimanded for refusing to rise to his feet when senior officers entered the room but this type of behaviour was dealt with simply by public reprimands. However, a serious reprimand was administered after the prison hospital was ransacked during a major disturbance in the camp.

Not only was Murphy involved in wrecking the hospital but he also removed a large selection of drugs, similar to amphetamines, to his own hut. A senior UVF officer came across Murphy as he was literally grading the drugs and demanded to know why he had them in his possession. Murphy replied that 'they might come in handy'. He was ordered to get rid of the tablets but refused. Eventually a 'Regimental Sergeant Major' was sent for and instructed to supervise Murphy in flushing the drugs down a toilet. Murphy, as we know, had an intimate knowledge of drugs as a result of his work at Crumlin Road Prison hospital, and it is possible that he had experimented with tablets during his time there.

Bates was also in trouble with his superiors over his refusal to undertake the duty of sitting on hut roofs for the purpose of receiving messages. This method of communication was used by the UVF to relay information to other Loyalist paramilitary groups, but also to the two IRA factions in the camp. Messages between the sworn enemies consisted often of no more than pieces of news from someone who had been granted the privilege of a visit to the outside world, or expressions of solidarity in relation to demands for better treatment or privileges in the camp. When Bates refused to take his turn at this game he was told bluntly that he would either get onto the roof or would be bodily removed from the compound. Not relishing the threatened punishment, he capitulated.

During political lectures when Spence and others talked of the moral stamp of approval necessary for a war, Murphy disregarded them. He was intoxicated with his youth, his power and with the status afforded by the use of a gun. He detested the lectures and the democratic socialist thinking which was beginning to creep into the rhetoric of the leadership. Attempts to examine the nature of the conflict in society, and the political solutions which might be sought, were of no interest to him.

The British Government was aware of the politicization which was going on within Long Kesh and the Secretary of State for Northern Ireland lifted the ban on the UVF and Sinn Fein to allow them to work towards a political dialogue. Much of the impetus for this sort of move emanated from the lobbying of clergymen on both sides of the religious divide. On the outside, the paramilitaries began setting up welfare offices and advice centres with a degree of government funding. It may have been a novel move by the Secretary of State for Northern Ireland, Merlyn Rees, but, like many of his decisions in relation to the paramilitaries, it proved to be naive.

In 1975, before Murphy was due for release there was a development which until now has never been revealed and which resulted in talks between the paramilitary leaders on both sides within Long Kesh. The leaders of the Loyalist and Republican groupings in the camp were becoming increasingly aware that they no longer held sway over events on the outside. Younger men who wished to do things their own way had taken over and they wanted no interference or advice from senior figures in Long Kesh. What worried Spence and those Republican leaders in the Kesh was that the sectarian war was getting out of hand. To understand the curious morality of this concern one must acknowledge that these men regarded themselves as soldiers fighting a war in which there had to exist some sense of honour. As a result of exchanges between the various compounds a coded message was sent to the

41

British Government requesting that the IRA and Loyalist paramilitaries be allowed to set up a conference in Long Kesh to resolve the sectarian war being waged outside. Such a conference, it was suggested, would also require the participation of paramilitary figures from outside the prison who were familiar with events currently taking place. Rees consulted the Governor of Long Kesh and agreed to a conference but stipulated that it should be held in secret within the prison. He also consented to the participation of others, provided they were not people wanted for crimes. The conference was given the title 'The Anti-Sectarian Assassination Conference'. Two members of each of the major paramilitary groups – the UVF, UDA, Official and Provisional IRA – plus one Catholic and one Protestant clergyman were invited to attend the first meeting. Half the delegates were paramilitary members from outside the camp. When discussion began, Loyalists suggested that in return for an end to the killing of Catholic non-combatants, the IRA should cease killing off-duty policemen and soldiers particularly members of the Ulster Defence Regiment which had been set up as a replacement of the 'B' Specials in 1970 as an integrated force of Catholics and Protestants to act in support of the British Army but had soon become a force populated mainly by Protestants because Catholics were under threat of death from the IRA for being members of such a body. Catholic members were easily identified to the IRA which lived within the Catholic Community. The Provos insisted they should retain the right to kill police and members of the UDR when they were on the streets wearing uniform. There was no dissent from this proposition. Likewise, each of the groups retained the right to shoot members of each other's organizations while the war continued.

Only one voice at the meeting failed to see the significance of any agreement with the IRA and it was that of Sam Smyth, a leading member of the UDA who was invited into the prison for the conference. He said that as far as he was concerned a three-year-old child or a seventy-year-old woman belonging to the Catholic community was a legitimate target. He was reprimanded swiftly by the UDA leader, Jim Craig from West Belfast, who was sitting alongside him and ordered him to keep his views to himself. Everyone present knew that the reference to women and children was enough to sign the speaker's death warrant. Three weeks later Smyth was assassinated by the Provisional IRA.

News of the conference has never until now been leaked to the media or the general public. Murphy was distinctly unhappy with the agreed arrangement between the paramilitaries. He was due for release within a month of the agreement and was anxious to get back into action. He had his own ideas on the way forward and made them known when he was released from Long Kesh on 13 May 1975.

3

A Killer Squad is Formed

The year 1975 brought considerable change to the UVF which, in turn, provided an atmosphere perfectly suited to the values and terrorist talents of Murphy and young men of his age, who believed that indiscriminate terror was the means by which they could exact revenge and change the situation. The only problem was that they had a leadership who, languishing in prison, were no longer in a position to control events. Since the dark days of the summer of 1972 Spence had sought to give the UVF a new political direction. The change in his own political attitudes was due in part to his attempts to read Irish history while in prison. He once recalled that when he first asked for an Irish history book the prison governor was so shocked that he enquired as to the reasons for such a request. The book, ironically, was Dan Breen's *My Fight for Irish Freedom*. Spence thus began a period of self-education, though he was quick to recognize that Dan Breen was 'good at kicking the truth about'. Spence also established contact with members of the Official IRA inside Long Kesh, and their political thinking which was developing along Marxist lines left an impression on him and led him to formulate a socialist policy for his own organization. It encouraged him in the view that the gun was not the only way to resolve the tribal warfare within his own society. At one stage he condemned sectarian killings from his prison cell and ordered that they cease forthwith. Spence's growing awareness of his working-class roots and how they reflected those problems which were germane to both communities is evidenced in this letter which was smuggled from his prison cell:

> One has only to look at the Shankill Road, the heart of the empire that lies torn and bleeding. We have known squalor. I was born and reared in it. No one knows better than we do the meaning of slums, the meaning of deprivation, the meaning of suffering for what one believes in, whatever the ideology. Insofar as people speak of fifty years of misrule, I wouldn't disagree with that. What I would say is that we have suffered every bit as much as the people of the Falls Road, or any other underprivileged quarter and in many cases more so.

This growing political dynamic within the UVF was resented by the younger element, who saw it as a capitulation to a left-wing philosophy shared by the enemy. The younger men believed that the leaders of the organization were becoming soft and that fine words would change nothing. They were scathing about Spence's view of a settlement based on working-class solidarity. They were also uninterested in the public statements and workings of the UVF's political wing, the Ulster Volunteer Party. This party had been set up in 1974 after Merlyn Rees lifted the legal ban on the UVF, in order to allow it to develop politically, much in the manner of the Provisional Sinn Fein. By the middle of 1975 Spence was well aware of the growing disenchantment within the ranks of the younger volunteers like Murphy, who had joined the UVF not for a political education but to lay their hands on guns. The UVF magazine *Combat* began warning its members to prepare for an autumn and winter offensive, saying that intelligence indicated that the Provisionals were about to launch a new campaign with weapons which they had been given by Third World and Soviet bloc countries. The magazine also made it clear that members of the security forces, including the police, were pleased with killings carried out by the UVF:

Our own intelligence sources together with those of the security forces indicate that we and other Loyalist groupings have restricted attacks to known Republican activists. Many of our contacts with CHARLIE and DELTA RUC Divisions have reported that the vast majority of grassroots constables, together with several Special Branch and CID personnel, were overjoyed at the result of our operations in recent times. As one constable put it, 'If the paramilitaries had concentrated on known Republicans years ago the war would have been won in 1972.'

Those in the UVF who were about to launch a new offensive took on the role of explaining, in advance, the logic behind their proposed actions:

We in the UVF hold that war is a relic of physical-force Republicanism and so long as Republicans, be they papists or socialists, are permitted to band themselves together for the purpose of seeking a physical force solution, then the Protestants of Ulster cannot hope to escape the horrors of war. And we further hold that the lust for Republican socialism or popish nationalism on the part of our enemies is so deeply rooted in the nature and instinct that nothing less than superior force will ever induce them to abandon their assaults upon the lives and liberties of the Ulster Protestants.

These thoughts represented an attitude which was much at variance with the views of Spence and his leadership, and this was further highlighted by the implicit reference to Spence in the following paragraph from *Combat*:

Having realized that we are in a war situation and that we have been forced, as a result of political compromise and treason, to engage ourselves in a war effort against our enemies, it must also be realized that the talk of humane methods of warfare and the rule of civilized warfare and all such homage to the sentiments of mankind are hypocritical and unreal and are only intended for the consumption of stay-at-home armchair generals. There are no humane methods of warfare, there is no such thing as civilized warfare; all warfare is inhuman, all warfare is

barbaric; the first blast of the bugles of war sounds for the
time being the funeral knell of human progress.

This was ironically the sort of hard talking that Lenny
Murphy and his kind were pleased to hear and not the
talk of democratic socialism or of working-class solidarity
emanating from the old men of the Spence leadership.
The young turks found justification for their terror policy
after an attempt at politicizing the UVF failed when the
Volunteer Party's candidate in the October 1974 election
polled only 2,600 votes in West Belfast. They were also
able to point to the IRA ceasefire of February 1975 which
was initiated after the Provisionals attended talks with
leading Catholic and Protestant clergymen. Such a ceasefire once again appeared to indicate the hand of British
ministers at Stormont Castle. In fact, it was believed within
the ranks of the Provisionals that following the failure of
the power-sharing executive at Stormont in the summer
of 1974, the British were prepared to consider withdrawal
from Northern Ireland and that a ceasefire would allow
them time to explore that possibility. This was a further
sign to the younger members of the UVF that Ulster was
in danger of being sold out. A casual observer might well
have thought that with the constant political blundering
and insensitivity of Merlyn Rees, together with the seem-
ing bankruptcy of British politicizing in Northern Ireland,
the Provos were right in their view that the British lacked
the political will to stay. Within the UVF there was certainly a fear that a sell-out was a distinct possibility.

Lenny Murphy's return to the Shankill Road and his
traditional stomping grounds of North and West Belfast
was greeted with satisfaction by many young men who
needed somebody to lead them in a new campaign.
Murphy decided to set up his own unit which would be
solely under his control and not that of the UVF Brigade
Staff in West Belfast. During the first month of his freedom he spent much of his time in the Brown Bear pub

on the Shankill Road, which he established as a headquarters and meeting place. In the same area he found
himself faced with a competing unit which operated from
the Windsor Bar and was run by a man of Murphy's
generation: Anthony 'Chuck' Berry. 'Basher' Bates was
also now on the outside and soon renewed his acquaint-
ance with Murphy, assuming a subservient role. Murphy
knew he needed more recruits in his team if he were to
have sufficient power to operate independently of the UVF
leadership. He reckoned he required fifteen or twenty, of
whom three or four would form an inner circle. A team
of twenty would offer him protection not only from the
orders of the leadership but also from 'Chuck' Berry's
Windsor Bar team. Murphy was fortunate in having alongside him two personal friends who were able to give him
a picture of the structure of the UVF in the Shankill area,
how it had changed while he was in prison, and who was
available for recruitment. Two men were to be his constant
support and his eyes and ears. They cannot be named
here for legal reasons and will subsequently be referred
to throughout this book as Mr A. and Mr B.

Mr A. and Mr B. were several years older than Lenny
and had remained closely in touch with him since his
school days. Mr A. was a cold, astute and ruthless character who did not have the flamboyance of Lenny, but one
thing they did have in common was a deep hatred of
Catholics and a desire to carry out a war of attrition. Mr
B. was two years older than Lenny and though not as
prominent a figure as Mr A., he also detested the other
community to the extent that he was willing to do whatever
Lenny asked of him. Mr A. and Mr B. were to be his
closest associates. Three others were chosen to form the
inner circle of the unit. These three other 'lieutenants'
had the distinction of also being well known to Murphy:
Bates and McAllister, who regarded Lenny as a hero, and
a third man, twenty-six-year-old William Moore, from 88
West Circular Road in Belfast. Moore was not well known

to the authorities, like Bates and McAllister, but he did have a criminal record dating back to 1966. However, his list of crimes was not comparable to that of the other two. Moore was a 'dark horse'; someone who possessed unknown potential and was not easily identifiable as a member of an illegal organization. This was considered a plus by Murphy who recruited him after a chance meeting in the Brown Bear pub. Moore knew of Lenny's past and was impressed by the way he gave orders and stood at the bar with a 9mm pistol in his waistband. Moore lived with his widowed mother to whom he was devoted, and was regarded by neighbours as a quiet, unassuming fellow. When he met Murphy in 1975 he was in the process of changing jobs and had acquired a black taxi of the type used in London. His previous job had been as a meat packer in Woodvale Meats on the Shankill Road. There he had had the good fortune to form a relationship with the daughter of the boss. It was she who had provided the money for the taxi, thus enabling him to leave his lowly position in the meat plant. Moore had been unhappy there and would have preferred carving the carcasses to packaging. He asked someone in the carving room to teach him how to use a knife to slice the flesh from the bone. Before he left the meat plant he stole several well-honed knives and a meat cleaver, which he kept at home as a souvenir of his time there.

Ownership of a taxi allowed him to become a member of the Shankill Taxi Association, and it is worth examining at this point the use of the London-type cabs known in Belfast as 'black taxis'. In the early seventies when street rioting was rife in Nationalist areas of Belfast and in particular on the Falls Road, rioters invariably hijacked buses and burned them to provide barricades and also to express distaste for the Belfast Corporation which owned and ran the City's bus service. Bus services were often withdrawn for days after rioting and many busmen were understandably reluctant to drive vehicles into the Falls area.

Not entirely for humanitarian reasons, the IRA decided to provide its own transport service called 'people's taxis'.

Essentially, the service was a racket, in that it was a clever means by which the IRA was able to establish on the one hand a 'no-go' area for buses and on the other provide a service which could be used to raise funds for weapons. Within months hundreds of black taxis were operating throughout Catholic West Belfast and each driver was paying a weekly levy to the IRA. Each time the illegality of the taxis was raised the Provisionals burned more buses which, in turn, resulted in an outcry for a transport service. Eventually British politicians at the Northern Ireland office decided for the sake of expediency and to prevent further burning of buses to allow the black taxi service to continue to operate freely. In time it became a legally bona fide service. The UVF decided to form a similar service that 'would be under the auspices of the Ulster Volunteer Force which has a public conscience and duty to the working people'. Thus, William Moore, taxi driver, was soon working under the 'auspices of the UVF'.

While forming his unit Murphy kept a low profile, as did Mr A. and Mr B., McAllister and Bates were the only members of the unit seen on the streets. Moore was rarely seen in their company. He plied his trade as a taxi driver and, when required, attended meetings in the Brown Bear pub. Murphy's low profile was maintained, with one exception. He assaulted a young Catholic in a late-night affray in a hamburger bar known as Ken's, not far from Belfast city centre. It happened a month after Murphy's release from prison when he enquired as to the religious persuasion of twenty-two-year-old John Paul Donnelly who was unlucky enough to find himself standing beside Murphy while ordering food. Even in public Murphy could not restrain himself from hounding Catholics. He and some of his cronies set upon Donnelly and left him badly beaten. On this occasion Lenny narrowly escaped being apprehended by the police. It was fortunate for

Donnelly that Ken's was close to the city centre and there were plenty of late-night revellers to witness the incident and prevent more serious physical damage.

By September 1975 Murphy had recruited types who would allow him to establish his dominance and thus assume a comparable role to that of 'Chuck' Berry of the Windsor Bar unit. Additionally, it would place him beyond the control of the UVF Brigade Staff. This autonomy, however, meant that he did not have access to the UVF's store of weapons. There were now twenty men under his command and a pattern was established for meetings in a room above the Brown Bear. The meetings were chaired by Lenny and his constant companion, Mr A. Some members of the unit were earmarked by Lenny and Mr A. for operational purposes. Their names are worth mentioning at this stage to illustrate the type of people with which Murphy surrounded himself. There was twenty-two-year-old Arthur Armstrong McClay who worked as a plasterer and who committed his first crime at the age of thirteen when he placed explosives in a letter box. He was not known to the police as someone involved in illegal activities until the time the butchers were caught. Another member of the team was twenty-four-year-old carpet salesman Benjamin Edwards, a flamboyant character with a taste for flashy clothes which earned him the nickname 'Pretty Boy' Edwards. He was a petty criminal. One member who did not immediately fit the pattern was a young man of Murphy's age, Norman Waugh. Waugh spent most of his teenage years delivering papers in the Shankill district and was well known. He was regarded as a reticent loner. He had a slight speech defect which made him self-conscious and his features suggested low intelligence, so that people in the district regarded him as 'not right in the head'. Waugh, the loner, found solace, acceptance and a new status by becoming involved with the Brown Bear unit and being seen in the company of hard men. Those who would previously have viewed him as a figure of fun began to

51

treat him with respect and caution. The eldest member of the team was thirty-one-year-old Edward Leckey, a shop manager from Battenburg Street off the Shankill Road. His life of crime began at the age of fifteen when he was found guilty of larceny and housebreaking. A year later he was again before the Juvenile Court admitting to nineteen charges of housebreaking and theft. His propensity for crime eventually led him into borstal training but it was only when under the control of Lenny Murphy that he became known to the police for UVF activities. Another dark horse in the group was twenty-two-year-old David John Bell from Cupar Street, the location for many sectarian confrontations of the early seventies.

There were two other misfits earmarked for special attention by Murphy and Mr A. They had all the necessary characteristics: a hatred of Catholics, a history of crime, and a malleable personality. The first was Edward McIlwaine, who lived at Forthriver Crescent in the Glencairn estate where Murphy created his own dumping ground for bodies. Twenty-two-year-old McIlwaine was a waster who found it difficult to settle in any job. He was a part-time member of the Ulster Defence Regiment, and confided to an associate that his motive for joining the UDR was to fight the IRA, though the more likely explanation was that he needed money plus the social status UDR membership accorded him. The youngest member of the Brown Bear team was William John Townsley who, though only fourteen, was a tough, mature individual. He was to prove a hard nut to crack in later interviews by the police.

By the end of September 1975 Murphy and Mr A. had put the unit together and believed the time was ripe to begin their own war irrespective of UVF policy. At that time the leadership of the UVF in the Maze believed that the pact with other groupings, which had temporarily broken down, should be reactivated, but in *Combat* magazine that month someone writing under the pseudonym

'Activist' expressed the thinking in circles frequented by Murphy and his gang:

> *Assassination:* A few illustrations will suffice to drive home these points. One concerns the public outcry over alleged sectarian assassinations. It is alleged by both Loyalist and Republican politicians that both the IRA and the UVF have been engaged in senseless sectarian murder campaigns. They say that the premeditated murder of another person, albeit an enemy soldier, shows a callous disregard for human life. They say that the assassination of a British soldier or an IRA activist is against the rules of civilized and humane warfare. The very same people will, however, calmly call for more soldiers and better equipment to wipe out the terrorists. They will call for the reintroduction of the death penalty for traitors and gunmen and calmly sit down by the trap door as it calmly swings open and sends another soul out into eternity. Now, I ask you what is the difference between the UVF Volunteer's bullet and the British soldier's bullet? What is the difference between a UVF man shooting a traitor or a gunman and the prospect of an executioner sitting in Crumlin Road Gaol hanging his victims by the neck until dead? Is the victim of the UVF man any deader than the victim of the British soldier? Is the victim of the hangman any deader than the victim of the gunman? There is no difference whatsoever when a gun is fired or a trapdoor opens, a life is lost and no amount of emotional ravings about the method of execution will change the verdict for the victim. War brings death and destruction and those who originate a war situation, be they politicians or gunmen, must be prepared to accept the fact that there is no humane or civilized way in which to fight that war.

It was emphasized later in the article that no UVF volunteer took pride in 'blasting several of his fellow human beings into eternity' but facts had to be faced: 'We must fight fire with fire, bomb for bomb, bullet for bullet,' argued the writer. The magazine also issued a warning to journalists, in particular to the Northern editor of the *Irish*

Times, David McKittrick, who was instructed to temper his comments about the UVF. It accused him of giving the IRA the names of new members of the organization's Brigade Staff by printing those names in his newspaper, and it threatened that if any of the people named met harm directly or indirectly McKittrick would be 'treated accordingly'. McKittrick, a fine investigative journalist, was aware in the autumn of 1975 that, in his words, a 'blood-thirsty' leadership had taken control of the UVF which was planning a new terror campaign.

The Brigade Staff called for a 'Big Push' for the beginning of October to give notice of their intentions. They were willing to risk such action even in the knowledge that it could lead to a renewal of the ban on the UVF which had been lifted in 1974. The organization preferred to demonstrate a return to traditional terrorist methods though this would force them underground.

Lenny Murphy received orders to plan 'something' for 2 October. The go-ahead was sufficient and he was determined to select his own targets irrespective of plans being drawn up by the leadership. In the last week of September he told his unit that he had chosen his target. It was to be Casey's Wholesale Wine and Spirits establishment in the Millfield area, between the lower Shankill and Falls on the edge of Belfast city centre. He chose Moore for his driver but assured him that his own taxi would not be used in the operation: a van was to be hijacked on the relevant day. Lenny said that he would lead the operation while two other members – twenty-one-year-old William Arlow Green and his nineteen-year-old brother, Thomas Noel Green – would be used as back-up. Murphy told them all that the motive was robbery. Three members of this special operations unit were detailed to watch the premises for several days to determine how to enter without attracting too much attention. Thomas Noel Green, a van driver, was told not to report for work on the morning of 2 October. He was to meet Murphy, Moore and William Green at Mr A.'s house off the Shankill Road.

When Murphy and the selected members of his unit met at 8.00A.M. on 2 October Lenny outlined his plan and told them that a van was at that moment being hijacked in North Belfast for the robbery and the owner would be held until the job was completed. Murphy produced a .45 pistol which he said was for his own use, then handed a .22 pistol to William Arlow Green and a .38 revolver to Moore. The plan was simple in that the spirits store opened early for business and was entered via a gateway which, when opened, would allow the hijacked van to be hidden in the premises until the robbery was completed. Murphy said that if there was trouble the guns would 'come in handy' but entry was to be achieved with the least possible effort. The van would be driven into the premises and a member of the team would close the gate behind them. William Arlow Green would tell the staff that he was there for a drinks order. Murphy and the others would then rush out of the van, usher the staff upstairs and demand money.

Four people were employed in Casey's: two married sisters, Frances Donnelly aged thirty-five and forty-seven-year-old Marie McGrattan, and two eighteen-year-olds, Gerard Grogan and Thomas Osborne. All were Catholics. Casey's was owned by a Catholic family and the premises were situated close to the Falls Road; all factors indicating the religious affiliation of the staff. Grogan and Osborne were helpers, selecting and loading drinks orders, while the two sisters conducted business directly with customers. At 10.00A.M. Murphy and his three associates left Mr A.'s house, got into a hijacked van and headed for Millfield with Thomas Noel Green in the driving seat. In the rear and out of sight lay Murphy, Moore and William Green. Within five minutes the van had reached Casey's and when it came to a halt Moore got out using the rear doors. He opened the gateway to allow the van in and then closed the gateway to the premises, screening off the vehicle from the roadway. Marie McGrattan was the first person to see the UVF men and asked if they were there for a drinks order. While she was chatting to Moore, Murphy and William Green eased themselves out of the vehicle and Murphy handed her a bogus order for spirits which was crudely written on a scrap of paper. Grogan, hearing the sound of voices, appeared in the yard and stood watching the four men who were facing Marie McGrattan. She suggested that her prospective customers accompany her to an upstairs office and walked ahead towards a staircase. She was followed by William Green and Murphy, who, before ascending the staircase, motioned to Moore to look after Grogan. Noel Green remained alongside the van to facilitate a quick getaway. The events of the fifteen minutes which followed illustrated Murphy's potential for barbarity. While Murphy made his way to the office, Moore chatted to the two young men in the downstairs storeroom, asking them their names and where they lived. Once inside the upstairs office, Murphy and William Green drew their guns. Marie McGrattan and her sister raised their hands and Murphy demanded to know the whereabouts of the office takings. Marie replied that there was no money on the premises because it was too early in the day to attract custom. Murphy became threatening and asked their names, which they gave. He demanded money again, and again was told there was none. At this point he told Green to keep the women covered with his .22 pistol while he searched the office. The search produced nothing and in fury Murphy told the two sisters to get down on their hands and knees on the office floor. He stood over Marie McGrattan, pointed his .45 Colt semi-automatic at her head and indicated to Green to do likewise to Frances Donnelly. Murphy then shot Marie through the back of the head and Green fired his pistol into the head of Frances. Before leaving the office Murphy ripped out the telephone, took the lock off the door and closed it tightly from the outside. As William Green made for the van, Murphy headed for the storeroom. On hearing the shooting, Grogan and Osborne panicked but were restrained by Moore who produced a gun from inside his jacket. Murphy was at Moore's side within thirty seconds and quickly enquired the religion of the two eighteen-year-olds in front of him. Immediately on hearing they were Catholics, he shot them both. The four UVF men got into the van and drove back to the Shankill area where the hijacked vehicle was set alight to eliminate fingerprints. The guns used in the operation were handed over to Mr A. for safekeeping.

At Casey's Thomas Osborne staggered to his feet with blood spurting from a bullet wound in his neck. He made it to the roadway at Millfield where he stopped a passing car which rushed him to hospital. He was to die three weeks later when an operation was performed to remove a blood clot caused by his wound. Before police were alerted to go to the premises Marie McGrattan's husband was on his way there to pick up a cash float which his wife had collected from the bank. The cash was intended for Casey's and for the McGrattan bar, The Brown Horse. When he arrived at Millfield there was no one to be seen in Casey's yard so he walked into the store where he found Grogan lying dead. He rushed to the upstairs office and, with the assistance of a police constable who had just arrived on the scene, broke down the door. A sickening sight met his eyes. His sister-in-law lay dead in the middle of the room and his wife lay dead behind the door, where she had crawled after she was shot. The money which Marie had told Lenny Murphy didn't exist was safely hidden in her car in the yard.

Noel and William Green were apprehended by the police and questioned about the Casey shootings but they refused to reveal the participation of Lenny Murphy or William Moore and, until now, the role played by them has not been known. The first to be arrested was William

Green, who broke down under questioning but lied about the part he had played in the murders. He didn't mention in detail the other players in the drama and stressed constantly that the killings were not planned as part of the operation; instead he claimed the motive was robbery. He told of Marie McGrattan being shot and added: 'The other fellow turned to the woman and I heard a shot. With the sound of the shot my gun went off and I saw blood spurting just in front of the young, black-haired woman.' He had the audacity to tell the police that the whole matter sickened him and he couldn't sleep for weeks. Nothing was further from the truth and the police knew it.

I obtained a copy of a private statement that William Green intended making when brought to court, in which he emphasized his shock at the shooting and attempted to lessen the role he had played in it. In the statement he refers to the moment when Marie McGrattan was shot and how, on hearing a loud bang which he wasn't expecting, he 'sort of jumped' and his gun went off. He says that on going downstairs he heard more shots just as he was getting into the van. At no time in any statement does he identify the men who were with him on that gruesome day. He says he was 'sick and giddy' after the shootings. The only semblance of truth in his account of the incident is contained at the end of his statement where he says that if he had refused to take part in the Casey killings he would have been threatened and forced to participate.

The truth is that the UVF leadership did not sanction the killings and Murphy did not reveal his true intentions until actually at the scene of the crime. Noel Green, who played a lesser role, told the police he did not know the identity of the men whom he drove to Casey's. Like his brother, he pretended not to know how many people were shot that day. He claimed he heard a shot and 'one of the fellas in the van told me that somebody was shot on the job'.

From all the evidence I have seen and the information

I have received from informants, it appears that the only persons apart from Murphy who knew what was intended that day were William Moore, Mr A. and Mr B. William and Noel Green eventually admitted their roles and were convicted. Their fear of Lenny Murphy prevented them naming the others.

On 2 October there were other examples of how the 'Big Push' was being realized. A photographer was killed in his studio on Belfast's Antrim Road and a woman was killed in a bomb attack on a Catholic-owned bar in the town of Killyleagh in County Down. Elsewhere scores of people were injured in shootings and bombings, with the death toll for the day reaching eleven. That night a four-man UVF team died near Coleraine, when a bomb they were transporting exploded prematurely. The UVF claimed responsibility for the day's violence and this incensed the Secretary of State who, two days earlier, had pointed out that proscription of the UVF would serve no useful purpose. However, on 3 October, under pressure from others in the Northern Ireland office and members of the mainly Catholic Social and Democratic Labour Party, Merlyn Rees renewed the ban on the UVF. The result was that the new leadership of the organization collapsed at a secret meeting held in the Shankill area on 12 October and the old leadership, with some changes, resumed power. Lenny Murphy by this time had his own unit firmly established and seemed beyond control. He operated as he wished and without fear of retribution either from the new leaders in his own organization or the authorities. He knew that within the UVF and within his own unit he was so feared that no one dared compromise him because of the terrible revenge he would exact on them or their families. He was secure, with Mr A. and Mr B. in position to guard his back, and was confident that the rest of his associates would carry out orders. Within three weeks of the killings in Millfield he was evaluating his strategy for the future. The policy outlined to his men was that, for every Protestant killed, a Catholic should be killed in revenge. He boasted of the terror he would instil in the enemy and expressed his conviction that the ultimate way to kill a man was to cut his throat. He now felt so secure that he could revert to type, to the days of 1972. He believed he was invincible, to the extent that he could publicize to his unit his intentions for the campaign he planned to wage against the other community. He told them that it mattered little who the victims were since all Catholics were 'scum and Republicans'. Sitting with Murphy one day during an exposition of his inner thoughts was William Moore, who still possessed the tools of his trade in the meat plant; he was aware that these would be of use to Lenny. Also present at the discussion were Mr A., 'Basher' Bates, 'Big Sam' McAllister, 'Pretty Boy' Edwards and 'Winkie' Waugh; names which run off the tongue like those given to foot soldiers in a Mafia 'hit' squad.

4

The Butchery Begins

The question being asked in the summer of 1972 and in the years leading to 1975 was whether the situation would reach new heights of barbarism. The UVF, UDA, Provisional IRA and Red Hand Commandos had in the past demonstrated again and again their potential for taking human life in a most ruthless fashion, but in 1972 both sides indulged themselves in the most grisly sectarian war of attrition against society yet. Few people stood back and examined the reasons for it but merely expressed sympathy with the condemnations made by politicians and clergy. No one sought to make the point that prejudice in a community invariably leads to anything ranging from ridicule to extermination. Northern Ireland has a society where prejudice is so deeply rooted that extermination rather than derision is the likely outcome when nothing is done to erode it. In most instances the victims of prejudice are not the combatants but the innocent. It is difficult, of course, to eradicate prejudice but serious and concerted attempts should have been made to replace it with tolerance and more positive attitudes within the churches and the educational system. Few people took the trouble to analyse the factors that contributed to the growing prejudice of the seventies, such as intolerance stemming from the patriotism underlying the two conflicting ideologies, and the literature which supported them. The classic work, *The Nature of Prejudice* by Gordon W. Allport, defines prejudice in a manner which is relevant to the situation in Northern Ireland: 'An avertive or hostile attitude towards a person who belongs to a group, simply because he

61

belongs to that group, and is therefore presumed to have the objectionable qualities ascribed to that group.' He goes on to make the point that this represents an antipathy based on faulty and inflexible generalization.

A renowned sociologist, Michael MacGreil S. J., made the same point in 1970 when considering this issue. He said that in prejudice there is a double assumption in that, first, the group is presumed to possess the negative qualities ascribed to it without examination and without taking the positive qualities into account. Secondly, the person is presumed to possess these qualities without the slightest effort being made to verify the presumption. In other words, the person and the group are denied a fair chance. According to MacGreil, prejudice is unfair, and is likely to be based on false generalizations.

In Northern Ireland Catholics often saw the whole Protestant and Unionist community as the oppressors and, obversely, Protestants believed that all Catholics were subversives and therefore Republicans. As a result, when the IRA began to destroy the fabric of Unionism, Catholics were seen by the Loyalist paramilitaries as the root cause of the evil.

In respect of the Shankill Butchers, there was another element, which was sadism. Many studies have indicated that sadists need aggression and I believe that in Northern Ireland the conflict provides the trigger for this aggression. It also allows misfits to find social acceptance by expressing the prejudice which is not just endemic but socially acceptable. It has been argued that a large percentage of the violence in Northern Ireland has not been political or religious. This is a simplification, for the political and religious background has made the violence possible, has often allowed it to be glamourized and has given it the status of being part of an ideological struggle. It has enabled many people who cannot escape prejudice to find a security within it and to accept its manifestations as a badge of patriotism. There are those who will scoff at the description of much of the conflict in Northern Ireland as politico-religious in character and yet much of the paramilitary literature which is referred to in this book was available to Lenny Murphy and his associates in late 1975 and its content supports my thesis, as the following extract from *Combat* magazine in the autumn of 1975 shows:

> The following areas have been marked down by the enemy for take-over: Cliftonville Road and Antrim Road. Soon, the whole of the Antrim Road from Carlisle Circus to Fortwilliam will be dominated. Stem the tide of Popery's penetration policies. The policy of the Papist Church is to buy as much property as it can in so-called residential areas and let it out at fixed rents to papists. The idea is to replace the Protestant population with Papists and Republicans.

It was against this background in late 1975 that Lenny Murphy began a new campaign of terror. In spite of the fact that a new Brigade Staff of the UVF had taken over, Murphy was determined to go it alone and to vent his hatred as he thought best. It is an indication of his single-mindedness, his sense of omnipotence and invincibility, that he ignored a plea from within Long Kesh to accept the orders of the new Brigade and not to wage war on any group except armed Republicans. Murphy had only one formula in his mind, which was that all Catholics were potential targets.

This instruction from Long Kesh was issued within days of the overthrow of the young leadership:

> The UVF, Red Hand Commandos and YCV [Young Citizen Volunteers] prisoners of war in Long Kesh fully support and applaud the actions of those senior officers who recently replaced the former Brigade Staff for the sake of the Loyalist people in general and the UVF in particular. For some time the name of the UVF has been abused. Rumours have been allowed to circulate to the effect that funds have been misappropriated and that gangsterism is

rife in our ranks. All this has served to damage our relationship with the people and we hope that the new Brigade Staff will soon set about the painstaking task of renewing our lost confidence. The new Brigade Staff are true Ulster Volunteers of long standing who have held responsible posts in the past, and who are completely competent. These men have our trust and our blessing to restructure the UVF. The sole aim of our organisation is to defend the Loyalist people against their enemies, at the same time stating that it is not our wish to wage war on anyone except armed Republicans determined to over-throw Ulster in order to force us into an Irish Republic.

The attempt in the statement to define the enemy and therefore the targets more clearly was in keeping with the Gusty Spence ethos but it did not appeal to Murphy. He decided that his operation would be kept secret, that he would neither seek orders from the Brigade Staff, nor inform them of his planned actions. There were those in the Brigade who knew of Murphy's freelance operation, though not in any detail. They were frightened to interfere.

On 23 and 24 November four young soldiers were murdered in South Armagh. The *Newsletter*, a Belfast-based daily paper, on 24 November dealt graphically with the killing of the soldiers and reported the tough talk of politicians on the need for increased security and stricter measures to deal with the IRA. On the same day Murphy called a meeting with Moore, Edwards and another member of the unit who had become a close ally, Archie Waller. Murphy demanded a response to the weekend violence of the IRA and stated it was time to hit a *Taig*. He called a meeting for that evening and requested that Moore bring along his taxi and his butchery knives. Murphy spent the rest of the day at his home in Brook-mount Street where he was now living with his wife and where, in the same street, his parents shared a home with his brothers William and John. Lenny's wife, the nineteen-year-old Margaret Gillespie, had married him in Crumlin

Road Prison on 5 May 1973 and she was a new dimension to his life on the outside. The ceremony was conducted before Lenny began his stint in Long Kesh and the officiating minister was the then Moderator of the Presbyterian Church in Ireland.

When Murphy met Moore and the others that evening he knew exactly where to seek a victim and it was of no importance that he would not know the identity of the target. A tour of the Antrim Road, he told the others, would undoubtedly lead to finding a *Taig*. Murphy drank with Moore, Waller and Edwards until after midnight before he resolved finally to make his move. He instructed that no guns would be carried on the job. Instead he chose the knives presented to him by Moore, on the grounds that if they were stopped and searched they could argue that Moore had used them in his previous job at the Woodvale meat plant. Murphy's criminal mind covered every eventuality, including the possibility that the taxi might be stopped by the police or the Army, in which case Moore would also say he was carrying passengers. A short ten-minute route was chosen on the grounds that the shorter the route the less likelihood there would be of them being caught once they had captured their target. The route Murphy mapped out took the team down the Shankill Road, across to the Crumlin Road and down the Antrim Road into Clifton Street with a shorter return journey. The importance of the route was that anyone walking after midnight would be easily identified at a distance and few people would be walking the streets at such a time. More importantly, any person in the vicinity of the lower Antrim Road and Clifton Street was likely to be a Catholic because the sectarian geography of the city determined that Protestants would not use those roads after dark. Murphy proved by this calculation his familiarity with the sectarian dividing lines.

The taxi with Murphy and the others aboard took the planned route with one or two slight variations devised by

Murphy. They avoided Clifton Street's main thoroughfare and entered an adjacent area of narrow and darkened streets such as Library Street and Union Street. Both streets were 150 yards from the bottom of the Shankill and less than one mile from Murphy's home.

Elsewhere in Belfast that night thirty-four-year-old Francis Crossan was travelling across the city from a club near his home in the Suffolk area of South Belfast to North Belfast, where his family had been intimidated out of their home one year earlier. On his way to the Holy Cross Bowling Club in the Ardoyne district he passed the spot where his brother Patrick, a bus driver, had been the victim of a sectarian shooting several years earlier. Crossan intended spending a few hours with friends at the Holy Cross and enjoying a few drinks. Sarah Ellen Murphy, no relation of Lenny's, remembers Crossan drinking quietly in a corner of the club. Another member of the club, John Greene, later told police that he chatted with Crossan who was not drinking heavily, just bottles of Guinness. Crossan left the club at ten minutes past midnight. There was no transport available to him so he made his way on foot towards Belfast city centre. It was a foolhardy thing to do but he seems to have been unaware of the danger.

Some time after 12.30A.M. Moore spotted a man walking down Library Street towards the city's main thoroughfare, Royal Avenue. It was Francis Crossan. Murphy told Moore to stop the taxi alongside the solitary figure, then Murphy, Edwards and Waller rushed out of the vehicle and Murphy hit Crossan over the head with a wheel brace. As Crossan fell to the ground his assailants dragged him into the taxi and drove off. Within minutes they were on the Shankill Road. Moore later revealed that Murphy kept hitting Crossan with his fists and the wheel brace and kept repeating: 'I'm gonna kill you, you bastard.' Edwards' recollection was that Crossan 'kept squealing the whole time'.

Murphy directed William Moore to drive to an alleyway

off Wimbledon Street in the Shankill district. By the time they reached their destination Crossan was quiet and Moore stopped the taxi to allow Murphy and the others to carry Crossan's blood-spattered body out of the vehicle. With Moore's assistance the four men carried him deep into the alleyway and dragged him along the ground until they were out of sight of the roadway. Murphy then took out a large butcher's knife and stood over Crossan who was lying on the ground breathing heavily, his eyes closed. Murphy set about hacking at Crossan's throat until the head was almost severed from the trunk. Finally, and triumphantly, he held the knife aloft. It was a demonstration by Murphy of the 'ultimate way to kill a man'. Murphy's clothes and hands were covered in blood and the interior of the taxi was also blood-smeared. Murphy ordered the others to accompany him to his home, where they washed out the taxi and removed their bloodstained clothing, which was later burned. The knife was carefully wiped clean and returned to Moore for safekeeping. Edwards and Waller remained in Murphy's house that night and Moore drove home.

Six hours after the killing an elderly resident of Wimbledon Street opened the back door of her house in search of her cat and saw what she thought was a tailor's dummy lying in the alley. On closer inspection she realized she was looking at a battered body. Francis Crossan was lying on his side, his pupils dilated and his head almost at right angles to his body.

The Scenes of Crime Officer who arrived to examine the area surrounding the body found pieces of glass in the alley and glass fragments protruding from Crossan's forehead. This was later confirmed to be from a beer mug which had been shoved into the victim's head, either in the taxi or while he was lying in the alley. The State Pathologist, Dr Thomas Marshall, was given the task, as on so many occasions in Northern Ireland, of establishing the cause of death and looking for clues which might assist a police enquiry. His report illustrates the extent of the brutality inflicted on Crossan in a short space of time and the intensity of the attack. Murphy's willingness to expose himself to large amounts of blood in a confined space, such as the taxi, adds another macabre dimension to his potential for brutality.

Death was deemed by Dr Marshall to be due to the throat wound which crossed the front of the neck below the chin and extended across the right side to the nape of the neck. The tissues of the neck were raggedly divided as far down as the spine, which was also incised. The root of the tongue was severed and the right artoid artery and jugular vein divided, with the result that massive haemorrhaging caused death. There were linear wounds on the head, one on the back of the scalp, a second above and behind the right ear, two above the right eyebrow, another across the root of the nose, a sixth across the tip of the nose and a seventh on the left cheek below the eye. Some of these were caused by a blunt instrument and others by a glass. One wound above the right eyebrow had glass embedded in it. There were also bruises and abrasions on the face, two depressed fractures to the right side of the skull due to severe blows with an object of a limited area. These blows would not have significantly accelerated death. There were other abrasions on the right shoulder, the left hip, the back of the wrists and hands and on the right side.

These findings indicate that three persons – Murphy, Waller and Edwards – had beaten Crossan in the rear of the taxi. Moore later confided to associates that he was also involved in kicking Crossan while he lay in the alley and seconds before Murphy produced the knife.

News of the murder was not given much space in the local papers but the evening edition of the *Belfast Telegraph* carried a headline on 26 November, 'Slaughter in Back Alley', and a photograph of Crossan's body covered in a blanket. There were several paragraphs describing how the body was found and the name of the victim. Little information was available to journalists and though, even in the Northern Irish context, it was a gruesome crime, it did not merit the coverage a similar crime in the United Kingdom would have done. From the little information available, there was nothing to indicate that this murder was to be the start of a campaign of killings of a similar nature. No organization claimed responsibility, even though it was the custom for paramilitaries to telephone newspapers after an act of terrorism. In this case Murphy was not in a position to speak for the UVF. To have done so would have exposed him as the murderer to the new leaders which, in turn, would have led to confrontation with the new Brigade Staff. Within twenty-four hours the killing of Crossan was a mere statistic, a victim like so many before him and soon to be forgotten. That is the way it is in Northern Ireland. A policeman is killed, a soldier, a UDR man, a Catholic or a Protestant. It is all part of the ritual of daily life and people learn to live with it. While they feel impotent to change it they thank God the victim was not someone they knew and not themselves. One group of people forced to face the tragedies head-on is the Royal Ulster Constabulary. They have to look at the reality of the carnage, reveal the ghastly truth to the families of the victims and, finally, they have to live with the detail until the murderers are found. Francis Crossan and others mentioned earlier were killed within the confines of the Charlie ('C') Division of the RUC, and the story of the murder squad detectives in that division is as central to this book as the story of the Shankill Butchers.

5

Charlie Division

'We're looking for somebody more brutal than the average terrorist and we'd better get to him.' Those words were spoken by Detective Inspector Jimmy Nesbitt when he addressed the nine other members of his murder squad on 26 November in the Tennent Street headquarters of the RUC's C Division, off the Shankill Road. Earlier that morning Jimmy Nesbitt had been in bed when he received a call from the duty officer in Tennent Street station saying that a body had been 'dumped on his patch'. When he arrived at the murder scene he was joined by one of his closest associates, Detective Sergeant Cecil Chambers just as the body of Francis Crossan was being loaded into a vehicle by mortuary personnel. Nearly fourteen years later Cecil Chambers, still remembers that morning vividly: 'It was a horrific sight and especially when the body was lifted off the ground because the victim's head was held to the trunk by tissue. I knew I was witnessing something different . . . a more personal type of killing.'

Jimmy Nesbitt shared that view and expressed it to the six detective sergeants and three detective constables who worked with him: 'I know this is something different from what we have seen before. It looks like the work of somebody different to the types we have come across. It represents for me a new degree of cruelty. We have seen victims who have been killed with concrete blocks, stabbed, shot or beaten to death but the sight of this victim stirs something inside me which makes me feel cold.' When I asked about that experience of fourteen years ago he said: 'Maybe it was the degree of cruelty represented in the broken body of the man but I knew right away that it was an example of a chillingly cold-blooded act. It was not like the experience of seeing someone who had been stabbed. I was convinced that unlike other killings where anger was represented in the way the victim was treated, in this case we were dealing with someone not just callous but clinical.'

Nothing at the scene of the murder indicated to Nesbitt and his team the whereabouts of the killers or where the victim was kidnapped. Aside from the fragments of glass the only signs of how Crossan got there was a tear in his trousers which suggested that the body, after being carried down the alley, was dragged for ten yards. The detectives were lost for any explanation of where Crossan met his death. The possibility of his having been set upon at the entrance to the alleyway was eventually ruled out. So where was he picked up by his killer or killers and why? These were the questions Jimmy Nesbitt realized it was imperative that his team address.

If the victim was abducted elsewhere and transported to the alleyway there was every reason to conclude that planning and transport were required which would strongly suggest the involvement of a paramilitary organization. If Nesbitt could determine where the abduction took place it might well indicate territory controlled by particular paramilitaries and therefore narrow the field of potential suspects.

Essentially, Nesbitt desperately required to know the motive for the murder, knowledge of how the body came to be in the alleyway, and whether he was dealing with a killer or killers. Finally, was the crime committed by a person or persons in the area covered by C Division, or was the victim murdered elsewhere and the body dumped in a place which would encourage the police to concentrate on the wrong neighbourhood? Nesbitt needed considerable manpower to seek answers to a wide range of questions. Primarily, there was an urgent need to establish the whereabouts of the victim before he was murdered which would necessitate numerous interviews and door-to-door enquiries.

It was difficult for Nesbitt to decide how to concentrate his effort because uniformed personnel would only be available to him for several days, after which they would be obliged to return to the difficult day-to-day policing of the Division. His murder squad staff were already burdened with a large number of unsolved killings and daily terrorist incidents. These obstacles were further compounded by the realization that members of the public were always reluctant to assist the security forces because of the fear of terrorist retaliation: he could not expect much public support in his investigation. He knew from experience that his questions would not be answered quickly, if at all. But without answers he would not be in a position to combat the menace he was now facing, the possibility that there was a maniac in the community, or that there was a paramilitary gang which was bringing a new horror to terrorist warfare.

Nesbitt was no ordinary policeman. He was in charge of a murder squad in an area which had always been riddled with crime, even before the present Troubles; but from 1969 onwards C Division was on the front line of two warring communities and more sectarian killer gangs than any other district in Northern Ireland. The responsibilities of the Division extended over a fifteen-mile-square area with a population of 150,000. The most important element in those statistics is that the majority of the violence occurred in an area of three square miles which contained every paramilitary group in the Province. Additionally, C Division represented a geography that was constantly changing due to continuing sectarian violence. Apart from the obvious dividing line between Republican and Loyalist strongholds, there were many roads and streets which were changing gradually and subtly and this was recognized and exploited by the paramilitaries. One of the major obstacles faced by Nesbitt and his team was lack of resources. By 1975 they were dealing not just with day-to-day murders and attempted murders but also a backlog of cases from 1970 onwards. By the beginning of 1975 there were 117 unsolved murders and in 1975 alone there were 34 murders and 153 attempted murders. Overall, in C Division, there were 2,911 crimes to be dealt with that year. Despite the overwhelming difficulties generated by this crime wave, the success rate of Nesbitt's team was almost a fifty per cent detection rate for murders that year and over thirty per cent in respect of attempted murders.

When criticism was levelled at the police, and in particular at C Division, some commentators forgot the relevant parallels which could have been made with police forces elsewhere in the United Kingdom. A reasonable comparison would be the police hunt for the Yorkshire Ripper, Peter Sutcliffe, and the manpower made available to the West Yorkshire, South Yorkshire and Lancashire police forces. Between 1975 and 1980, using computers, which C Division in Belfast did not possess, the police in the Ripper enquiry interviewed 250,000 people, wrote 23,000 statements, visited 26,000 homes and checked 175,000 vehicles. The following warning was placed on 6,000 hoardings: 'The man next to you may have killed twelve women'. Newsagents were asked to distribute two million copies of a brochure giving details about the murders and reproducing what were then thought to be samples of the Ripper's handwriting. In 1977 there were 304 full-time detectives working on the case. At one stage fifty detectives were assigned the task of tracing a £5 note which was found at the scene of one of the murders. Five thousand men were interviewed, including Sutcliffe. Special telephone lines were installed to encourage the public to assist the police in the hunt for the Ripper and as a result almost 900,000 calls were received. The overall enquiry cost £3 million.

By comparison the Tennent Street murder squad operation was limited to ten men and did not have the budget, public support or manpower to match even remotely the Yorkshire enquiry. But in the person of Jimmy Nesbitt the RUC had a man who was not simply dedicated to his job but was undoubtedly the most professional detective in Northern Ireland. He dreamed of being a detective when he was very young, and says, 'I read everything about detective work that I could get my hands on. I was fascinated with the details about murder cases and I followed accounts of every trial in the newspapers.' There was nothing in his family history that would have encouraged or prepared him for life as a policeman. He was born on 29 September 1934 to James and Ellen Nesbitt, a couple in their late twenties who had one other child, three-year-old Maureen. James Nesbitt senior was a hardworking electrician and both he and his wife were regarded by neighbours as a friendly and respectable couple. The family home was a neat terraced house on Belfast's Cavehill Road which was, at that time, regarded as a middle-class neighbourhood. The Cavehill Road is within North Belfast and ironically a short distance from the area where the young Jimmy Nesbitt would later be involved in tracking down the Butchers.

In 1939 James and Ellen sent their son to the Model Primary School on the Ballysillan Road not far from their home. He remained there until 1946 when he transferred to Belfast Technical High School were he excelled as a dedicated and intelligent pupil. His parents shared the hope that he would go to university but it was not to be. At the age of sixteen Jimmy decided that he preferred to find a job and an exciting lifestyle. He says of that decision: 'I simply wanted to get out into the world and make something of myself. I was itching to do something interesting.' His first job promised a great deal. He was employed as a representative for a linen company and offered the prospect of international travel to sell the company's products. He says: 'It didn't really turn out as I intended. I was employed as a trainee sales representative and promised everything but after seven years I decided that I had to move on and the career with the prospect of realizing my need for an exciting challenge was that of a policeman which had always fascinated me, anyway.'

His fascination led him into the RUC in 1957 as a uniformed constable and his first duty was in the border police station of Swatragh. If it was action he liked, he soon gained experience because the IRA campaign of attacking border police stations was at its height. Jimmy Nesbitt was given the responsibility of guarding the police station at night. On his first night-duty an IRA unit attacked the station and a member of the Special Constabulary standing alongside him was shot. Nesbitt fired back and repulsed the attack. For this display of courage he was given his first commendation in the force. It was awarded for 'acting in a manner not expected of someone of his rank and in a fashion which showed zeal, ability and intuition expected of a person of higher rank but with similar opportunities'.

He spent twelve months in the lonely Swatragh outpost and was awarded a second commendation for repelling another IRA attack. These examples of courage and initiative resulted in the young constable being moved away from the stresses of life in a lonely police station in a border battle zone to duty in the town of Coleraine in County Londonderry. The transfer occurred in 1958 and his superiors in Coleraine soon appreciated his attention to detail and allowed him to help with detective work. In this way he 'got a real taste for it'. However, he was obliged to wait another three years before his aspiration to be a detective was realized. In the years after 1961 Detective Constable Nesbitt worked conscientiously, but he was not simply content to be a detective constable. He had faith in his own abilities to do greater things and anxiously awaited promotion. His superiors encouraged him to return to the uniformed branch of the service because there was little prospect of advancement in CID. Instead, Nesbitt opted to play a waiting game. His commitment to his work was total and he constantly impressed others with his professionalism. In 1967 he married Marion Wilson, who understood his passionate commitment to his job. She appreciated, too, that they would never have an ordinary nine-to-five lifestyle. Within four years he was celebrating promotion to Detective Sergeant, and the birth of his first child. Events in Northern Ireland were changing rapidly and he found himself being transferred to a station in the centre of Belfast. Within two years his exceptional abilities were rewarded with further promotion to Detective Inspector and he was moved to the front line and Charlie Division.

Several months before his arrival in C Division an assessment was made of his ability which makes interesting reading and illustrates why he was being assigned to one of the most difficult jobs in Belfast: 'He stimulates interest among his colleagues, often drawing on his personal experiences and marrying theory with practice. He is thoroughly sound and reliable and upholds the best traditions of the Royal Ulster Constabulary. He brings great credit to the Force.'

He was also bringing to his new post at Tennent Street station experiences of the Northern Ireland conflict which had earned him no fewer than sixteen police commendations. Over several years the number of commendations would reach an amazing sixty-seven; unheard of in any police force in the United Kingdom. The only police officer ever to have received a similar number of commendations was a spy catcher in the Special Branch Division of Scotland Yard, with a total of thirty-two.

Nesbitt's arrival in Tennent Street in September 1973 was greeted with some suspicion, as might be expected when a senior officer enters a new area. He observed that some of the detectives were engaged in petty bickering which centred on arguments about who should take statements from suspects or interview criminals. Inevitably those men who took the statements from suspects were likely to be credited with success if those statements provided admission of guilt whereas the detectives responsible for the initial investigation were overlooked. Nesbitt, in his quiet way, soon eradicated this problem. He tactfully conveyed to his detective squad that the prime factor in their detective work was to put a terrorist behind bars and that the whole murder squad and not a single individual of C Division received the credit. He was able to instil a camaraderie within the ranks of the six detective sergeants and three detective constables under his command. He encouraged cooperation and the belief that success would derive from teamwork. He stressed the importance of a proper filing system in the squad's large office and insisted it be kept up to date at all times. It would provide the necessary method of checking and double checking so that nothing could ever be left to chance. He introduced action sheets which could be filled out with accuracy and exactitude and instructed that notebooks were not to be discarded. Files were to be kept on every incident and these would be checked daily by himself and the Station Collator to ensure that every investigative task was carried out satisfactorily and to ascertain whether certain matters required further scrutiny. Nesbitt also possessed a keen sense of humour and this attribute endeared him to his men. It was an invaluable asset in a situation rife with stress, fatigue and constant threat.

It was noticeable to the Divisional Commander that Nesbitt commanded immediate respect from the men under him and this was more attributable to demeanour than to physical presence. At five feet ten inches, always casually dressed, with a thick angular face and a cigarette permanently jammed between his lips, he looked anything but the part. He could more easily have been mistaken for a journalist, with an anxious expression constantly creasing his brows. This description belies his quiet confidence and a toughness which was brought to bear when the situation demanded it. He was not to be trifled with but he was willing to recognize ability and to praise it. He soon made clear his view 'that there were horses for courses' and that he would assign men to roles which best suited their talents. When necessary, he would remove men from tasks to which they were ill-suited. The detective sergeants and constables in his midst were all in their early thirties but were battle-hardened, some of them having spent most of their careers in C Division. A facet which impressed those under Nesbitt's command was his willingness to share success with them. He led by example and took on any task, however menial. This, on occasion, required a twenty-four-hour day. He constantly emphasized the importance of the team and the need for reliance on each other until they became inseparable as a unit.

When I first met Jimmy Nesbitt during the course of researching this book I was particularly struck by his shyness which I concluded derived from being constantly closeted within a police force which afforded him little opportunity to meet other professionals. He appeared to be a man burdened by the violence around him and exhibited an introverted personality which was offset by his sense of humour. His humour, I deduced, was his way of distancing himself from the horror of the brutality he had witnessed. Northern Ireland has produced a brand of humour which outsiders would define as 'black' and Nesbitt's humour fitted precisely into this category. It could be defined as a mechanism for helping people cope with the terrible tragedy of the Conflict. At our first meeting, he told me a story which reflected this sense of humour:

There was a guy who lived in the Shankill area and I knew he was a thug who represented a public nuisance. Like clockwork he got drunk every Friday night and fought with

anyone who crossed his path. One Friday night in June
'75 he made his usual foray into a Loyalist club off the
Shankill Road and by midnight he was predictably drunk
and abusive. He sought trouble and ended up fighting
with other customers in the club before he returned home
battered and bruised.

Now, this guy lived with his mother and she told me
that, the morning after this affray, she made her son breakfast and he duly arrived at the dining table. He began
pouring himself a cup of tea when his mother turned to
him and said:

'What happened to your ear?'

'What ear?' he asked.

'Your left ear,' she added.

At that point the guy discovers that one of his ears is
missing. Someone had bitten if off the previous night.

Nesbitt assured me of the veracity of this story and pointed
out that it illustrated some of the people he was obliged
to deal with in C Division.

Aside from his humour, the sharp, drawn features and
the lines which creased his brow bore testimony to a man
who lived with considerable stress but possessed the ability
to cope with it. I harboured the thought that this man who
resembled the archetypal newspaper news-editor required
a constant level of stress for fear that if it was not there
he would be deprived of the adrenalin and the dynamic
for dealing with the difficulties of his job.

Another characteristic which struck me forcibly on that
first meeting and during subsequent meetings was his
ability to recall events in great detail. It was, I believe,
indicative of a man who constantly filed the significant and
the trivial in the event that somewhere, someday it could
prove useful or invaluable. The minutae mattered to Nesbitt. He was a man always in control but with a friendliness
and generosity that was deceptively disarming. His lifestyle
was one of respectability, much like that of his parents.
His constant smoking was not matched by heavy drinking.
At weekends he shared one or two bottles of wine with

his family at mealtimes and that was the extent of his alcohol indulgence. If there was a Presbyterian ethos lurking in his life, like many who are born into the Protestant tradition in Northern Ireland, it was only evident in his work ethic because, aside from that, he was a man with a contemporary image and a defined realism. During my research I met many of the men who worked with him and each of them held him in awe as one would a hero. They showed him respect and called him either 'Sir' or 'Boss'.

Within his team there were several detective sergeants who established a very close working relationship with their boss. In particular there was Cecil Chambers, a quiet and extremely talented investigator. Alongside him were two other men, Jim Reid and John Scott, who were to figure prominently with Nesbitt in the Shankill Butchers enquiry. Scott was a tough-talking, no-nonsense detective from a rural background who possessed a fine mind for detail, names and faces, and who was singularly devoted to his work. Reid was a self-assured man with a thorough knowledge of the paramilitaries.

After Nesbitt had been with the Division for several months he noted a fascinating dimension to the lives of the detectives around him. Like himself, they did not exhibit signs of stress except when removed from the Division. During working hours the adrenalin flow was high and there were no signs of fatigue, boredom, dissatisfaction or irritation.

The murder by the IRA of twelve policemen from the station and other life-threatening situations were regarded as part of the job. 'The real problems,' says Nesbitt, 'were dealing with the families of victims and conveying news of tragedy to the living.' He adds: 'There were times when it really hit me hard, not simply seeing the bodies but witnessing the heartbreak and tragedy of the living and knowing that in those people it would remain.' The same view was expressed by John Scott and Cecil Chambers, both of whom spent many hours consoling the fathers, mothers, girlfriends and boyfriends of those who had died tragically. Though dealing with death on a daily basis, there was nothing cynical about his men, says Nesbitt. He witnessed only zeal and a determination to end the killing. Members of his team wished to be included in an investigation even should this mean being called from home after a succession of fourteen-hour days.

When a killing occurred the murder squad was assisted for at least three days by other members of CID and the uniformed branch. Every effort was made to swamp an area where it was suspected the terrorists operated. After this period of assistance the murder squad would revert to team work and the other members of the Force returned to dealing with ordinary crime.

In Nationalist areas there was no awareness of the difficulties facing the C Division police officers whose job it was to track down sectarian killers. Firstly the police were countering a constant IRA campaign, sectarian killers on the Nationalist side, plus killings by the UVF and UDA. There were those in the Nationalist community who believed that because most members of the RUC originated from the Protestant community the task of tracking down Loyalists should be easy. This was far from the truth, as illustrated by an episode in C Division shortly before the arrival of Jimmy Nesbitt. One evening, while two policemen were walking down the Shankill Road they were approached from behind by two armed men who forced them into a Loyalist bar. The two policemen were Sergeant Trevor Gray and Constable Malcolm McConaghy. McConaghy was well known around the Shankill for regularly pounding the beat. However, at this time he was not very popular with some members of the UVF, having apprehended one of their members who admitted committing 164 driving offences. The criminal in question was Stewartie Robinson who was notorious for stealing cars and driving them through police and Army roadblocks. He was infamous for having driven a stolen car into Tennent Street, where he waited outside C Division HQ for police to chase him. The job of catching him was eventually given to the man in C Division who was regarded as something of a whiz-kid driver: Constable McConaghy, who raced cars in amateur events. He eventually caught Robinson, who had become the most fired-on terrorist in Northern Ireland because of the number of times he crashed through security cordons. His capture made McConaghy a marked man by the UVF. On the night in question the young constable was treated in a manner which demonstrated the difficulties of policing on the Shankill Road. McConaghy and Gray were held at gunpoint while surrounded by men drinking and deriding them. They were ordered to get down on their hands and knees and bark like dogs, then they were forced to run around the confines of the bar imitating chickens. After-wards they were taken to a backroom and interrogated about police activities in the area. McConaghy was singled out for special treatment and was removed to a toilet where he was told to spreadeagle himself against a wall. A shot was fired between the gaps of the fingers of one hand and excretia was shoved in his mouth. After several hours the two policemen were released with a warning that they could at a future date find themselves in a 'wooden box'. The experience was to prove too much for McConaghy and he later left the Force.

The greatest obstacle facing detectives was the fact that members of the public who genuinely advocated support for the police were, in the event, too frightened to pass on any information they might have about terrorists. Jimmy Nesbitt says that his men viewed terrorists as criminals and it was unimportant which community had spawned them. 'They were all criminals to us and our job was to get them.' He adds, 'When we went into Catholic areas we discovered that most of the people there were glad to see us. They would quietly shake your hand, but were too frightened to help. On both sides the ordinary people would have liked us to change their lives but they couldn't help us for fear of their own lives and the lives of their families. That was the sad part of it all. When someone whispers that it is good to see you in their district, they do it in a way in which they cannot be seen or heard.'

In Nesbitt's company there were no hidden agendas, only the discussion of tactics, and never any examination of the political situation, even outside the place of work. He says: 'We lived for the job. My wife showed me sympathy when I was called out at all hours of the morning and the same with the wives of the other lads. It was the job, the squad, and the recognition that when we were successful we all shared it and celebrated together.'

This single-mindedness can be seen in one piece of detective work which Jimmy Nesbitt undertook shortly after he arrived in C Division. While at home one morning he was contacted and told a body was lying at the rear of the Windsor Bar off the Shankill Road. The body was that of a man who showed signs of having been badly beaten and shot. Nesbitt rushed over to find that in fact the Windsor Bar itself was the murder scene. There were obvious signs that the body had been upstairs in a back room of the premises and later in a toilet. A considerable quantity of blood was found seeping from the floor of the toilet and through the ceiling to the bar below. The rear yard of the bar was also stained with blood in a manner which indicated that the victim was dragged from the bar into the yard and then to the alleyway at the rear. There was no identification on the body and it was removed to the mortuary for an autopsy. After public appeals failed to produce the name of the victim, a young man in his early twenties, the corpse lay in the mortuary for over a week. Meanwhile Nesbitt became obsessed with his attempts to discover the identity of the deceased. He contacted journalists in the hope that their underworld contacts might reveal something about the victim. It was through

this procedure that a freelance photographer approached
Nesbitt and told him that he had seen a photograph in a
Scottish newspaper of a young man reported missing. The
description of the missing young man fitted the description
of the deceased.

Within twenty-four hours of receiving this information
Nesbitt knew that the victim was twenty-two-year-old
Edward Donnelly from Hamilton in Scotland, a former
member of the British Army. Nesbitt contacted Donnelly's
parents and decided to take on the case himself to ensure
that this would not remain yet another unsolved crime.
He discovered that Donnelly had been discharged from
the Army and appeared before Hamilton Sheriff's Court
on 5 June 1974, when he was sentenced to three months
in a Young Offenders' Centre for possessing a small quantity of explosives which he had stolen while in uniform.
There was still no apparent Northern Ireland connection
but Nesbitt kept digging and teasing away at the story. He
next visited London, where Donnelly had gone to enlist
as a mercenary after his discharge. In London it was
revealed that Donnelly offered his services for the war in
Angola and, when turned down, went to France to join
the Foreign Legion but returned after a fortnight bearing
only a Legion cap badge. The story appeared not to fit any
Northern Ireland crime pattern. In the victim's clothing
Nesbitt found a crudely drawn set of unnamed streets. He
speculated that they could be London streets but could
turn up nothing to substantiate this theory. Weeks of painstaking research were then spent on uncovering the method
used by Donnelly to travel to Belfast and finally it was
firmly established that he had been a passenger on the
Stranraer–Larne ferry. Nesbitt turned to his team for
assistance and together they discovered a lorry driver who
had given a lift to the young man. He revealed that Donnelly first asked him if he was driving to the Irish Republic
and, when told he would be travelling in the opposite
direction, the young Scotsman said he would be happy to

accept a lift. He told the driver he was a mercenary, had previously served seven years in the British Army and two years in the French Foreign Legion, and was willing to fight for either side in Northern Ireland provided the money was right. Donnelly dismounted from the lorry at a roundabout close to Toomebridge in County Antrim.

With this information in their possession the murder squad contacted haulage companies and uncovered another driver who picked up Donnelly at Toomebridge then left him at the King's Hall on the outskirts of Belfast. A picture was being pieced together but there was nothing to explain the presence of the crude map found on the body. A public appeal for anyone who had seen Donnelly in Belfast was answered by two young girls and a middle-aged man. The girls told how they met the young ex-soldier at the King's Hall and he asked them for directions to UDA Headquarters. They suggested he take a bus to Sandy Row near to Belfast city centre. They drew a crude map giving directions and this was the map found later on the body. However, they gave wrong information regarding the location of UDA Headquarters. The middle-aged man met Donnelly close to the Shankill area. Donnelly asked him for directions to UDA Headquarters and was directed to the Windsor Bar. This was another error, which was to cost Donnelly his life. The Windsor Bar was not a UDA haunt but UVF and was a dangerous place to be. In the bar Donnelly talked to UVF men about wishing to fight for the UDA. His Catholic-sounding name and his harebrained scheme signed his death warrant. He was tortured under interrogation by members of the UVF before being shot through the head. No trouble was taken to hide the body nor the evidence that he had been killed in the bar. The killers were confident that no one who had been present would talk because they were all guilty by deed or association.

Nesbitt was not to forget this particular case because it symbolized for him the many bizarre and peculiar aspects of crime in Northern Ireland. It showed that survival in Belfast depended on an acute awareness of the geography of the city.

The problems of the murder squad were not solely confined to the activities of Loyalist paramilitaries, though that would change with the emergence of the Butcher campaign. There were the ever-pressing demands of trying to cope with an increasing campaign by the Provisional IRA, based mostly in the Ardoyne area which sat in the middle of what was largely Loyalist territory. On the Republican side there were young men very much in the mould of Lenny Murphy who grew up knowing nothing but violence and who were more concerned with the power of the gun than with any special knowledge of the conflict they were promoting. Within their tribe they were Murphy's counterparts and, equally, their hatred of the other community was so intense that events around them triggered them into action.

One such young man came to the attention of Jimmy Nesbitt, and the facts of the case are as indelibly printed on his mind as those crimes committed by the Butchers. The young man was called Norman Robert Patrick Basil Hardy. He was a bricklayer who in 1974, at the age of sixteen, was killing Protestants. He was the eldest in a family of seven children, four boys and three girls aged between five and fifteen. His parents separated when he was fourteen and his father, a merchant seaman, left the family to live in England. Robert Hardy left school at fifteen and lived with his family in the Ardoyne district, working as an apprentice bricklayer. His involvement in violence came to the attention of the RUC and Army when he was fourteen years old. As a member of A Company in the Provisional IRA's 3rd Battalion he was used primarily as an assistant in serious crimes. He was found guilty of riotous behaviour in 1973 and was detained in borstal for six months. On his release he resumed his role within the IRA and was found in possession of explosives the following year; this time he was placed on probation for two years. But this was not to be the end of his terrorist activities, even though the court was advised that because of his youth he was influenced by older people and was prepared to change his ways and thus deserving of clemency. On Saturday 23 November 1974 several Catholics were murdered and this was the catalyst for a train of reaction. Hardy went in search of two friends his own age, Joseph Todd and Michael Donnelly, who were also involved with the IRA. He told them he intended retaliating for the murder of Catholics. He later admitted that he brought them round to his way of thinking by pointing out to them that it was their duty to assist in an operation. He described the likely consequences if they refused to cooperate, then sent them to hijack a car in the Ardoyne, knowing this to be an area where a car owner would be frightened to report a stolen car immediately. Meanwhile, Hardy went to a Provisional IRA arms dump, to which he had access, and lifted two hand guns and ammunition. The three teenagers got into the hijacked car with Hardy in the front passenger seat and Donnelly as the driver. Hardy handed a gun to Todd and told Donnelly to drive up the Crumlin Road in search of a 'Prod'.

Hardy later told Jimmy Nesbitt the story of the events which followed:

'We came down the Crumlin Road past the Edenderry Filling Station. We turned into a side street near the Crumlin Picture House and into another street which brought us out again onto the Crumlin Road and past the Edenderry Filling Station. We reversed back into the Filling Station. I saw an attendant come out of the office and me and my mate dashed out and put him back into the office. There was a young girl in the office. We took them both into an office on my left. I told them both to lie down. The fella said to take the lot and I thought he meant to take the money. The fella lay down flat but the girl knelt down. There was a short space of time while I was considering to shoot the girl or not. Both of us then opened fire at the same time. I emptied my gun and there were about twelve shots fired in all. These murders were not done on behalf of a political organization. They were not politically motivated murders. It was just a rash decision on my behalf.'

Before he made this statement admitting his involvement, and in the knowledge that Todd and Donnelly had already been charged, Hardy had shown a different side to his character. He had proved difficult for the detectives interviewing him until Nesbitt took over.

Like Murphy, Hardy chose a route where he knew only Protestants would be found walking; he did not know the identity of his victims and did not wish to know. His statement, however, omits some very important details. Firstly, he provided himself with two 'standby' victims should he have found no suitable target walking the street because he knew that two young Protestants worked in the petrol station and they could be killed if Hardy was unable to find a 'suitable' and innocent person walking on the public thoroughfare. Secondly, he directed the car into the filling station and decided to kill the occupants. His victims were Heather Thompson, aged seventeen, and John Thomas McClean, aged twenty-four. Hardy never explained why he hesitated before shooting the girl six times. She, for her part, did not lie on the floor like her colleague but, possibly out of a sense of humility, knelt down and bowed her head. One can only speculate as to the effect of seeing a young girl in a prayer-like posture. Did it stir something deep within Hardy or was it simply that she reminded him of the females in his own family? Whatever the effect, it did not restrain his actions. To Nesbitt, the image of Heather Thompson lying dead on the floor when he arrived on the scene was deeply moving. He says he had difficulty erasing the memory. Perhaps he was beginning to understand that in C Division he was dealing with what he himself called the 'chilling dimension to terror'.

Hardy, who ended up being detained at Her Majesty's Pleasure, was also believed to have been directly involved in the killing of another innocent Protestant, James Carberry, who was shot dead and whose body showed evidence of torture. One has to ask how many more people would have died if Hardy had not been caught and whether he would have been one of the Shankill Butchers if he had been born a Protestant, less than one mile away.

In late 1975, after the Crossan murder, Nesbitt and his squad went about their daily work unaware that Lenny Murphy was being sidetracked by an internecine UVF feud which would postpone his sectarian assassination plan, if only for a matter of months.

6

A Public Execution

The new leadership of the UVF in West Belfast was determined, at an early stage, to rid itself of the legacy created by the previous leadership and it sought to do this by exercising greater control over UVF volunteers, particularly those who were using membership to practise the extortion of protection money from shopkeepers. A decision was also taken to stamp out petty crime, particularly offences such as housebreaking and larceny which were responsible for bringing the UVF into disrepute and eroding its power base with the Protestant working-class community. The new leaders quickly made it known that they wished to hear from anyone who was being intimidated or being forced to hand over money to members of the UVF. Leaders of UVF units were told that volunteers who strayed from the rules would be severely dealt with irrespective of their standing in the organization. Ironically, the Brown Bear team's activities were not scrutinized during this putsch against 'criminal' elements. Murphy was asked to help in the clean-up operation to root out the 'undesirable elements'. He was soon given an opportunity to demonstrate his willingness and it provided a welcome diversion from his real purpose of killing Catholics. It also distanced him from the rumour and whispering taking place in the Shankill area following the killing of Crossan.

Murphy's part in the clean-up began several days after the killing of Crossan. He was asked to investigate a burglary which had taken place on the Shankill Road. An elderly spinster living at 161 Shankill Road was awakened in her bedroom during the night by three intruders. She was threatened until she revealed the whereabouts of a small amount of cash which she kept in her home. Before the robbers made their getaway they tied up the old lady, who remained in that condition until a neighbour entered her house twelve hours later. The crime shocked the ordinary people of the Shankill and representations were made to both the UDA and UVF by local residents who wished an example to be made of the culprits.

The leadership of the UVF saw this as their first opportunity to demonstrate their intent to stamp out crime and thus enhance their reputation. Lenny Murphy and Mr A. were called to a meeting of the UVF Brigade Staff and told to find the 'criminals' responsible for the robbery and punish them. The Brigade Staff provided a list of twelve men in the neighbourhood who had a history of petty crime. Some of those on the list were members of the UDA and Murphy was told that should the culprits be found to be UDA members they should be handed over to that organization, which was equally anxious to see the matter resolved. Before the meeting ended, a UVF staff officer arrived with a description of the burglars which he claimed came from a police source who interviewed the victim of the robbery. With the description fixed firmly in his mind, Murphy left the meeting certain he knew the identity of the criminals. He was, however, faced with a difficult problem if his theory as to the identity of the thieves was indeed correct. He confided to Mr A. that the three men he had in mind were members of another UVF unit and that it might be judicious to involve that unit in the search for the culprits, rather than the Brown Bear team taking independent action. This was a shrewd decision on the part of Murphy since the team he had in mind was the Windsor Bar team which would not brook lightly any interference in their affairs. Murphy and Mr A. conducted a brief meeting with the leader of the Windsor Bar team at which Murphy sought agreement that no matter whence the culprits derived they should be dealt with. This cleared the way for Murphy to operate freely and he made no mention of the fact that he believed he knew the identities of the men being sought.

His next task was to inform his own men about his intentions and prepare a plan of action. That same day he retired to the upstairs room of the Brown Bear and called an *ad hoc* meeting of his volunteers. Firstly he told them that he was sanctioned by the Brigade Staff to apprehend the criminals who robbed and assaulted the old lady. Discussion followed as to the means of punishment. One suggested that the three should be 'breeze-blocked' (a form of punishment favoured by the UVF and UDA for their members: concrete blocks were dropped onto fingers and, in the event of a serious crime, onto the head); another volunteer suggested it should be a 'head job', implying that the three should be shot through the head. Murphy vetoed these suggestions and pointed out that it was the wish of the Brigade Staff that the punishment be restricted to kneecapping: a practice which has been used by all the paramilitaries in Northern Ireland but primarily by the IRA. Thousands of men, young and old, have been subjected to this form of punishment. When it first began, victims were shot through the front of the kneecaps and in most cases recipients of this barbarous punishment were able to walk again after surgery. As a result, the paramilitaries changed their methods and shot victims through the back of the legs, thus blowing out the knee-caps and crippling the victims for life.

Kneecapping was a punishment used on joy riders, drug-takers, thieves and sex offenders. Other forms of punishment were beatings with baseball bats or the use of an electric power drill on the kneecaps. A bizarre dimension to such punishments was revealed to me by Jim Nesbitt, who was given this account of a kneecapping by the victim: 'I was pissed one night and was on my way home when I looked into a bar and thought that it would be fun to scare the hell out of all the people in there. I had a gun on me at the time so I took it out, walked up to the door, opened it, and fired a few rounds into the bar. It was a UDA pub and members of that organization complained to my superiors in the UVF and demanded that I should be punished. I was court-martialled and thought I was gonna get a "head job" but they believed me when I told them I was pissed and had not intended on killing anybody. I was relieved when they told me that I was only going to be kneecapped. I knew the guys who were given the job of shooting me so I was certain that they would not do me too much damage. The only problem was that they came to collect me at a bar on a Sunday and I was wearing a new suit which I had just bought in Burtons. I asked them if they would let me pull up my trouser legs so that the suit would not get damaged as well. They were kind about it and allowed me to do this before they shot me through the knees.'

Murphy told his volunteers that the men they sought would be shot through the back of the knees to create the maximum damage. He gave his unit twenty-four hours to find the men he believed to be guilty, and ordered that they be brought to the Brown Bear for interrogation. Within the specified time Murphy returned to the Brown Bear where his men were holding the suspects. They were Roger McCrea, Edward Bell and the infamous joy rider, Stewartie Robinson.

When Murphy walked into the upstairs room of the Brown Bear, Bell, McCrea and Robinson were seated in chairs surrounded by members of the unit. Murphy approached the three suspects and demanded to know if they were guilty of the robbery. At first the three were reticent and denied any knowledge of the crime. Moore stepped forward and said he had evidence from an associate that the three of them had bought drinks in the Windsor Bar from the proceeds of the crime. When this allegation failed to elicit a response, Moore, McAllister and Bates harassed the three hostages and began beating them, but to no avail. Murphy opted for stronger action; he produced his 9mm Browning pistol from inside his jacket and pointed it at Bell then slowly placed the barrel against his forehead. Deliberately and slowly he repeated the exercise with McCrea and Robinson. He then stepped back and warned the three that he would give them thirty seconds to admit their guilt or he would shoot them. No one doubted that the threat was genuine. Robinson broke down and admitted that he was involved, but demanded mercy on the basis that the old lady had not been hurt. The other two, hoping to impress upon Murphy the mild nature of the crime, echoed Robinson's statement. Murphy was unimpressed and ordered Moore, Bates and McAllister to continue the beating while others held down the three suspects in chairs. Murphy ordered several volunteers to go downstairs to the bar and fetch cardboard and string so that placards could be made to be hung around the necks of the 'criminals'. His intention was that each placard should carry details of the crime committed by the three so that when they were discovered after having been kneecapped it would be apparent to all that the punishment was for robbery and other crimes. It was known that the media would carry details of such a shooting and this would serve as a deterrent as well as demonstrate that the Brigade Staff was making a determined effort to clean up the Shankill. The placards, when eventually prepared, read: 'Shot for crimes against the Loyalist people'.

Moore was told to fetch his taxi and drive it to the front of the Brown Bear so the three 'criminals' could be transported to a disused garage some half a mile away, where the punishment would be administered. The firing party chosen by Murphy consisted of Archie Waller, Sam McAllister and William Arlow Green. Green at this stage was enjoying his freedom before being caught and sentenced for the killings at Casey's Wine Lodge. Mr A. was asked to give a gun to each member of the firing party, who were told to travel in a separate vehicle. Lenny elected to travel in Moore's taxi so that he could hold Robinson and his associates at gunpoint until they reached the venue for the shooting. When Murphy, his captives and the firing party met at the garage a curious ritual ensued, masterminded as always by Murphy, with Mr A. present. The three thieves were ordered to hang the placards around their necks. They were then told to lie face downwards. Murphy addressed the firing party and told them to open fire on his orders. Waller was made to stand over Robinson, McAllister was led to a point where he was looking down on Bell, and Green was given the task of shooting McCrea. Murphy stood by with his pistol in his hand ensuring that everything was satisfactory. At the moment when Murphy ordered the weapons to be cocked, Robinson panicked, rose quickly to his feet and ran towards the garage entrance. Murphy was slow to react but Waller responded quickly and shot Robinson in the back. Some twenty seconds elapsed while everyone stared at Robinson lying face downwards with blood oozing onto the garage floor. Murphy, determined not to be side-tracked from the task in hand, brusquely ordered McAllister and Green to proceed with the kneecapping of the other men. This having been achieved, members of the unit other than the firing party were told to take Robinson's body and dump it in a nearby alley in the hope it would be seen as a crime unconnected with kneecapping. Murphy walked over to McCrea and Bell who were writhing on the floor and warned them not to reveal that Robinson had been shot dead or they too would be hunted down and shot. He ordered his men to return to the Brown Bear and left the two injured men to crawl to the roadway for assistance.

Murphy knew the killing of Robinson was not within his remit and would be construed as a failure to obey orders. Furthermore, Robinson was a member of the

Windsor Bar team and its volunteers would take a serious view of the killing. It is an incredible fact that, within the subculture of a paramilitary world, punishments of varying degrees were applicable according to the gravity of the offence. When it came to their respective terror campaigns no such gradations applied to the atrocities committed.

When the Windsor Bar unit discovered that one of its members had been shot dead, an enquiry was quickly carried out to find the culprits. It did not take much time to deduce that the kneecappings and the murder were connected. It became common knowledge that Murphy and his men were responsible, but no one was willing to point the finger at Murphy personally. While I was writing this book it was suggested to me by a member of the UVF that Murphy put it about privately that Archie Waller murdered Robinson during a personal quarrel, but the truth of that claim remains unknown. However, Murphy kept up the pretence that he ordered the kneecapping of McCrea and Bell but knew nothing about the demise of Robinson. He was summoned to a meeting of the Brigade Staff at which the leader of the Windsor Bar unit was present. He told those present that Bell and McCrea had admitted their guilt in relation to the Shankill Road robbery but when quizzed about the death of Robinson, he replied that the death was in no way connected with the activities of his men. One is forced to ask why Lenny Murphy's answers were believed. The fear he inculcated, from Brigade Staff members down, was such that no one dared to accuse him of lying. However, the leader of the Windsor Bar team was an unusual exception. He did not accept Murphy's explanation and conducted his own clandestine enquiry. McCrea and Bell were visited in hospital and questioned about the episode. They did not divulge precise details of what occurred in the disused garage other than admit it was Murphy and his associates who carried out the kneecapping. However, someone did leak an important detail about the shooting of Robinson:

Waller was named as the trigger man. Retribution was swift, following a sanction from Brigade Staff to kill Waller. Sanction was granted on the basis that Waller alone should be shot since any further revenge action might lead to a feud within the organization.

Within a day of Brigade Staff agreeing to the killing of Waller, a three-man assassination squad was dispatched from the Windsor Bar to find Waller and shoot him without indulging in the preliminaries of interrogation and torture. They found him seated conveniently behind the wheel of a car in a Shankill Road side street with McAllister as his front-seat passenger. The three-man team approached Waller's car on foot but before they reached the vehicle McAllister got out of the car and ran away. Waller did not react but sat in the car while the hit-squad produced guns. One of them walked to the window beside Waller and shot him at point-blank range, killing him instantly. It is a strange fact that Waller did not move after McAllister hastily left the vehicle. Could Waller have thought that the men approaching his car were in search of McAllister? Had McAllister deliberately and conveniently given him that impression? Had Murphy used McAllister to set up Waller because he knew that someone had to pay the penalty for shooting Robinson?

McAllister knew the identity of the men who approached the car and was able to tell Murphy who fired the fatal shots, which indicated that McAllister had watched the murder from a safe distance. News of Waller's death was conveyed to Murphy in the Brown Bear where he was drinking with some of his associates. Moore later recalled that Murphy behaved like 'a madman' when McAllister described how Waller met his death. Waller was, after all, one of those who tortured Crossan before Murphy cut his throat. Murphy reacted to the news by calling for a meeting of all the members of his unit. Moore, McAllister and Bates were told to travel around West Belfast and contact every volunteer, making it clear that the meeting was

mandatory. Mr A. and Mr B. were the first to arrive at
the Brown Bear and were informed that the shooting of
Waller could not go unpunished since this could lead to
other members of the UVF in West Belfast quickly getting
the idea that the Windsor Bar team were a law unto
themselves; when the whole unit was assembled, Murphy
reiterated this view. There is little doubt that Murphy saw
this episode as a test of his power as a self-styled leader,
not only in the eyes of those under his command but also
other Shankill UVF units. During the meeting Murphy
was agitated, gesticulating with his Browning pistol and
demanding retaliation. One man who was present
described the scene as being almost like a prayer meeting
except for the pistol display by Murphy. McAllister was
asked by Murphy to give a detailed account of the manner
in which Waller was 'executed' and to name those responsible. While the unit sat enthralled, McAllister described
how he was sitting in the car but had managed to escape
within seconds of Waller being shot. No one sought to
ask why Waller remained seated in the car, seemingly
oblivious to his imminent death. Murphy controlled the
meeting to the extent that when McAllister named Waller's killers as Noel ('Nogi') Shaw, Dessie Balmer and
Roy Stewart, Murphy allowed individual members of the
unit to express their anger and lay plans to avenge Waller's
death. Murphy, in essence, allowed the temperature to
heighten without offering an opinion and finally called the
meeting to an end with the express wish that all members
of his team should meet during the afternoon of Sunday
30 November, at the Brown Bear. Murphy left the Brown
Bear in a black mood and allowed his men to remain there
to drink and smoulder with anger over the killing of one
of their own.

If one examines Murphy's behaviour at the meeting,
there are several factors to be borne in mind, one of
them an incident unseen by the men under his command.
Murphy was not willing to advocate action against the

three men named by McAllister until he had thoroughly examined the possible consequences with Mr A. and Mr B. in private. This was because the man who pulled the trigger during the Waller killing, Nogi Shaw, was expendable, as was Balmer, but Stewart represented a threat because of his close relationship with the leader of the Windsor Bar team. Again, a curious morality was operating, in that Stewart could be spared because he had worth in terms of someone in authority and yet the other two could be sacrificed though their deaths might well create a more serious feud. Murphy concluded that to kill two in revenge for Waller's death would assert his authority to a point which would preclude retaliation. If he were also to kill Stewart he would be inviting the prospect of all-out war with the Windsor Bar unit simply because the leader of that unit viewed highly his friendship with Robinson.

Murphy did not make it clear to his men that the Stewart factor was an obstacle in his thoughts nor did he point out that he had no intention of seeking approval from the Brigade Staff for avenging Waller's death. He was determined to prove to his men that no one could stand in his way when his power was threatened. Prior to the meeting on the following day, Murphy changed the venue from the Brown Bear to the Lawnbrook Social Club. This was a shrewd move to avoid detection on the Shankill Road where there was a remote possibility of a response from the Windsor Bar team. Also, Sunday was traditionally a quiet day with most shops closed on the Shankill Road and any unusual activity would quickly be noticed. The Lawnbrook Social Club was in a discreet location and, unlike the downstairs bar of the Brown Bear, entrance could be restricted to his unit members by means of a telephone request to those who officially looked after the club.

At 2.00P.M. on Sunday 30 November Murphy addressed all his men in the lounge of the Lawnbrook and told them the three men involved in the murder of Archie Waller would be 'wiped out' that day. While this announcement was being made most of the men in the room were either drinking or ordering drinks at the bar. Murphy added that he was not concerned which of the three had pulled the trigger; as far as he was concerned they all had to die. What he did not reveal to his men was that he had arranged for someone to contact Stewart to tell him not to be in the vicinity of the Shankill for forty-eight hours, by which time, as Murphy saw it, the matter would be resolved. Moore, McAllister and Bates were told to leave their drinks aside and take Moore's taxi to the Windsor Bar and once inside the premises they were to pick up any of the three being sought. They were warned not to cause a scene in the bar but to request, with adequate persuasion, Shaw, Balmer or Stewart to leave with them on the basis that 'Lenny wished to talk to them'. Murphy knew that on the strength of his reputation most members of the UVF would accede to such a request and would understand the penalty for refusing. In the event, only Shaw was to be found drinking alone in the Windsor and was forcibly removed without interference from anyone. He was bundled roughly into Moore's taxi and driven to the Lawnbrook. When they arrived outside, McAllister demonstrated his physical strength by dragging Shaw from the taxi while Moore and Bates rushed into the club to inform Lenny they had been successful in apprehending one of the men wanted by him. As Shaw was dragged into the club, drinks were abandoned and he was set upon, kicked and beaten by those who fought to get closest to him. After several minutes, Murphy and Mr A. intervened and requested that Shaw be carried to the front of a small wooden stage normally used by musicians. Murphy placed a chair on the stage and Shaw was then strapped to it. The stage overlooked the whole of the club and its drinking environs and while Shaw was being tied to the chair Murphy summoned his men to leave the bar and move closer to the stage. Most of the twenty or so men obeyed, taking their drinks with them. Murphy left the stage for several minutes and returned brandishing a Browning pistol. While the others waited in anticipation, he walked to the front of the stage and to within a few feet of Shaw. He addressed the assembled drinkers telling them that the man in front of them was Archie Waller's killer. Not content with this assertion, Murphy said it was time to interrogate Shaw and commenced striking him several times across the head and face with the pistol butt. He continued beating Shaw to a background chorus of 'kill the bastard'. When he received an admission of guilt he told Shaw he was going to be killed. By now, eighteen-year-old Shaw was crying both with pain and fear while Murphy and Mr A. discussed whether straws should be drawn to select the man to pull the trigger. Straws were eventually drawn but the young man selected to be executioner indicated unwillingness. Murphy reacted angrily by telling the unwilling man that he would be dealt with later. He turned to the others and said, 'I'll fuckin' show you all how it's done.'

On hearing these words Shaw broke loose from the binding on his wrists but was unable to free the strapping round his ankles. Murphy remained unconcerned and slowly drew back the carriage of his pistol, releasing a bullet into the chamber. Shaw instinctively put his left hand to his temple as Murphy casually levelled the gun at his head. Murphy pulled the trigger of the Browning and the first bullet went through Shaw's wrist. Four more bullets followed in quick succession, forming a circle of holes in the side of Shaw's head and sending the chair and victim crashing to the floor. Shaw died instantly, one of the bullets remaining lodged in his brain and the others exiting the skull and impacting against the wall at the back of the bar. Murphy stood motionless for at least one minute looking down at Shaw. He finally turned to those watching and said, 'Clean up the fuckin' mess.'

Mr A. undertook the task of disposing of the body by first sending a volunteer to hijack a black taxi in which the body could be transported to an area sufficiently well removed from the Lawnbrook. Other volunteers were dispatched to find cloths to wash the floor and the stage where blood was spilled. Meanwhile Murphy stood at the bar, drink in hand, watching the cleaning-up exercise. Mr A. joined him and they discussed whether or not the body should be covered until the taxi arrived. Mr A. suggested putting the body inside a linen basket as this would facilitate removal from the club and avoid arousing the suspicion of passers-by. Murphy agreed to this, and Shaw's body, in foetal position, was shoved into a basket taken from the club's storeroom. The lid was closed while those present continued drinking. Moore was given the job of driving the taxi with the linen basket aboard. He abandoned both taxi and linen basket in an alley off Urney Street, almost a mile away in the Shankill area.

When Moore returned to the Lawnbrook, Murphy told him to take Bates and McAllister and search for Stewart and Balmer. They were to be shot where they were found. Within hours they located Balmer and shot him in the stomach but he survived. Stewart was not found and no further action was taken against him.

Shaw's body was discovered by police from C Division at 6.25P.M. that same day and immediate forensic examination indicated that he was killed 2.6 hours earlier. It is interesting to note the coding formula used by medics to establish the time of death. The formula is the body temperature of the deceased subtracted from normal body temperature and divided by 1.5. In the case of Shaw it was thus:

$$\frac{99F - 95F}{1.5} = 2.6$$

Close examination of the body revealed the terrible

beating Shaw had received, though Moore was later to attribute the injuries to a 'kicking'. The injuries were in fact substantial:

Scalp: 4 serious lacerations.
Face: lacerations and considerable bruising.
Neck: bruising.
Trunk: patchy bruising.
Right and left upper limbs, right and left lower limbs: considerable bruising and abrasions.

The pathologist's report also included two details concerning tattoos on the deceased, which are significant only inasmuch as they indicate something of the character of Noel 'Nogi' Shaw. On his right lower limb was a tattoo containing the words 'Long Kesh', and on the front of his thigh just above the knee was a drawing of a Thompson sub-machine gun with the letters 'UVF' tattooed on the outer side of the right calf.

When the body was found it was transported along with the taxi to Tennent Street police station where both were examined by Jimmy Nesbitt, who discovered four spent 9mm cartridge shells at the bottom of the linen basket. Nesbitt deduced that the place where the body was dumped indicated that it was a Loyalist paramilitary killing, since Shaw was known to be a member of the UVF.

In the weeks following, Murphy lay low and encouraged his men to do likewise. He also stressed the need for vigilance for fear that a member of the Windsor Bar team should seek to continue the feud. Eventually the Brigade Staff issued orders that the feud was to cease, since they had come to recognize that Murphy was not likely to back down in face of threats from any source.

Christmas 1975 passed without incident though Murphy had not forgotten his real purpose in life and was constantly stressing to Moore and the others that once New

Year arrived the Shaw episode would have been forgotten and they then 'could get back to killing *Taigs*'. On the evening of 9 January 1976 Murphy met Moore for drinks in the Burning Bush Club in Ceylon Street off the Shankill Road. He told Moore there was a special job to be done that night, but there was an obstacle concerning his wife Margaret and one of her friends. It transpired that Murphy had promised to collect Margaret and her friend from a club on Belfast's Shore Road to drive them home. Murphy foresaw the difficulty of extricating himself from his wife's company and for this reason he wanted Moore to pick up the women and drive them home. Moore agreed to this and Murphy cautioned him not to allow himself to be persuaded to bring them to the Burning Bush but to take them directly home to Brookmount Street. He was then to return quickly to the Burning Bush as he was needed for an operation later that night.

When Moore arrived at the club where the women were drinking he told Margaret Murphy that Lenny had instructed him to drive her home and that her friend was welcome to join her. Margaret became suspicious and insisted that Moore drive her to the place where Lenny was drinking. She believed her husband was having an affair with another woman and it was her intention to confront him about it in public. Moore stressed that Lenny was engaged 'in business' and did not wish to be disturbed. Margaret Murphy, however, was not to be deterred and prevailed upon Moore with cajoling, and eventually threats, to take her to meet Lenny. Moore relented under the pressure and drove her and her friend to the Burning Bush. When they arrived Lenny was standing at the bar talking to associates and there was no woman near him. He addressed a terse 'hello' to his wife and instructed her to leave the bar and walk home because he was busy. Margaret Murphy did not argue with her husband and meekly left the premises with her friend.

Lenny took Moore aside and pointed to two men drinking at the bar who he said were members of the Ulster Defence Regiment. He singled out one of them, describing him as a frequent visitor to Loyalist bars and added that this man was always armed. He told Moore that he intended killing a *Taig* and that it would be preferable to use a 'clean weapon'. This contention about a 'clean weapon' exemplifies his ability to analyse, in advance, the risk of using a UVF weapon which, if forensically tested, might link him to other murders which he had or had not committed. He explained his thinking to Moore and pointed out that UVF men had been apprehended with guns used in other operations and a forensic test on the weapons had been enough to convict them of murders committed by others. In his opinion, he told Moore, it was better to get caught with a 'clean weapon' so that if apprehended before a murder they would simply be charged with theft and firearms possession or, after a murder, with only one killing.

According to Moore, Murphy told him that it was his intention to take the UDR man's gun, though questions arise about this account in the light of subsequent events. However, it is interesting to look at Moore's account of events as they developed once Murphy decided to steal the UDR man's gun. Moore says that Murphy took one of the UDR men into the toilet of the club, threatened him, took his weapon and fired a shot close to his head. The UDR man in question was John McFarland Fletcher from Belfast, a twenty-one-year-old sergeant and this is the account he gave to the police:

At 2.30A.M. on 10 January I was in the toilet of the Burning Bush with a friend, John Lockhart, when two men came in. Each man had his face covered with a scarf and one of them pointed a pistol at my head and pushed me back. He then searched me and took my issue Walther pistol and holster from the waistband of my trousers. He then turned me round and put the gun to the back of my head and pushed me out of the toilet and then through the door and onto the street. He made me lie down on waste ground at the side of the club. He asked me who I was, where I lived, and I think I told him. There was a shot fired close to my head while I was lying on the ground, head down. I was then put into the back of a black London-type taxi and made to lie face down on the floor. I was driven off by three men, the driver and two in the back with me. I was taken to a house where I was questioned. I was then taken to the taxi and driven around for a while and then released. The person who attacked me in the toilet was five feet nine inches with darkish hair nearly shoulder-length. He was wearing a black three-quarters-length leather coat. I only got a glimpse of the other fellow and I would not be able to describe him. I am sure the person who stole my gun had spoken to me while I was drinking in the club. After they released me I went straight to the police station at Tennent Street. When I was released by these men I was told that if I said anything about what had happened I would be shot.

This statement was not made until almost one month later and prompts many questions. The man was after all a regular visitor to Loyalist clubs in the Shankill area and he spoke to both Moore and Murphy at the bar and accepted drinks from them. He was in a position to describe them. His description of Murphy was misleading and he failed to describe the other 'assailant'. Moore confirms that Murphy deliberately picked a quarrel with the UDR man, removed the gun from him and fired a round close to his head but he makes no mention of taking him to a house or driving him around in a taxi.

It is possible that the UDR man was indeed driven to a house, probably Murphy's. He did not report the theft of the pistol for three hours, which allowed Murphy time to use it. In 1988 the same UDR man was imprisoned for the theft of weapons from a UDR armoury housed in a British Army base at Holywood, outside Belfast. At his trial he pleaded that his actions resulted from mental instability caused by his imprisonment by the Shankill

Butchers in 1976. At the time of his trial this plea went unnoticed and journalists were unaware of the details concerning the episode so there remain unanswered questions about this matter, such as why no attempt was made at the time to examine closely the credibility of a UDR sergeant who drank in a Loyalist para-military meeting place while armed. Murphy told Moore that he wished to be driven to North Belfast and in particular the Cliftonville Road area where they would shoot a *Taig*. It is interesting to note that Murphy felt confident that he could be driven by Moore through a sensitive area of North Belfast while armed with a pistol, but it was perhaps frustration that spurred him to take such action. After all, his lust for killing had not been satisfied since the shooting of Shaw. 'I'm goin' to kill a *Taig* and the best place to find one is in the Cliftonville Road,' he told Moore before they set off from Brookmount Street.

The Cliftonville Road had been a killing ground for Loyalist paramilitaries in 1972. This came about because of the violence of the early 1970s when Catholics were burned out of their homes. This in turn created fear in both communities to the extent that many Protestants moved out of North Belfast and displaced Catholics moved in. In subsequent years Protestant families continued to feel threatened by an expanding Catholic community in the district, with the result that the Cliftonville Road became virtually a Catholic ghetto. Until the beginning of the present conflict in 1979 the road had been a middle-class area housing mostly Protestants who began to witness increasing violence in several Catholic districts which bordered the Cliftonville Road. The road also provided easy access between Catholic and Protestant ghettoes which, in turn, made it dangerous. However, once the majority of residents were Catholics the area became a killing ground for roaming gangs from the UDA and UVF.

Murphy, with his history of killing going back to the early seventies and his geographical knowledge of Belfast, was aware of the potential the Cliftonville Road offered. A favourable feature for a killer was the fact that the road was only minutes from the Shankill and other Loyalist strongholds and it rose steeply, the brow of it providing a panoramic view and thus an excellent way of spotting the presence of Army or police patrols. Another advantage from Murphy's point of view was that the district was controlled by RUC Division D, where he would not be as readily identifiable to police patrols as a UVF suspect.

As requested by Murphy, in the early hours of that morning, Moore drove him along the Cliftonville Road and through adjoining streets and avenues in search of a victim. The time was such that the only people likely to be walking the streets would be drunks returning home, and drunks were easy prey.

At 3.30A.M. Murphy asked Moore to make a final sweep of the Cliftonville Road in a last ditch effort to find a victim. As they drove down the road towards Manor Street Murphy saw a blind man feeling his way along the pavement with a white stick and with a dog leading him. He told Moore to stop so that he could get out and shoot the man but, simultaneously, Moore spotted another figure one hundred yards away. He pointed out the figure to Murphy who immediately forgot the blind man and asked Moore to drive slowly along the road. They both quickly realized that the person was in fact female but Murphy insisted 'she would do'. The girl was twenty-one-year-old Deirdre Assumpta McQuaid, who had left a party at a friend's flat on the Cliftonville Road. At the moment he spotted her, Moore was unaware that her husband, Ted, was urinating in a nearby garden.

Deirdre McQuaid, in her account of the events which followed, neglects to mention that she argued with her husband about the route they should take on their way home. She makes no mention either, probably due to embarrassment, that she was standing on the Cliftonville Road waiting for her husband while he urinated. This waiting period allowed Murphy and Moore the opportunity to drive past and assess the situation. In retrospect there was little Deirdre McQuaid or anyone could have done to prevent what happened. She later gave this account to police:

> There were quite a number of people at the party and Ted and I were dancing, having an odd drink and chatting to people. Ted knew most of the people there as quite a lot of them worked with him at the Department of Health and Social Services. At about 3.30A.M. Ted and I decided to go home. I left Ted to get his coat and I walked slowly downstairs and onto the pavement at the front of the house. I noticed a black taxi driving slowly past on the opposite side of the road. It turned left into a side street and disappeared from view. It reappeared from a side street opposite where I was standing and turned right before driving down the Cliftonville Road. Ted arrived and he and I began walking down the Cliftonville Road. The taxi suddenly came up the road again. I told Ted I thought this was strange because the taxi had driven up the Cliftonville Road a short time previously. Suddenly the taxi drove past us going in our direction and I saw it stop a short distance in front of us. I said to Ted about the taxi but he did not seem to be alarmed. Ted was between the taxi and me. The door opened and a young man got out and started walking towards us. He was swaying about as if he was drunk and I said to Ted, 'It's okay, he's drunk.' Suddenly he put his left hand inside his jacket and pulled out a small gun which he pointed at Ted and started firing. He never looked at me but kept shooting at Ted. Ted fell to the ground but he just kept shooting. I threw my handbag at him but he jumped into the taxi and drove off at speed. I went to Ted and he said, 'Run, Deirdre!' I started screaming for help and ran back to the flat.

This account illustrates the unfortunate victim's naivety with regard to the district in which he was walking that night and his neglect of his wife's suspicions about the taxi. Had he listened to her he might be alive today. Deirdre McQuaid also failed to mention that she argued with her husband about the constant presence of the taxi and this could explain why, at the moment the taxi stopped alongside them, he was walking slightly ahead in angry mood. However, once shot, his thoughts were for the safety of his wife. One can only guess why Murphy did not kill Deirdre McQuaid. He was not, in fact, drunk when he alighted from the taxi. This pretence was a ploy to allay any fear Ted McQuaid might have had so that he would not have felt the need to run away. It gave Murphy time to take aim. His aim was good and the first bullet struck Ted McQuaid on the chin and the second on the chest. Four subsequent bullets were fired into him as he lay on the ground.

A nightwatchman in a nearby school witnessed the shooting but proved an unreliable witness when he described the murderers' getaway car as a dark blue mini. A patrol of British soldiers was quickly on the scene and placed a cordon around the prone figure of Ted McQuaid. The soldiers found themselves harassed by revellers from the party who, on learning that their friend had been shot, arrived on the scene and tried to remove Ted McQuaid – although seriously wounded he was still breathing. An ambulance was summoned and arrived within ten minutes but Ted McQuaid died on arrival at the Mater Hospital a short distance away.

Moore later tried to distance himself from the crime by pointing out that he dissuaded Murphy from shooting the blind man, hoping perhaps to create the impression that to do so would have been a greater crime than killing Deirdre McQuaid and her husband. This once again illustrates the bizarre perceptions which often motivate killers in a conflict such as that in Northern Ireland. Murphy on this occasion was prepared to shoot anyone, man, woman or child, or a blind man, as long as he could reasonably establish the religion of the victim, whereas Moore was prepared to make a distinction, not from any normally understood sense of morality but within the definition of a 'fair target' in battle-hardened Northern Ireland terms. The distinction which Moore sought to emphasize says a great deal about prevailing views within paramilitary circles and how such views often find expression in the way society itself views terrorism. Frequently in Northern Ireland people are willing to condemn vociferously those crimes which directly affect their own community but are passively silent when the other community suffers grief. Generally there is too much tacit acceptance of violence, and condemnation becomes an intrinsic part of the conflict and loses positive effect except, perhaps, when a crime of such proportion is committed that it cries out for denunciation. Such an example would be the IRA bombing of Enniskillen. Yet UDR personnel, police, Army and civilians from both sides are killed daily. It could have been a subconscious awareness of these features of his society that made Moore dissuade Murphy from killing the blind man. This incident expresses for me the complexities of this particular society.

The two events of 9 and 10 January 1976 were connected and the RUC should have recognized the fact within twenty-four hours. The reported theft of a pistol and a spent .22 cartridge at the spot where McQuaid was shot should have, at the very least, aroused suspicion. Fletcher says he told police about a black taxi being used in his abduction, as did Deirdre McQuaid. From my investigations I found that no such connection was made. I enquired whether Deirdre McQuaid had been shown mugshots of suspected terrorists, since Lenny Murphy would have been on file, and the police told me it was quite likely. A range of such photographs would have been prepared by RUC Headquarters and made available to detectives in D Division so that she would have had an opportunity to identify the killer.

It is difficult so many years on to verify what happened

and I have no reason to doubt the RUC version that such a procedure took place, although I was unable to trace Deirdre McQuaid and speak to her. She was the one person who would have been able to identify Murphy and the description she gave to the police was more accurate than the one supplied by Fletcher. My contention is that once again there was a distinct lack of communication and exchange of information between D Division and C Division. Fletcher was interviewed in C Division and Deirdre McQuaid in D Division, and it was not until some of the Butchers were caught that it became clear that the Fletcher incident and the McQuaid killing were linked.

Nowadays the exchange of information between RUC Divisions is collated on a very professional basis with a collator for each area passing information to other Divisions. All information is then fed into a centralized computer. Murphy demonstrated that he knew exactly how the police operated and he was aware, in my view, of the failings within the system.

The Nationalist/Republican analysis will conflict sharply with the theses that mistakes were made by the police simply because of a failure of communication. The alternative thesis may well suggest a sinister motivation though other events to be described in this book will provide the substance and truth for my argument that the failure to connect the McQuaid/Fletcher episodes was because of human error. There is reason to believe, as I now do, that if Jimmy Nesbitt and his team in C Division had been in possession of the facts of the McQuaid killing they would immediately have connected it with the Fletcher incident. Possibly the most vital piece of information provided by Deirdre McQuaid concerned the use of a black taxi. The fact that this was not immediately part of the analysis of the murder squad at C Division is a sad reflection on the manner in which information was evaluated and processed.

I asked Jimmy Nesbitt about this matter and specifically

for the number of Moore's taxi. He was unable to supply this information because the files relating to that period would not now be available in relation to car numbers. He also pointed out that the Motor Tax Office, which is now computerized, would be unlikely to have the information I required. I discovered this to be the case. My reason for seeking the registration of the taxi was to confirm whether Deirdre McQuaid was supplying vital evidence when she told them she believed it began with the letters DIY. If this had proved accurate, then the police had the opportunity to trace it. It will now never be possible to know whether Deirdre McQuaid had been correct, as Moore's taxi was later destroyed in a junkyard.

7
Murder Most Foul

On 6 February 1976 two teenage gunmen, members of the Provisional IRA, laid an ambush for policemen patrolling the Cliftonville Road. As two constables were making their way along the road before midday, they were shot from close range. One died instantly and the other died in hospital two days later. On the evening of the shooting Murphy and Moore went to the Long Bar on the Shankill Road where they were served drinks by Robert 'Basher' Bates, who was working there as a part-time barman. The conversation between the three centred on the shooting of the two policemen, and at Murphy's instigation they arrived at the conclusion that it demanded retaliatory action from them. Murphy had no love for the police, but the fact that most members of the RUC are drawn from the Protestant community encouraged him to see the attack as one on his own kind. This belief has been present in the thinking of Loyalist paramilitaries since the beginning of the present Troubles and has never been fully recognized by the Provisional IRA. The non-recognition of this reality by the Provisionals when waging their campaign of terror is conveniently to ignore the racism and sectarianism of their own ethos, which indirectly gives impetus to Loyalist paramilitaries who slay Catholics.

The Provisionals credit their campaign with the inheritance of romantic Nationalism and ideological imagery and ignore the fact that the shooting of a policeman or a UDR man is a direct blow aimed at the community which shares the same part of the island of Ireland as they themselves. They refuse to accept that their actions in this respect

114

breed an atmosphere in which gangs such as the Shankill Butchers develop and thrive. No doubt members of the Nationalist community might argue that my analysis provides a convenient explanation for Murphy's attitudes and actions. I would say, instead, that many of Murphy's actions must be evaluated in terms of the extreme prejudice which had developed within him since childhood and which found an outlet in acts so violent that they could only have been committed by a psychopath. His psychopathy made him unique only in the methods he chose for slaying his victims. Around him were others, on both sides of the conflict, who could be described as temporarily abnormal; some simply misfits who, thanks to the war situation, could achieve a degree of acceptance within their own community. Murphy sought to glamorize violence by the use of fear and power. In contrast there were others, such as Spence, who were developing an ethos rooted in a concept of Britishness rather than Irishness. This ethos was in opposition to Murphy's 'For God and Ulster' mentality which contained the belief that Ulster was Protestant, and Catholic was evil.

Moore and Bates, Murphy's companions in the Long Bar the evening the two policemen were killed, shared his intense hatred of Catholics. The three were exemplars of the brutalizing effect of prejudice but equally they had themselves contributed to that process by their dehumanization of the enemy. After discussing how to retaliate for the deaths of the policemen it was decided they should take Moore's taxi and drive to the area surrounding Library Street, where they had apprehended Crossan. When Moore later described how the decision to retaliate was taken he said they simply got into the taxi to travel across the city to buy chips. Moore frequently relied on this explanation when later he talked to detectives. It was as if he wished to give the impression that the killings just happened, and were not premeditated. It was the defence of a mass murderer seeking to distance himself from the atrocity.

The three left the bar and went down the Shankill Road, with Moore driving and Murphy and Bates in the back seat of the cab. As they turned into Millfield, Murphy continually issued directions to Moore on which route to take so that they circumnavigated the area. It was Moore's task to spot anyone who happened to be walking in the neighbourhood and relay the information to the rear of the cab. The person seen on this occasion was some fifty yards away and was described by Moore as 'a wee man'. He was in fact five feet four inches tall, and was wearing a short overcoat with a fur collar, and blue trousers. He was fifty-five-year-old Thomas Joseph Quinn, a road-sweeper by trade. Quinn was a lonely man and a heavy drinker who was to be seen frequently wandering home drunk or walking aimlessly through the city centre. Those who knew him regarded him as a sad and pathetic person who had mentally disintegrated after the death of his wife in 1974. He had a son and daughter who rarely visited him and he did not converse with his neighbours. On the night in question he was making his way home after drowning his sorrows for hours in a city bar.

Murphy instructed Moore to drive alongside the unsteady figure on the pavement, who was oblivious to the sound of the approaching taxi. When the taxi drew along-side Quinn, Murphy leaped out and hit the drunken man over the head with a wheel brace, sending him sprawling onto the roadway. Murphy called to Bates to help him lift the injured man into the taxi. Bates obeyed and Quinn, who was moaning in pain, was lifted bodily and placed on the floor of the cab, which was then driven off by Moore in the general direction of the Shankill Road.

At Murphy's command, Moore drove to the Lawnbrook Social Club. I have since discovered that they stopped outside Murphy's home in Brookmount Street where Murphy got out, went into the house, and returned within two minutes. It seems reasonable to assume that they stopped to collect the murder weapon though this was never admitted by Moore or Bates when they were later questioned by detectives. On the way to the Lawnbrook Club, Murphy and Bates administered a severe beating to Quinn which culminated in multiple injuries but was not sufficient to cause death.

When the taxi finally came to a halt outside the Lawnbrook, Murphy got out and went into the club, where he spoke to Benny 'Pretty Boy' Edwards who was working there as a part-time barman. According to Edwards' testimony, Murphy told him that they had an IRA man outside in Moore's taxi and 'we're gonna do the bastard so how would you like to come along and help us?' Edwards accepted the invitation without question and quickly sought permission to leave the bar.

Edwards' first impression of Quinn when he joined Murphy in the taxi was that he was 'seeing a small boy'. This was due to Quinn's diminutive figure and the fact that his face and head were covered in blood and his features distorted to such an extent that his age was not apparent. With Edwards on board, Moore drove towards the Glencairn housing estate via the Shankill Road, taking a route which provided a clear view ahead and the opportunity for a quick getaway should an Army or police roadblock be encountered. Why did Murphy and the others feel they could travel this route and take the chances they took, unless they believed there was little surveillance in the area? After all, they were four men in a car with a butcher's knife and a badly beaten man. It may have been that the security forces did not have the manpower to cover the area properly at that time. Two hundred black taxis travelled the Shankill every day, though it must be said that any vehicle, particularly taxis of this type which had been used previously in acts of terrorism, would surely have attracted attention. The question is seemingly unanswerable. There are no statistics available or security forces' files to indicate the degree of surveillance which existed in the Shankill area at that time. One can only conclude that terrorism dictated that there was never sufficient manpower to police the district properly, that Murphy and his associates were adept at finding gaps in the surveillance which did exist, or that the security forces failed to recognize the manner in which the killers operated and the fact that they were so close at hand. It is impossible to find out whether there were patrols on the Shankill on the nights the Butchers operated or whether manpower on those occasions was not available. Murphy and his associates knew intimately the geography of their area and it is possible that there were occasions when they set out in search of victims but had to abort their missions because of the presence of security forces. One such mission undertaken by the gang will be dealt with later in this chapter and it illustrates that Murphy would abandon an operation for several days until he was sure that there would be no Army or police presence to thwart his plans.

Murphy, Bates and Edwards beat Quinn as they travelled towards Glencairn but, before they completed their journey, Murphy produced a butcher's knife and drew it across Quinn's neck, making an incision eight centimetres long which cut the subcutaneous tissue below the jaw, causing bleeding but not death. Murphy used the knife several times in this manner before the taxi stopped at Forthriver Way in the Glencairn estate, at which point he placed the bloody knife in an inside pocket of his leather coat and pointed to a gap in a line of cast-iron railings several yards from the taxi. He suggested they carry Quinn through the railings where they would be out of sight of the roadway and of anyone who happened to pass or be looking out of a bedroom window. Bates, Murphy and Edwards lifted the now unconscious Quinn from the taxi and Murphy told Moore to drive around the estate for five to ten minutes as a means of avoiding suspicion should there be a security force patrol in the vicinity. Moore obeyed the instruction and said he would return to pick up the others beside the gap in the railings. Quinn was carried through the railings and down a narrow path which led to a shallow, muddy bank. Murphy and Bates held the victim's upper body, and Edwards held his feet, but after travelling twenty yards in this fashion Edwards became tired. Quinn was dragged for a further ten yards until they were all out of sight of the roadway, though there was sufficient light from street lamps to allow them to see clearly. Quinn was laid on his back on a grassy bank and Murphy produced the knife and hacked at his throat while Bates and Edwards looked on. The wound which finally killed Thomas Joseph Quinn took considerable physical effort because it extended back to his spine. There is every reason to believe that Bates and Edwards participated in the final demise of Quinn because of the number of wounds to his throat. Murphy had brought along Edwards for the express purpose of 'blooding' him. Bates and Edwards, however, later attributed the throatcutting to Murphy. This was recorded in police interview notes in which they refused to name him as the killer but simply said that Quinn's throat had been cut by a man 'they did not wish to name'.

Moore drove around the Glencairn estate as instructed and returned to collect the others at the specified time, which was approximately 1.00A.M. on 7 February. The four of them travelled to Murphy's house where they all washed out the inside of the taxi to remove the blood stains and Edwards and Bates were supplied with a change of clothing. Murphy took their bloodstained clothes saying that he would have them laundered and returned within several days.

At 7.00P.M. that day Jim Campbell, then deputy editor of the *Sunday News* in Belfast, was sitting in his office when he received a telephone message from a male caller claiming to be 'Major Long of the Young Militants'. The caller told Jim Campbell that the body of a 'militant

Republican' could be found on a grass bank at Forthriver Way and that the killing was in retaliation for the murder of the policemen on the Cliftonville Road the previous day. The caller was Lenny Murphy and by claiming responsibility for the killing of Quinn in the name of a non-existent grouping he was distancing himself from the crime in the event of questions being asked by the UVF leadership. The use of the pseudonym 'Major Long' was a curious choice since the previous evening he had been drinking in the Long Bar with Bates and Moore. A journalist later described the use of the bar's name as a 'vital piece of evidence', which he alleged was ignored by the police. It should not be assumed, however, that if Nesbitt and his team had connected the Long Bar with the use of the pseudonym 'Major Long' it would have led them to the Butchers. Bates worked there on a part-time basis but most of the meetings with Murphy were held in the Brown Bear or the Lawnbrook. Additionally, the Long Bar was frequented by many members of Loyalist paramilitary organizations and it would have taken considerable luck to have eliminated everyone who drank there with the exception of Bates. At this stage of the campaign by the Butchers, luck was at a premium as far as Nesbitt and his team were concerned. The Butchers did not leave witnesses and the only witness who might have proved crucial, Deirdre McQuaid, was not part of the C Division investigation.

Quinn's killing confirmed Nesbitt's growing fear that he was dealing with a 'most chilling dimension to terrorism'. He says: 'Suddenly there was a fear in my mind that we were possibly dealing with a maniac or maniacs who would do this again and again. The worst thing was that there were no clues. We didn't even know where Quinn was picked up and, despite public pleas, no one came forward to tell us they had seen him in the hours before he died. In Glencairn we talked to many people but no one saw anything. It was the usual story of a brick wall.'

A forensic science team visited the scene of the murder but nothing unusual originated from their investigation. The body of Quinn was found lying face downwards, indicating that he was rolled over and down the shallow bank after his throat was cut. The wet and muddy conditions made a thorough examination of the scene difficult. A comb was found near the deceased but ownership was never established. Fingerprint experts carefully examined the area but came up with nothing, and footprints were also examined and copied but all to no avail. Nesbitt needed only to look at the body to deduce that it was another sectarian killing but the brutality of the killers made the difference. He also knew very quickly that he was dealing with more than one person because of the number of footprints in the vicinity of the crime, the physical effort required to transport the body to the site of the murder and the extent of the physical injuries inflicted on the victim.

The murder of Quinn happened at a time when Murphy was planning the mass murder of Catholics in one incident. He contemplated killing a group of Catholic workmen in retaliation for the murder by Provisionals of ten Protestant workmen on a bus, in what has become known as the 'Kingsmill Massacre'. This occurred after the killing of five Catholics by the UVF in January 1976. Within one week of the murders at Kingsmill in County Armagh, Murphy had laid the groundwork for an attack on a lorry which ferried Catholic and, unknown to him, Protestant workmen to Corry's Timber Yard in West Belfast's Springfield Road.

Murphy received a tip-off from an associate who worked in the timber yard that Catholic workmen from the company travelled on a truck to Corry's each morning and their route took them through the Shankill district. Murphy borrowed Moore's taxi every morning for three weeks and followed the lorry as it made its way from Carlisle Circus on the Antrim Road to the Springfield Road, travelling for part of the way along the Shankill, where the lorry driver stopped at the same time each morning to buy a newspaper. On most of his trips Murphy travelled alone, but on a few occasions he was accompanied by either Moore, Bates or Mr A.

The lorry picked up Protestant and Catholic workers at Carlisle Circus, some of them seated in the cab and others on the open area at the rear of the vehicle. It is conceivable that Murphy knew there were Protestants aboard and this did not concern him. His fanatical hatred frequently obscured his judgement and allowed him to dismiss any petty hindrances which might arise, such as the fact that Protestants might have to die to enable him to kill a large number of Catholics.

He decided that if he was to attack the lorry successfully the place to do it was outside the newsagent's shop known locally as Adair's, which was situated at the corner of Cambrai Street and the Shankill Road. The day before the killing of Quinn, Murphy called a meeting with Moore, Bates and Mr A. and told them 'the hit' on the lorry would take place the following morning at approximately 7.45A.M., when the vehicle stopped outside Adair's. He instructed Moore and Bates to travel in Moore's taxi to his house for 7.00A.M., where they would find him with Mr A. and the four of them would drive together to a 'safe house' to collect weapons.

The following morning everything was arranged but the attack on the lorry was aborted because of the presence of soldiers in Cambrai Street. The lorry did not make another journey until Monday, but it was in the intervening period that Murphy kidnapped Quinn and murdered him.

Monday was set as the day when another attempt would be made on the lorry but there were several factors which Murphy omitted from his calculations. During his trips when he followed the lorry he failed to take note of the faces of the men on it. One week before the attack on the vehicle the Catholic workmen who regularly travelled on

it decided to use an alternative route and different transport. A newspaper report later attributed their decision to
the fact that they had noticed a black taxi following the
lorry through the Shankill. However, this was not the
case. They were apprehensive about travelling through a
Loyalist stronghold each day and, at the end of January,
they were offered alternative means of travel which did
not include the Shankill route. Murphy, unaware of this,
laid his plans for Monday 9 February.

As before, Moore and Bates travelled to Brookmount
Street and picked up Lenny and Mr A. They made their
way in the taxi to a 'safe house' nearby and were given
a Thompson sub-machine gun and a MkI carbine (an
American rifle of Second World War origin). They
returned armed to Murphy's home and Bates, Moore and
Mr A. waited while Murphy went to hijack a car. The
hijacking was not simply a spontaneous decision by
Murphy but one which he had planned meticulously. The
car he had in mind, a Ford Cortina, was parked in the
same place each morning. It was owned by a postman who
delivered letters in the Ceylon Street area and who parked
the car before making his deliveries, the timing of which
Murphy noted accurately. Ironically, the postman was
Nathaniel Cush, a part-time member of the UDR who
died in 1987 when the Provisionals booby-trapped his car
outside the main postal sorting office in the centre of
Belfast.

Murphy calculated that if he stole the car the theft
would not be obvious to the owner for at least an hour,
which was sufficient time for him to attack the lorry and
then abandon the Cortina. The gang of four drove in the
stolen Cortina to Cambrai Street, to a position where they
were afforded a clear view of the corner shop and the
Shankill Road. They did not have long to wait, and with
predictable punctuality the driver of the lorry, Henry
McClelland, parked outside Adair's and went into the
shop to buy a newspaper. On the lorry were six other

people: McClelland's son, Harry, Mary Johnston and Raymond Carlisle were crammed into the cabin, and on the open rear of the vehicle were Archie Hanna, Louis Magee and James Wylie.

Archie Hanna also dismounted from the lorry and followed Henry McClelland into the shop to buy a sandwich. On seeing the two men enter the shop Murphy told Moore to drive slowly down Cambrai Street and then reverse the Cortina until it was close to the rear of the lorry. Murphy cocked the Thompson, easing a round into the breach, and handed the carbine to Bates who loaded the weapon and put it in a firing mode. Mr A. handed each of them a black woollen scarf which they tied around their faces thus obscuring the nose, mouth and chin. As Moore brought the Cortina to a standstill Murphy was first to get out, followed by Bates. Archie Hanna was busy clambering back into the lorry's cabin as the two gunmen stepped off the pavement onto the road to face the length of the lorry. Henry McClelland was walking out of the shop when he saw the two gunmen and he shouted instinctively, 'They're Prods. They're all Prods'. His split-second reaction in defining the threat emanated either from a long-harboured fear about driving Catholics through the Shankill or because his knowledge of the conflict warned him that on the Shankill Road only Protestants would confront him brandishing guns and preparing to shoot his workmates.

His warning was in vain. Murphy opened fire with the sub-machine gun, followed by Bates who fired single rounds from the carbine. When Murphy first fired his weapon it was switched to automatic fire and jammed after five shells were discharged. He took the carbine from Bates and handed him the Thompson. Bates made his way back to the Cortina while Murphy continued to spray the lorry with bullets, discharging eighteen rounds in total. He then made his way to the hijacked car and Moore drove the car away at speed.

They drove to Glencairn where Murphy, Mr A. and

Bates got out. Moore was told to abandon the Cortina at Forthriver Way, return to Brookmount Street and pick up his taxi, then operate in the usual manner of a cab driver for the remainder of the day so as not to arouse suspicion. Murphy and Mr A. separated from Bates and left the weapons with an associate in Glencairn.

Meanwhile, on the lorry Archie Hanna and Raymond Carlisle were dead and Louis Magee and James Wylie were injured. Magee and Wylie survived after lengthy hospital treatment, though Wylie suffered from bouts of acute depression long after his physical wounds had healed. A medical report in April 1976 recorded that Wylie was 'suffering from considerable mental trauma and was finding it difficult to sustain interest in any subject for any length of time'. This condition persisted for a lengthy period.

Louis Magee had shown great courage and here is his account of the shooting: 'I turned my head to the side and saw a masked man who appeared all black to me. He had something long in his hand and was in a crouched position. I saw sparks coming from what he had in his hand. I tried to hide behind a battery when I saw what he had in his hand because I realized it was a shooting. Then I felt something hit my head. I thought I was a goner so I lay still pretending I was dead. When I was lying there I felt a bullet hit my left leg and another bullet tear into my left forearm. I thought they were gonna try to finish me off. I jumped up and off the back of the lorry. I knew I couldn't run so I crawled underneath the lorry and lay there until the shooting stopped.'

At lunchtime that day Moore called at Murphy's home just as the BBC radio lunchtime news was revealing details of the attack on the lorry. The news stated that the dead and injured were Protestants. Moore says that Murphy 'went mad' and threatened to shoot 'twice as many Catholics' to counterbalance those they themselves had killed on the lorry. Moore's account suggests that Murphy did not wish to believe that he was guilty but preferred to see it as a crime which called for revenge. I am more inclined to think that Murphy suddenly realized that he had made an error of judgement and that to obscure his participation from the UVF leadership he would have to make it known that he intended to retaliate. Moore did not understand Murphy's reaction because he was overwhelmed by its ferocity, to the extent that Moore adds that Murphy 'went berserk' and had to be restrained by Mr A. Murphy did not reveal to anyone outside his circle of associates that he was the man who had committed the killings. Instead, he made it known in UVF circles that he attributed the murders to a Provisional IRA murder squad and he wished for revenge. Whether the UVF leadership actually believed this or not, they took no action to investigate the shooting or to accuse Murphy of being responsible.

It was among the members of his unit that Murphy felt vulnerable on this issue and it was never mentioned again in his presence. His ferocious outburst of anger during the lunchtime news was the only occasion on which he talked about it. The threats made during that tirade were eventually put into practice.

Murphy remained inactive for two weeks following the lorry killings, but during this time he had a conversation with Moore, Bates and McAllister which reveals how he coped with the cut-throat killings. He told them the best way to 'handle it' was to keep doing it so that the memory of seeing one individual dying faded with the next killing. This may well have been fanciful theorizing on Murphy's part articulated for the benefit of his gang, since it is clear he did not actually suffer from bouts of depression or remorse; the reverse was nearer the truth. It was he who said on another occasion that the ultimate way to kill was to cut someone's throat. Murphy perceived himself as macho and cavalier and wished to impress this image on others.

On the evening of Saturday 26 February 1976 he was

ready to demonstrate his personal thesis on ways of coping with the use of the knife. As with most of his crimes, the plans were made over a drink in a bar and on this occasions it was the Long Bar. In his company were Bates, Moore and Mr C. who, like Mr A. and Mr B. cannot be named here because, like them, he has never been charged with the Butcher killings and remains a free man.

At some stage in the evening Murphy invited two women to join him, and bought them drinks before encouraging them to linger with him and his associates. (The women have never been charged and for obvious legal reasons cannot be named here. One of them has since gone to live in Canada.) Murphy held court until midnight, expressing his views about the political situation and concluding that the only way to change it was to create terror among the 'enemy'. At 1.00A.M. the four men and two women boarded Moore's taxi, with the women in the front seat alongside William Moore. When Bates was later asked why they all got into the taxi he trotted out the rehearsed response that they were intending to travel across the city to buy chips. Bates knew only too well what lay ahead, since Murphy had made clear his intentions before they left the Long Bar. Moore says that when they were all in the taxi Murphy told him to drive to the Library/Upper Donegall Street area to 'look for a *Taig*'. They took a route similar to that taken on the nights they abducted Crossan and Quinn and made the same detours through the darkened side streets of the district.

That night, twenty-four-year-old Francis Dominic Rice, an unemployed labourer, spent much of his time drinking with friends in a Catholic social club on the periphery of Belfast city centre. He played a few games of snooker and decided to lay down his cue when he saw a girl, Margaret, whom he had known for six years, enter the club. He joined her and remained with her and some of her friends until midnight, at which time she said she wished to go home. Francis asked Margaret if he could walk with her to the taxi stand. Margaret agreed because, as she later confided to detectives, she was 'fond' of Francis. They walked together to within fifty yards of the taxi depot, where they talked casually for a few minutes and Francis kissed Margaret goodnight. Margaret's memory of Francis was that he was not drunk and would have been capable of defending himself if attacked. His journey home took him through Union Street, past the junction with Library Street and into Upper Donegall Street, from where he intended making his way to Carlisle Circus and the Antrim Road. As he walked into Upper Donegall Street, Moore's taxi pulled alongside him and Murphy leaped out of the vehicle brandishing a wheel brace. Rice tried to escape but was felled from behind and staggered onto the roadway. Bates rushed from the taxi and helped Murphy drag Rice, who by now was slightly dazed, into the vehicle. Moore drove off into Upper Library Street and onto Peter's Hill and the Shankill Road.

As the taxi travelled slowly along the Shankill, Murphy, Moore and Bates kicked and punched Rice while the two women watched from the front seat and Moore from the rear-view mirror. Murphy stopped the beating and searched Rice to ensure that he was a Catholic. Rice had on his person a membership card for a club situated in the predominantly Nationalist New Lodge Road district, and Bates later told detectives that when Murphy found the card it 'sealed Rice's fate'. Personally, I do not think it made any difference, because he was already injured before Murphy searched him and found the card. Rice might well have revealed his religion under torture and therefore finding the card would not have been of any great consequence.

Murphy instructed Moore to drive to Brookmount Street where Murphy left the taxi, entered his house, and returned with a butcher's knife. The taxi was then driven in the direction of the Lawnbrook Club and, at Murphy's insistence, to Esmond Street. During this journey Murphy taunted Rice with the knife and cut him about the throat and sides of the neck while he was being held down on the rear seat. Mr C. sat on his chest and Bates held his arms. Moore admitted later that while Murphy was in his house getting the knife, Bates and Mr C. beat Rice and Mr C. told him he was going to be killed.

When the taxi reached Esmond Street Murphy gesticulated to indicate that he wished Moore to pull up at the entrance to an alleyway. Rice was conscious, Murphy having ensured that the throat wounds were not fatal, and he was moaning with pain. Murphy told Moore that he was going to 'finish off' Rice and that he would require the assistance of 'Basher' Bates and Mr C. and that, while he was doing this, it would be safer for Moore to drive the women around the neighbourhood and meet up with him and the others at the far end of the alleyway. Rice was carried deep into the alley and dragged a short distance before being laid on his back. He was kicked by the three killers before Murphy set to work with the knife. It took Murphy several minutes before he hacked through his victim's throat until the knife touched the spine. Shortly afterwards the gang, including the women, were on their way to Forthriver in Glencairn, where Murphy, Mr C. and the women took their leave of Moore and Bates. Moore went to Bates's home where they cleaned the interior of the taxi and Bates changed his clothing.

An elderly woman whose house overlooked the alley found the body at 8.00A.M. when she ventured outdoors to put rubbish in her dustbin. She told police that during the night she had heard voices with Belfast accents and the sound of a 'heavy vehicle', which reminded her of the noise made by black taxis on the Shankill Road.

Jimmy Nesbitt swamped the Esmond Street area with uniformed policemen together with members of his own murder squad and members of CID who were temporarily released from other duties. The only person who was able to provide assistance was the elderly lady who found the body.

Nesbitt was in no doubt that he was dealing with a crime committed by the murderers of Crossan and Quinn because of the similarities and the frenzied nature of the attacks. He now had an avenue which required urgent investigation and that was the possibility of the use of a taxi in the killing of Rice. He immediately assigned men to trace the names of all taxi drivers on the Shankill Road. He reckoned that if he could narrow down the number of taxi drivers to those who could be described as suspects, he could have their taxis forensically tested. The selection was related to those drivers who had been observed 'acting suspiciously', and a shortlist was drawn up on the advice of members of the murder squad and other detectives within the CID. The taxis under suspicion were brought to Tennent Street during the course of one day. There is no figure available for the number of taxis called in by the RUC, but Nesbitt says that Moore's taxi was amongst them. Nesbitt's tactics were flawed, as he himself was aware, since the first taxi driver to be contacted by police would pass on word to other members of the Taxi Association and news of the police operation would be common knowledge within a matter of hours. This was inevitable in a small neighbourhood such as the Shankill. Nesbitt believed the chance was worth taking on the basis that even a speck of blood might be detectable under forensic examination. Why was Moore's taxi one of those selected for examination in Tennent Street Police Station? In what way had he been acting suspiciously? The police answer to these questions is simply that he was assessed as a person who was 'seen acting suspiciously'. I believe that Nesbitt was forced because of the lack of manpower, because of the time it would have taken to test every taxi and because of the fact that such a massive operation would have alerted the guilty party, to settle for a random selection. According to Nesbitt, the examination of

Moore's taxi revealed nothing of value to the police. The examination was, however, valuable to Moore. Murphy ordered him to dispose of the vehicle as quickly as possible. He took it to a scrapyard and had it destroyed and within twenty-four hours had replaced it with a beige Mark II Cortina, registration DIA 9477. Police documentation on the testing of the taxis has since been destroyed and I have no reason to doubt their assertion that Moore's was examined.

News of the third cut-throat killing generated bizarre speculation in some sections of the Press and tabloid imagery featured strongly. Significantly, the word 'butchers' found its way into the journalistic language of Northern Ireland, though the description Shankill Butchers was not used until several months later. Nesbitt found a greater significance in the use of the word 'butchers' because the expert *post mortem* analysis carried out by Dr Thomas Marshall, the State Pathologist, suggested that a butchery knife was likely to have been the murder weapon, and from this information it occurred to Nesbitt that the murderer or murderers could be butchers by profession or employed in the butchery trade. Nesbitt and other members of the C Division murder squad visited most of the butchery premises in the Shankill area and spoke privately with the owners in the hope that someone might have come to their attention. Enquiries were made as to whether knives were missing or stolen but, as with other enquiries, Nesbitt's team was out of luck. With hindsight one may feel entitled to ask why Moore was not investigated after his taxi had been forensically tested, since he previously worked as a packer in Woodvale Meats; surely a vital clue with regard to the cut-throat killings. It is easy to frame such a question in retrospect and the response from the RUC is simply that at the time Moore was cleared of suspicion following a detailed examination of his taxi. There was at the time a serious problem *vis-à-vis* resources available to the police. The number of terrorist acts being committed within C Division alone called for large-scale facilities and manpower, and those which were available were plainly inadequate – a shameful situation. I examined the register for the hours worked by the Tennent Street murder squad during February 1976 and I was shocked by the frequency of twelve-to-sixteen-hour days worked by Nesbitt and his men. In one three-week period, Nesbitt's diary shows that he worked 336 hours, which is almost three times the hours anyone would expect to work in a normal job.

During those three weeks Nesbitt and his team 'called in markers on all the informers they used in West Belfast'. Nesbitt adds: 'We interviewed every informer and, I shouldn't say this, but we went close to making promises. Christ, we were determined to solve those killings. When we got nothing from the touts, something I considered unusual, I knew we were dealing with either someone who was running a very tight operation or someone who scared the hell out of everybody in the Shankill area. We even brought in a leading member of the UVF on a false pretext and tried to persuade him to deal with us, but he offered nothing.'

Many hours were spent after midnight by Nesbitt, Detective Inspector John Fitzsimmons who worked in CID, and members of the murder squad such as Jim Reid, Cecil Chambers and John Scott, considering means of solving the cut-throat killings. It was Nesbitt who finally came up with a novel but dangerous scheme to trap the Butchers and he called it 'Operation Knife Edge'. His plan was to place policemen on the streets in plain clothes and have them behave as drunks. He further planned covert surveillance at Forthriver in Glencairn. The evidence of Margaret McKee about the route taken by Rice after he left her on the fateful night convinced Nesbitt that he had to concentrate on the Library Street and Carlisle Circus area. He was aware of the risks to his men because a lone policeman could be shot from a passing

car or set upon by 'ordinary' criminals. Although a policeman used for these purposes could be wired with a microphone, protection would necessarily be some distance away
if the operation were to succeed. There was always the
possibility that in this situation he might not have the
chance to use his hidden microphone since a few seconds'
delay could lead to the killers escaping with a victim.
Nesbitt's scheme was given approval at the highest level
within his own Division but he made a request that the
role of playing the drunks should be given only to those
who volunteered. In the event, both uniformed men and
detectives made themselves available in large numbers.
Others offered to be part of the back-up teams which
would afford the best protection possible from a discreet
distance. The prospect of many extra hours being involved
in this work did not deter the large number of volunteers.

Nesbitt set about producing large maps on which he
placed whatever information was available about the cut-
throat killings. He insisted that everyone be briefed,
including those men who would not be part of the finer
workings of Operation Knife Edge, and he provided a
separate register so that every policeman going on duty
recorded that he had briefed himself on the available data
on the killings. Any new information gathered while on
duty, such as people or taxis observed to be behaving
'suspiciously', was added to the register at the end of duty.
The register was then signed. Nesbitt examined this log
daily in the hope that a pair of eyes might have seen
something of relevance to the enquiry.

The central thrust of Operation Knife Edge was the
use of policemen as decoy victims and it was undertaken
on as many nights as available manpower permitted. The
decoy was dressed shabbily, was wired with a hidden
microphone to a hidden back-up team, and armed with
the standard issue Walther PPK. Considering the speed
with which Murphy snatched his victims, this was a daring
and risky venture. It proved to be unsuccessful and was

abandoned in favour of normal police methods after several months. D Division also cooperated in the project and made personnel available, but like C Division they finally jettisoned the scheme.

Nesbitt also sought to warn the public of the dangers of walking through troubled areas or unlit streets in North and West Belfast. He enlisted the help of Bill McGookin, Head of the RUC Press Office, and appeals were made through newspapers and the broadcasting media to create a public awareness of the dangers faced by late-night drinkers. Inevitably it was people walking home late at night from pubs and clubs who were most vulnerable. In some instances the absence of late-night buses or a lack of money to pay for a taxi from a reputable company gave victims no alternative but to commit the folly of walking through dangerous areas.

Another factor is that people in a war situation adapt and become anaesthetized. They are aware of danger but come to accept it as part of life, and thus, through lack of prudence they offer themselves as victims.

As for Murphy and his gang, they must have been constantly aware of the slightest increase in security force activity. There was a sufficiently large number of people involved in paramilitary activities in West Belfast to note the frequency of police patrols and pass on such information to every pub or club in the Shankill area.

One factor which I believe was missing in Nesbitt's thinking at the time, though it may not have proven crucial, was a psychiatric evaluation of the crimes, together with a profile of the type of people most likely to be guilty of the killings. Dr Alex Lyons, who is familiar with the nature of political violence, has, since this period, continued to study the character of the conflict and the types of personalities involved. He works at Purdysburn Psychiatric Hospital on the outskirts of Belfast and has produced fascinating material on the subject. I found it interesting to note that in one of his papers he indicated that he did not have full access to material necessary for his studies and he hoped that in future the Northern Ireland Office might see its way to relax the rules on access to information about murderers and their crimes.

The singular dimension to the cut-throat killings which called for psychiatric evaluation was the use of a knife in a political conflict, and the fact that there was no substantial history of similar murders within the general parameters of Ulster terrorism. There is, however, sufficient evidence to show that the knife has been used by those on the fringes of paramilitary organizations: people out of control and therefore not subject to the kinds of discipline imposed by the majority of terrorist groupings. This thesis, if accepted, would have led Nesbitt and his team to search for people who appeared to act independently of any para-military authority or exhibited an autonomy outside their known role within a particular organization.

In a study by Dr Lyons it is also pointed out that alcohol plays a large part in the lives of sadistic murderers. Murphy was not an exceptionally heavy drinker, though some of his companions were, in particular McAllister and Bates. Murphy's actions were not the result of alcohol consumption, but the use of alcohol played a significant part in the lives of many of those within his unit. The pub was a constant feature of their daily lives and Murphy behaved as if he owned and controlled the Brown Bear Bar. The reason for such a defiant proprietorial attitude should have aroused suspicion and been investigated.

It is of value to note that a study by Dr Lyons and a colleague, Dr H. J. Harbinson, on the differing aspects of political and non-political murder in Northern Ireland shows that non-political murderers offend late at night and at weekends when most alcohol consumption occurs. This does not apply to political murderers who operate during daylight hours. The two psychiatrists also discovered that travelling, using a car or a motorcycle, is a method favoured by political murderers together with a choice of victim with whom they are unacquainted.

On the basis of their study and with the benefit of retrospective analysis, it is possible to categorize the Lenny Murphy unit killings as both political and non-political. In terms of their actions, I tend to favour the non-political definition, though I would not apply this definition to their attitudes, thoughts or conditioning.

8

The First Mistake

At 1.20A.M. on 2 March Lance Corporal John McIntosh was in charge of a mobile military patrol travelling in a Land Rover along the Shankill Road towards the city when he saw two men emerge from the Bayardo Bar. He decided to check them out and he did so with the assistance of three other members of his patrol. While he was questioning the two men as to why they were on the road at such a late hour Lenny Murphy emerged from the Bayardo with 'Basher' Bates and another man. The other man cannot be named here for legal reasons but will subsequently be referred to as Mr D. Lance Corporal McIntosh was informed by Murphy and the others that they were going to a club nearby and the lance corporal released them from questioning. However, he watched as they walked down the Shankill Road and into Downing Street which housed a Loyalist club. Half an hour later the lance corporal again saw Murphy, this time in the rear of a bronze-coloured Ford Cortina car heading up the Shankill Road towards the countryside. There were three other men in the car but the one who caught the soldier's attention was Murphy. The Cortina was also observed by a member of an RUC mobile patrol who noted the registration number as AGE 6J.

About two minutes later another military patrol saw the Cortina stop in Crossland Street off the Shankill Road. Murphy got out of the car and went into a shop, a premises known to remain open until 2.00A.M., returning within three minutes. The windows of the Cortina were steamed up and the soldier was unable to identify the other occupants. Before the Cortina was driven away, Murphy and his gang shouted abusive taunts at the military. There were in fact four occupants in the car; the fourth man cannot be named for legal reasons but will be referred to as Mr E.

The Cortina was frequently used by Mr E. though it was the property of UVF Welfare Association in the Rathcoole housing estate. This estate is situated on the Belfast Lough shoreline, ten miles from Belfast. At 2.50A.M. two Catholic women, twenty-five-year-old Mary Murray and twenty-eight-year-old Margaret McCartney were travelling along the Cliftonville Road in a car. They were both returning from a dance in the town of Ballymena in County Antrim and Mary Murray was the driver. Both women lived off the Cliftonville Road and knew the dangers present in the area but felt safe because they were in a car. As they reached a point close to where Ted McQuaid was shot, Mary Murray was startled by headlights from behind, which were being switched on and off in quick succession. This was a method used by police and Army patrols to signal cars to stop. Knowing this, Mary Murray slowed down to a stop. As she pulled into the side of the road she saw a bronze Cortina draw alongside. Suddenly shots were fired from the other car and Mary was hit by three bullets, one in the right shoulder and two in the lower chest region. As the Cortina sped away up the Cliftonville Road, Mary fought to remain conscious and drove the car to her friend's house, from where she was taken to hospital. Margaret McCartney had a lucky escape because bullets had passed over her head and shattered the rear windscreen.

The Cortina made its way to the top of the Cliftonville Road then to the Ballysillan Road and it was obviously the driver's intention to make for Glencairn. Unknown to the gunmen, a military patrol was positioned on the Ballysillan Road. Murphy was prepared for any eventuality, and sat in the rear of the car reloading the automatic pistol which he had used to shoot Mary Murray. The military mobile patrol on the Ballysillan was in position due to the quick thinking of Gunner Michael Mallinson of J Battery of the 3rd RHA Regiment. While on patrol in the Cavehill Road area he heard the shots fired by Murphy and ordered his men to head for the Ballysillan area in anticipation of the gunmen making for Glencairn. This is his account of what happened after he established a vehicle checkpoint on the Ballysillan Road:

> We had just set up the checkpoint when we saw a car travelling at speed towards us from the Cliftonville/Old-park direction. Our Land Rover was sitting at an angle to the pavement, blocking the path of this car. The four flashers on our vehicle were indicating our presence. I was standing at the front-near-side of the Land Rover and I saw this car move across towards the centre of the road. Sergeant Davenport jumped into our Land Rover and moved it into the centre of the road to offer no opportunity for the oncoming vehicle to pass us. As the car approached, I stood in the centre of the road but the car passed, half on and half off the pavement. I could see three or four dark shapes in the car at this stage. I ran round the back of the Land Rover to the front and as I did so I heard two shots being fired at us from the car. The car continued along the Ballysillan Road towards the Cavehill Road junction. I immediately took aim at the rear of the car which had regained its own side of the road and was approximately 100 yards from me. I fired one aimed shot. Another shot was fired by a second member of the patrol. The car continued on its way and we jumped into the Land Rover and followed in hot pursuit. The car disappeared out of sight along the North Circular Road and when we reached the Antrim Road it was not to be seen.

The two bullets fired by the patrol struck the Cortina but none of the occupants was hit and Murphy ordered Mr E. to drive to Lowood Park off the Antrim Road, which offered easy access on foot to Loyalist districts on the Shore Road. When they reached Lowood Park, Murphy set the Cortina alight, hid his gun in a hedge and made off on foot to the Shore Road. On the Shore Road he stole a Fiat car which was parked in the Mount Vernon housing estate. The four men drove back to the Shankill.

Meanwhile, residents of Lowood Park had been awakened by the sound of men running towards the Shore Road and telephoned the police, who arrived quickly to find the car still burning. Murphy and the others, it seemed from a first inspection, had left no clues. The fire in the car was put out and the surrounding area searched. Police on the spot decided to make a further search at daylight and residents were warned that if they noticed any suspicious objects they should avoid touching them and await the arrival of a police forensic team.

At 4.05A.M. Corporal Frank Harnett, a member of a mobile patrol, was at the junction of Percy Street and the Shankill Road when he observed a red Fiat car approaching him. He stopped the car and inside found Murphy, Bates and two other men. He ordered Private James Robertson Gunn to detain Murphy and released the others. No reason was ever offered as to why Murphy was immediately arrested and the others allowed to go free. An explanation which might explain this anomaly is that Murphy was known to the soldiers as a terrorist or his name was on a suspects list which all patrols carry with them. Private Gunn handed Murphy over to Constable Innes at Tennent Street, who kept him in custody but did not interview him. While Murphy was in Innes's custody he made the first mistake of his career, which he recognized after the event. This is how Innes remembered the episode: 'During the time I was guarding him he requested to go to the toilet. I went into the toilet with him but as the urinal was blocked he went into one of the cubicles. I heard the toilet being flushed. On hearing this I rushed over and looked into the cubicle and saw Murphy drying his hands which were still wet and he was also wiping the sleeves of his jacket with toilet paper. I immediately took him back into the Enquiry Office.'

Murphy's intention in washing his hands and his jacket was to remove lead residue, which accumulates on hands or garments which have been close to a gun being fired. Here was another example of the important details Murphy had learned during the time he spent listening to the evidence in terrorist trials in Crumlin Road courthouse. This time he was observed attempting to rid himself of evidence and Constable Innes was well aware of what he was trying to do. Innes put a call through to Nesbitt who told him to hold Murphy in custody until he arrived at the station. He also told Innes to contact the Forensic Department to have Murphy's clothing tested and swabs taken from his hands. At 7.00 A.M. Reserve Constable Roy Suitters assumed the role of guarding Murphy and was present when a member of the Forensic Team arrived. Roy Suitters told me: 'Before the chap from the Forensic Team addressed the accused, Murphy told him, "I've washed my hands". Murphy was then asked by him if he had been wearing the same coat that day and Murphy replied that he had. When the chap from Forensic left the room Murphy turned to me and said, "That's the first mistake I've made".'

Immediately after Murphy's arrest instructions were issued from Tennent Street for the arrest of Bates, Mr D. and Mr E. who had earlier been released by the military patrol. As with Murphy, swabs were taken from their hands and their jackets were removed. They, however, had more time than Murphy in which to consider their position and had changed clothes. Nevertheless, each of them washed their hands in Tennent Street. They were not observed doing this but admitted to having done so when questioned by members of the Forensic Team.

A member of the RUC Scenes of Crime Team told Murphy that his jacket was being removed for forensic testing, to which Murphy replied, 'I was working with batteries and lorries when I was wearing that coat.' Even at such a late stage, and knowing the mistake he had made, Murphy tried to concoct an explanation for the presence of lead residue. The reference to lorries and particularly batteries, which contain lead, was a shrewd piece of thinking on the part of a professional terrorist such as Murphy.

When Nesbitt and Detective Inspector John Fitzsimmons arrived at the station that morning they discussed the presence of Murphy. There was, however, a further development to the saga which intrigued them both: the discovery of an automatic pistol in the hedge at Lowood Park. It was found at 8.30A.M. by Sergeant John J. Darnbrough, a member of J Battery of the 3rd RHA Regiment. The search had begun at 7.00A.M. and it had taken forty-five minutes to recover the gun from inside a hedge behind a six-feet-high concrete wall. Sergeant Darnbrough concluded that the gun had not been thrown there but carefully concealed.

News of the find was relayed to C Division and in particular to Nesbitt and Fitzsimmons who, at this time, were discussing with others the manner in which to approach the interrogation of Murphy. They knew they had the right man from the reports of sightings of Murphy and his gang, the evidence of the soldiers at the roadblock and the two women on the Cliftonville Road. Murphy was questioned briefly but, as John Scott says, 'He was a man who never gave you an alibi in case you might break it. He gave you nothing.' Nesbitt and his men concluded likewise after a short interview with him because he simply told them that they would have to prove any allegations they wished to make.

When news reached Nesbitt of the find of the 9mm Llama pistol he decided that there was an alternative way of cornering Murphy. He ordered that the pistol find should be properly recorded but the discovery should not be made known to Murphy. Murphy, he told the others, should be released. Nesbitt was well aware that there was no prospect of breaking Murphy under questioning. There was no guarantee that the forensic evidence would be sufficient to link him to the gun and the shooting of Mary Murray. So Nesbitt and Fitzsimmons decided to postpone Murphy's release for several hours until certain other factors were established, such as: would the three bullets taken from Mary Murray match the rifling on the Llama pistol and, if so, would Murphy's clothing provide a positive test?

Even if all these factors came together, Nesbitt knew it might not be enough to sustain a strong case. What he needed most was to link Murphy to the pistol in a way that strengthened the evidence against him. There was little prospect of bringing a conspiracy case and no chance of getting Bates, Mr D. or Mr E. to admit guilt. The prospect of releasing Murphy intrigued Nesbitt because he believed Murphy was likely to return to Lowood to retrieve the weapon from its hiding place.

He waited several hours for the forensic experts to do their work until finally he was informed that the bullets removed from Mary Murray did match the rifling grooves on the pistol and lead residue had been found on the sleeves and in the pockets of Murphy's coat. No traces of lead were found on the swabs taken from Bates, D. and E., nor on their clothing, and they were released. Murphy was also released though Nesbitt knew that twenty-four hour surveillance of him was virtually impossible. His plan was to place surveillance on the spot where the gun was found so that if Murphy did come to retrieve it a waiting patrol car could be alerted. At 8.15A.M. the following day, 3 March, Murphy drove to Lowood Park alone in a lorry and the following is an account of his behaviour as observed by one of the residents of Lowood Park: 'I saw a lorry parked outside 27 Lowood Park and my attention was drawn to the vehicle because it seemed to be slipping backwards as if the handbrake had not been properly applied. There was no one in the cab. I looked beyond the lorry and saw a man bending down, rummaging through the hedge surrounding the garden of number 27.'

Several residents of the street who were anxious about the events of the previous day were on the alert and witnessed Murphy searching the hedge, but there was one other person in the street who must, for security reasons, remain anonymous but who was there, at the instigation of Jimmy Nesbitt, to wait and observe. He radioed the police to tell them that the man they wanted was searching for the gun.

A schoolboy delivering papers at the time also saw Murphy and gave Nesbitt this account of what he saw: 'I was delivering papers when this lorry stopped beside me in Lowood Park. The driver was the only person in the lorry and he got out by the passenger door. He looked up and down the street several times before going to the hedge at number 27. He got down on his knees and searched among the leaves and roots of the hedge with both hands and shook it very hard. After this he walked into the garden and searched the other side of the hedge. When I saw him first start to search the hedge, I stepped up to number 37 and hid behind the hedge there and watched him. He had black curly hair, was of medium height and well built. He was wearing a Wrangler jacket and jeans. The jeans were turned up at the bottom and were a whitish colour and he was wearing black boots. After he searched the hedge he got into the lorry and drove away.'

Within two minutes of Murphy leaving Lowood Park his lorry was flagged down by an RUC mobile patrol and he was detained by Reserve Constable Gerard Donohue, who took him to Greencastle Police Station on the shoreline of Belfast Lough. From there he was transferred to Tennent Street Station, where Nesbitt and members of his murder squad were waiting for his arrival. Detective Sergeant Wilson and Detective Constable Woods were given the task of testing Murphy once again under questioning. Their notes of the interview represent the only record on police files of how Murphy dealt with the interrogation process. Detective Sergeant Wilson put the questions to the accused:

Q. Account for your movements on Wednesday night, March 10.
A. I finished work about 4.30P.M.
Q. What did you do then?
A. I got my supper and went out about 8.30 or 9.00P.M.
Q. Where did you go?
A. I went to the Lawnbrook Club, and seen the Morecombe and Wise Show.
Q. How long did you stay there?
A. I left about 8.50 or 8.55.
Q. Where did you go?
A. The Long Bar where I seen Basher Bates.
Q. Did you stay there long?
A. No, I stayed there until about 10.15 and I went to the Four Step and had a couple of games of pool.
Q. What did you do then?
A. I left it and went down to the Long Bar.
Q. What time was that?
A. About 10.55.
Q. How long did you stay there?
A. About ten or fifteen minutes. I went to the Loyalist.
Q. Who did you go to the Loyalist Club with?
A. Basher Bates.
Q. How long did you stay there?
A. About half an hour or so.
Q. Where did you go then?
A. I met Chuck Berry and he invited me up to his club for a drink.
Q. What way did you go up?
A. We walked up.
Q. Did you leave the club at any time?
A. I heard someone say that [Mr E.] was being lifted. Bates and a lot more of us ran down the stairs.
Q. What did you do then?
A. We went over to the soldiers and were talking.

145

Q. Where did you go after that?
A. We went back to the club.
Q. What time did you leave there?
A. I don't know what time. I was drunk. We were going over to a house in Moscow Street to get a lift when we met a friend and asked him to give Basher a lift to the West Circular and he said 'aye'.
Q. Did you both get into the car?
A. The three of us did.
Q. Who was the third person?
A. [*In this answer he mentions Mr D.*] We were stopped at the junction of Percy Street and the Shankill by the Army and they detained me.
Q. Were you in a bronze Cortina any time on Wednesday night or Thursday morning?
A. No, I don't think so.
Q. Were you in Crossland Street that night?
A. I don't know.
Q. Were you in Cliftonville Road early Thursday morning?
A. Definitely not.
Q. Was it Lowood where you stopped yesterday?
A. I don't know, but it was off the Antrim Road.
Q. What were you doing there?
A. I was going to the tiphead but I got a puncture.
Q. Where did you get the puncture?
A. I don't know. When you are driving a lorry you can feel when you get a puncture.
Q. Where did you stop the lorry?
A. When I turned right on the Antrim Road I heard her bumping and turned into a street on the left and then I turned left again and stopped. I got out and went round the back of the lorry to look for the puncture. I got on my knees and looked under her and checked for bricks between the tyres. I saw the back right outside wheel was flat.
Q. What did you do then?
A. I looked for a phone and I decided I would risk it and go back to the yard in it.
Q. Did you go back to the yard?

A. No. I got into the cab and drove onto the Antrim Road where I was stopped by police.

Q. What happened then?

A. They took me to Greencastle and then Tennent Street.

Q. What number is the lorry?

A. I don't know. It is not my lorry.

Q. Did you speak to anyone when you were out of the lorry?

A. No.

Q. What did you do when you got out of the lorry?

A. I looked around the lorry, below it and kicked the tyres.

Q. Did you touch a hedge or damage it?

A. No.

Q. Were you near a hedge when you stopped the lorry?

A. No. I never went near a hedge.

The questioning technique used by Detective Sergeant Wilson was deliberate and was employed in the hope of trapping Murphy, who would not have revealed anything under normal interrogation, hard questioning or verbal game-playing. Nesbitt had briefed Wilson well and was now able to take advantage of the risk which had paid off, namely having released Murphy in the hope that he would return to the scene of the crime. This he had done and was now answering questions while quite unaware that he had been watched as he returned to retrieve his gun. He was also questioned about the ownership of the lorry but was able to point out that he was working for Smyth's Haulage in West Belfast.

At 8.30p.m. that same day Detective Sergeant Wilson again saw Murphy but this time preferred the charge of his attempting to murder Mary Murray and Margaret McCartney. Murphy replied, 'Not guilty'. The following day he was also charged with possessing a firearm with intent to endanger life. Again, he replied, 'Not guilty'.

Both Nesbitt and Fitzsimmons felt it right to charge Murphy and this can be seen in a recommendation which

Fitzsimmons sent to the Chief Superintendent in C Division: 'While the evidence is circumstantial, it is strong and I would submit that Murphy has a case to answer. He is a known thug who has been interviewed on a number of occasions regarding sectarian murders. On one occasion he stood trial but was not convicted. I would suggest, therefore, that, circumstantial though the evidence may be, every effort should be made to bring this man to justice and I would recommend that he be proceeded against.'

The revelation in Fitzsimmon's recommendation that Murphy had been questioned on other occasions about sectarian murders is one which raises questions. It puzzled me because my enquiries did not reveal any evidence to support such a claim. If it were to be believed, then I should be obliged to conclude that Murphy had been suspected of sectarian murders. If this were so, why had he not been questioned about the cut-throat killings prior to his arrest on 13 March? I wondered whether Fitzsimmons had made a mistake by asserting this on paper, or perhaps he had deliberately stated this fact knowing it to be a falsehood and hoping that it would support the case for proceeding strongly against Murphy on the charge. I checked police files and documents prepared for the case against Murphy and reached the conclusion that Fitzsimmons was not lying. His comments were of course contained within private police memoranda on the Murphy case but this being so I still see no reason why Fitzsimmons would have fabricated this piece of supportive evidence to strengthen his recommendation. I also asked Jimmy Nesbitt if he could unearth from internal police documents any details which would indicate that Murphy was ever interviewed about the cut-throat killings. He replied that Murphy was questioned on 13 March 1976, the same day as he was charged with attempted murder, in respect of the killings of Crossan, Shaw, Quinn and Rice. Detective Sergeant John Scott confirmed this and added that Murphy had laughed when it was put to him that he had killed the people named by Inspector Nesbitt. I have no reason to doubt this but feel that Nesbitt, rather than being convinced, was merely going through the routine procedure of putting to a known killer crimes which had occurred in C Division. Ted McQuaid had been killed in D Division and Nesbitt did not include his name in the list put to Murphy. There is no answer available as to why Fitzsimmons claimed that Murphy had been questioned about sectarian killings prior to 13 March, since I have no evidence from police files to support this.

As time passed, Nesbitt had the opportunity to dwell on Murphy, examine the evidence, contemplate Murphy's demeanour during interview and recall how he had handled himself during the Pavis enquiry. No further cut-throat killings were occurring and Nesbitt began to feel certain that he had the cut-throat killer behind bars. Nesbitt was so sure of his hunch that he interviewed Murphy while he was on remand in Crumlin Road Prison. Murphy, as usual, played the joker and laughed off the prospect of his being the butcher.

While Murphy was waiting to be brought before the court there was no attempt to trace his associates, although the police knew that Bates had been with him on the night of the attempted murder of the two women. The explanation from the police is that they believed they had the cut-throat killer behind bars. Also, the burden of work, due to increasing terrorism, would not have permitted a large-scale enquiry, plus the fact that proper surveillance of Murphy's known associates would have been impossible in the Shankill area. While writing this book I discovered that the police were not allowed access to the Rumford Street Loyalist club and could only have gained entry if they had called for an Army assault on the place. Here again is a serious example of the RUC not having the necessary technical resources and manpower to mount an operation which would have identified and led to the arrest of the remainder of Murphy's unit.

Murphy was visited once a week in prison by Mr A., who relayed Lenny's orders to the unit which met weekly in the Brown Bear. The most significant of these was that the campaign was to continue but the cut-throat murders were to cease until such time as he ordered them to resume. Murphy knew that Nesbitt felt he had the right man behind bars and he busied himself devising means of throwing the police off the scent. He decided to bide his time and act when he saw fit. He was, however, determined to convince Nesbitt that he was not the knifeman. He was still in charge of the unit and had one trump card up his sleeve which he was convinced would fool even Nesbitt.

9
Murder Deal

Smithfield is a shopping area on the edge of Belfast city centre and has traditionally been a neighbourhood frequented by people from both sides of the community. It is essentially a market place with the features of a flea market. New goods are sold alongside junk and bric-à-brac. It is situated one hundred yards from the entrance to the Shankill Road and part of it borders the Castle Street extension of the Lower Falls District. Most adults in Belfast would be able to recall their first childhood visit to Smithfield, probably to look at the animals in pet shop windows or in cages on the pavement. The pubs in the area have both Catholic and Protestant clients. One such pub, the Chlorane Bar, provided a lively atmosphere both downstairs and in its upstairs lounge. Aside from passing trade, the Chlorane also catered for a regular clientele who frequented the premises after the surrounding shops closed each evening at 6.00P.M. It provided a welcome opportunity for people of both religions to drink together, not a regular occurrence in a city of ghettoes.

At 10.00P.M. on Saturday 5 June, Roland Cargill arrived at Smithfield Bus Station to discover that the bus to take him home would not depart until 10.30P.M. He decided to pass twenty-five minutes in the Chlorane Bar in nearby Gresham Street. When he walked into the downstairs public bar he ordered a drink and looked around the room. He noticed at least ten other people drinking and chatting, some in groups of twos and threes. Roland paid for his drink and sat alone at a table in the middle of the room within sight of the entrance to the bar. Also in the

151

bar were Robert Emerson and his brother John, who were sitting at a table under the staircase which led to the lounge. Robert remembers that he and his brother always sat in this spot. When they first arrived they noticed forty-seven-year-old Daniel McNeill from Percy Street in the Shankill area sitting alone at a table. Robert and his brother were soon joined by two other acquaintances: Frederick Graham and his girlfriend, Pat Mahood. Sitting at the rear of the bar between the storeroom and the gents toilet was forty-five-year-old William Greer who was relaxing after a hard day's work in the security service of the Royal Victoria Hospital in Belfast. His recollection is that everyone in the bar was in a happy mood; most of those present were regular customers and therefore casually acquainted. The subject of politics was studiously avoided by drinkers in this bar because the topic risked causing offence between customers of different persuasions.

Frederick Graham and Pat Mahood were sitting on a bench seat facing the main bar when they noticed the Emersons and exchanged greetings. Frederick and Pat also noticed Daniel McNeill sitting on his own and ordered a drink for him which the barman delivered to his table. McNeill, unlike others in the Chlorane, was believed by police to have UVF connections though he certainly was not an active member of the organization.

Also in the bar were Francis Carrothers, Samuel Corr and John Martin and, like the others mentioned, they were Protestants.

The owner of the Chlorane was sixty-four-year-old Jimmy Coyle, who was serving behind the bar and was on first-name terms with all his customers. He was a Catholic, and sitting in the bar that night was a fellow Catholic, forty-five-year-old Edward Farrell, whom Jimmy knew well.

At 10.00P.M., less than half a mile away from the Chlorane, Mark Hagan was driving his black taxi along the Shankill Road with one passenger on board. He was signalled to stop by two youths outside the Long Bar. He remembers expecting them to be prospective customers, and there was nothing to suggest that they were intent on hijacking his vehicle. However, once the youths were in the taxi one of them leaned over to the driver's seat and told Hagan that the taxi was being commandeered. Hagan and his earlier passenger were taken to the Windsor Bar with a warning that they would be held hostage there for half an hour. I believe that they were both told that in no circumstances were they to provide identification of the hijackers to the police nor to offer information on the identities of the men holding them hostage in the Windsor Bar.

Before 10.00P.M. Charles Bolton was cycling through Belfast city centre, making his way home after an unsuccessful evening trying to pick winning greyhounds at the Dunmore Park racing track off Belfast's Antrim Road. As he entered Gresham Street he noticed a black taxi drawing to a halt outside the Chlorane Bar. He felt intuitively that something was about to happen and got off his bike. His recollection of what took place was later given to police:

> Four men got out of this taxi and walked to the door of the bar. The light was on in the hallway of the bar and outside it was getting dark. The men walked in single file from the taxi into the bar. They seemed to go upstairs and I noticed that the last of the four men pulled on a bright coloured hood as he entered the front door leading to the bar. When the four men were inside, the taxi took off. I think it went in the direction of Smithfield Square but at any rate it soon returned, going against the traffic signs which indicated that Gresham Street was a one-way system and stopped outside the Chlorane. Before the taxi returned I heard clicks coming from inside the bar. I spoke to a man walking along Gresham Street and told him that I thought a robbery was taking place. I climbed onto my bicycle and went to a nearby Army Post and told soldiers there what I had witnessed. I also told them that the taxi was not using its headlights and that the four men were

all about five feet ten inches in height, well built and in the twenty to thirty years age group. They were all well dressed. One had shoulder-length hair, brown in colour, and was wearing a brown suit. He was the last man to enter the bar. The other men also wore suits. The taxi driver was an elderly man who was thin-faced and wearing glasses. I would not know him or the four men who walked into the Chlorane.

Roland Cargill remembers ordering a second drink and walking from the bar to his table when four men burst into the downstairs bar:

> They came in in Indian file and were wearing balaclava helmets. The helmets were a yellow colour and looked as though they were made from a chamois-type material. I noticed almost immediately that the two men leading this group were carrying handguns. The first one said to everyone, 'All right, Prods to one side and Catholics to the other.' I rose from my seat until I was almost at eye level with this man and I said to him something like: 'It's not going to be this sort of carry on?' He turned towards me and put his gun in my ribs and asked: 'What are you?' I said that I was a Prod and why should that matter. He then pulled the gun from my ribs and put it to my head. I assumed that I was going to be shot and I pulled my head back. He just fired the gun and shot me through the nose. I remember nothing else until I found myself lying between two other men on the floor and there were pools of blood everywhere.

Robert Emerson and his brother John were chatting to customers at another table when Robert witnessed the masked men entering the bar. He remembers it in this way:

> One of the four men asked whether there were any Prods in the bar and I told him that I was one and he ushered me towards the bar counter. At the same time two male customers came out of the Gents'. When they saw the gunmen, they tried to go back into the toilet but the gunman warned them not to do so. I was standing with

my back to the gunman and my brother John was alongside me. The gunman pushed me down the room towards the toilet and as this was happening the two fellows who had been in the Gents' made a dash for the toilet and the gunman started shooting at them. When the shooting started, my brother got down on the floor and shouted to me to do the same. When the shooting stopped, John could not get to his feet and he told me he had been shot in both legs. I was not injured but the following day I found two bullet holes in the bottom of my right trouser leg and two bullet holes in my cap.

John Emerson believes the gunmen were wearing linen money bags over their heads and remembers that each bag had holes cut for the eyes, nose and mouth. He says that everybody in the bar stood quietly when the gunmen entered.

Some of the bags worn by the gunmen were a yellow colour and others a darker colour. All the gunmen were armed with pistols. One big fellow with a yellow mask and wearing a grey-checked sports jacket and dark trousers said: 'All Protestants to the bottom of the bar.' The Protestants moved to the bottom of the bar beside the toilets and the Catholics went to the top of the bar. There were two men in front of me at the Protestant end of the bar when the gunmen started shooting at us. The two men in front of me went down and I pretended I was shot and fell with them to the floor. Initially there were six or seven shots fired and then there was a short lull. I lay on the floor pretending to be dead. One of the gunmen came over to me and pointed his gun down at me and fired three shots into my thigh, knee and below my right ankle. I lifted my head and had a look round and saw men lying shot all over the place.

One of those seen emerging from the toilet, who then attempted to return to seek sanctuary, was the security man from the Royal Victoria Hospital, William Greer. He says, 'When I heard one of the gunmen asking about Prods I thought that Prods were going to be shot and I ran into the toilet, sat on the floor and placed my feet against the door to prevent it being opened. Several shots were fired through the door and I was hit on both sides of the neck and on my right leg.'

Francis Carrothers remembers that the shooting began after Edward Farrell told the gunmen that he was a Catholic. Jimmy Coyle, who was standing behind the counter of his bar, also told them he was a Catholic.

Frederick Graham and Pat Mahood believed the gunmen were members of the Provisional IRA, once they had enquired if there were Protestants present in the bar. Carrothers says that he saw a man running towards the toilet. The man was Edward Farrell who, unlike Frederick Graham, believed the gunmen to be Loyalists and tried to escape. One of the gunmen shouted to him to stop. Farrell was unable to get into the toilet because William Greer was inside with his feet against the door. Farrell was shot twice in the back as he reached the toilet door. The same gunman then turned to Jimmy Coyle who was standing behind the bar counter, his arms by his sides, and shot him once at point-blank range through the heart, killing him instantly. Frederick Graham remembers closing his eyes when Jimmy Coyle was shot and waiting for the gunmen to kill him.

After the shooting the gunmen walked coolly out of the Chlorane and climbed aboard the waiting taxi, which was positioned so that it could drive into North Street, less than 100 yards from the bottom of the Shankill Road. This short journey necessitated them passing a small Catholic enclave, Unity Flats. As the taxi sped past Unity Flats two Catholic youths were walking along the pavement and heard three shots being fired from the taxi. One of the youths, Francis Fury, says he was not sure whether the shots were directed at him and his companion or whether they were just fired at Unity Flats generally. He also confirms that an Army foot patrol was near at hand but took no action to return fire at the taxi.

The other youth, Liam McCarville, was convinced at the time that the shots were directed at him and Francis Fury. He gave police a detailed description of the taxi driver: 'The driver was thirty-eight to forty years old. He was stoutly built and had shoulder-length curly black hair. He had a big pointed nose, sharp features and two wrinkled cheeks. I would know this man again. The windows of the taxi were down on the side facing me but I did not see the other persons in the taxi.'

John Emerson's son-in-law, Edward McGreevy, was drinking with his wife in the upstairs lounge of the Chlorane on the fateful evening and he gave this testimony to police the following day:

> My wife and I were beginning to drink our first one of the night when I heard thuds coming from the downstairs bar. They sounded like the noise of someone hammering with a wooden mallet. My wife and I were only in the lounge about seven or eight minutes when I heard the first thuds. There was a pause and then more of the same sounds. When I first heard the noises, the barmaid, Sheila, went to the food lift which linked the lounge to the downstairs bar and shouted something. I think she was calling for Jimmy Coyle to answer to explain the noises. When she got no reply she went to the top of the stairs outside the lounge and looked downwards. I saw her place her hand over her mouth. The other barmaid rushed across to her and as a result of something that was said I jumped to my feet and rushed downstairs and into the bar. When I entered the bar the first thing I noticed was a pile of bodies down at the bottom of the bar. I noticed smoke and the smell of sulphur in the air. I saw my father-in-law, John Emerson, lying on the floor and I remembered that my wife had followed me into the bar. I didn't wish her to see the whole mess and I pushed her out and told Robert Emerson to look after her. I phoned the police and they arrived very quickly.

The first policeman on the scene was George Robert McElnea who was attached to the RUC Special Patrol

Group in Tennent Street Station. The record on police files for that night indicates that he arrived at the Chlorane at 10.07P.M., several minutes after the shooting. He went into the downstairs bar to discover a pile of bodies close to the gents' toilet and he counted eight injured and dying men. A seriously injured man, now known to have been fifty-three-year-old Samuel Corr, staggered towards him. Constable McElnea placed him on a bench and rendered what help he could.

Three people lay dead in the bar: Jimmy Coyle, Edward Farrell and Daniel McNeill. Samuel Corr died before ambulances arrived and John Martin, one of the injured, died two weeks later.

Alan McCrum, a Scenes of Crime Officer, arrived in Gresham Street fifteen minutes after the shooting and removed spent bullet cases from the floor of the bar. These indicated that .45, .32, and .22 calibre weapons had been used by the gunmen, and the position of the spent cases led him to conclude that guns had been fired at the rear of the bar.

At 10.35P.M. Mark Hagan and his passenger were released by the men holding him hostage in the Windsor Bar. He walked to Tennent Street Station and reported the hijacking of his taxi. The vehicle was not found until 8.30A.M. the following morning in a cul-de-sac in Beresford Street off the Shankill Road. When all the bullet cases – twenty-four in all – were removed from the bar the RUC's forensic department was able to conclude that the .38 calibre cases were fired from a 9mm K-calibre pistol with a barrel rifling of six grooves, right hand twist. They ascertained that the .45 shells were not, in fact, fired from a pistol but a revolver. All the .9mm cases were fired from the same pistol, as were the .22 cartridges but the .45 cases indicated that two weapons of this calibre were discharged.

The attack on the Chlorane Bar was a joint operation between the Brown Bear and Windsor Bar units, though the only central figure from the Brown Bear team to take part in the killing was Robert 'Basher' Bates. On this occasion the attack was sanctioned by the UVF leadership in retaliation for an explosion earlier that day at the Protestant-owned Times Bar in Belfast's York Street, in which two Protestant men were killed. This explosion, which wrecked the bar, was carried out by the Provisional IRA.

The decision to attack the Chlorane Bar was taken because of the proximity of the premises to the Shankill Road. The hit could thus be carried out speedily and the geography of the surrounding area afforded a safe getaway. It could be argued that, in a city beset with terrorism and constant security patrolling, the gang on this occasion was taking a great risk. However, they well knew that their base was less than five minutes away. Also Murphy's confidence had been bolstered after the shooting of Mary Murray which had proved it was possible to make an escape in difficult circumstances, such as with an Army patrol close at hand. Additionally, the gang's use of a taxi provided a few important seconds in which soldiers or policemen had to decide whether it was carrying ordinary members of the public or terrorists. The terrorists were also well aware that once they reached the North Street junction with the Catholic enclave of Unity Flats they would have a view of the Shankill Road ahead where, in the event of a police or Army roadblock, they could make a diversion. Public comments to the effect that there was insufficient security activity on the night of this slaying, 5 June, do indeed seem justified. However, the counter-argument put forward by the police, then and now, is that if the life of the city is not to be disrupted twenty-four hours a day, security must be on a random basis. This view is based on the knowledge that terrorists rely on precise details of police and Army movements and that they calculate the risks attached to their operations accordingly. As we have seen, Murphy did take risks, some calculated others not, and later in this book I will show that there were many occasions when the Butchers were searching out victims and the security presence did, in fact, prevent them from achieving their aims. There were also instances where they snatched people who were able to fight them off and escape.

A statement which Bates later made to Detective Sergeant Cecil Chambers from Jimmy Nesbitt's murder squad reveals how the attack on the Chlorane Bar was planned and executed. It is one of two statements made in respect of this crime and one in which Bates claimed he wished to tell the 'whole truth'. There are people mentioned in the statement who were never charged and it has never before been printed in a newspaper or magazine. For legal reasons names will be omitted from it here. Three of the men who took part in the attack have been referred to already as Mr C. (in connection with the killing of Rice), and Mr D. and Mr E. (in connection with the attempted murder of Mary Murray and Margaret McCartney). For other names mentioned by Bates, including those of leading figures in the UVF and members of the Windsor Bar unit, I have again substituted letters of the alphabet.

On the evening of 5 June 1976, I was working as a barman in the Long Bar. From 6.00P.M. to 8.00P.M. I was given a break and went home to my mother's for tea. When I was in my mother's I heard on the news that the Times Bar in York Road had been blown up and people killed. When I returned to the Long Bar to carry on work, I was approached by Mr F., known as Bunter. He told me I was to take part in a job in retaliation for the bombing of the Times Bar. He told me to stand by. Mr F. then left the bar and a short time later when he came back I was standing alongside Mr G., Mr D., Mr C. and Mr H. Mr I., at that time the Battalion Commander of the UVF, and Mr J. who was the Provost Marshall in the UVF, were also along with us. Mr F., who was a Military Commander in the UVF, told us that we were to hit the Chlorane Bar in Smithfield. We all went to the Windsor Bar. Mr J. arranged to get masks and handed me one. It was a yellow-coloured money bag with holes for the eyes in it. Mr I. arranged to get the guns. He arranged to get one from the Lawnbrook Club and this turned out to be a .45 snub-nosed revolver. He got another .45 revolver from the Loyalist Club in Rumford Street. Mr G. had his own .9mm pistol and a .22 pistol. Mr D. took the .22 pistol. There was two .38 revolvers in the Windsor Bar at the time but they had no ammunition for them. I was given one of the .45 snub-nosed revolvers. Somebody else in the Windsor Bar had ammunition and they loaded both .45 revolvers. It was arranged that Mr G. would be in charge of the team and Mr D. was his second-in-command. Mr H. was told that he was to do the driving and Mr C. and I were to make up the team. Somebody arranged to get a black taxi and when we were told to leave around 10.00P.M. the taxi was sitting in Mansfield Street. Mr H. drove and the rest of us were in the back seat. We drove down the Shankill Road into North Street and straight into Gresham Street. Mr H. pulled up right outside the Chlorane Bar. We all put our masks on and got out. We all went through the front door. Mr G. shouted on everyone to stand up. When they all did, G. said: 'Catholics to one side, Protestants to the other'. At this point somebody walked out of the toilet. G. told him to come on in but the man got behind the door again. G. fired at him. Everybody started to fire then. I pulled the hammer back on my gun and pulled the trigger but it wouldn't fire. The rest were firing continuously. G. then said: 'That's it'. We all ran back to the taxi. The taxi had turned by this time and was facing North Street. Mr H. drove the taxi back to Beresford Street where we all got out and left it. We all returned to the Long Bar. On the way back up from the Chlorane, I told G. and D. that my weapon hadn't fired. Mr I. and Mr J. were waiting on us outside the Long Bar. Mr I. took me back to the Windsor Bar and to the rear of it. He took the .45 revolver from me and began testing it. He pulled the hammer backwards and forwards several times before the weapon fired. He told me to go back to the Long Bar. I waited in the Long Bar a while with Mr C. I saw Mr I. setting up a 40oz bottle of vodka for G.

and D. This was their payment for doing this job. A short time later Mr C. and I went home. I want to point out that Mr G. was in charge of his own team and it was the most feared unit in the Shankill area. G. had charge of about fifty men in all. This was another situation when it was impossible for me to refuse to carry out orders. I had no choice but to do what I was told as reprisals would have been taken against me or my family.

Like all the statements made by Bates, one is able to detect in them a man who does not know the meaning of truth. There is a deliberate attempt to distance himself from the crime committed; to make it appear as if it had happened by accident and his participation had been minimal. Bates did not take into account when making his statement that forensic evidence would show that two .45 revolvers had been fired. In the statement he cleverly concocts a story about his gun not firing and how eventually it was tested and proven faulty. He also omits to mention the shooting from the taxi as it sped towards the Shankill Road after the killings in Gresham Street.

In other respects he is accurate and particularly in relation to those he names. Mr G. was, in fact, the leader of the Windsor Bar unit. However, his description of this unit as 'the most feared' is a tactical move on his part. Again, it seems to be an attempt to weaken his own culpability by the suggestion that there were others more ruthless than his own unit members. We know that Lenny Murphy did not fear the leader and members of the Windsor Bar unit though he acknowledged they were capable of confronting him, as at the time Waller was killed. The manner in which the guns were acquired again shows the labyrinthine methods used by Loyalist paramilitaries and how all their actions were closely associated with bars and clubs.

Bates, however, neglects to mention that Mark Hagan, together with his passenger, was held hostage in the

Windsor Bar. He deliberately avoids the fact that he was an integral part of the planning and implementation of the operation. His description of the use of the taxi provides an interesting insight into the way in which the unit operated: when the gang boarded the taxi, the four who were armed deliberately sat in the back of the vehicle leaving the driver alone at the wheel. Such an arrangement was to give the impression of a normal taxi ferrying passengers on the Shankill Road and would not, therefore, arouse suspicion.

The hit squad did not intend to kill Protestants in the Chlorane, though they knew that Protestants would be present, as is evidenced by Mr G.'s order to the Chlorane customers when he entered the bar. Once the shooting started, however, the religion of the drinkers present mattered little. The scene in the bar was one of fear, panic and confusion, and it would seem that some of the gunmen panicked too. Bates and Mr G. were exceptions.

Not surprisingly, considering what the victims of the attack had endured, their accounts of the incident are confused. With the aid of forensic evidence, and information from a source which cannot be disclosed, I have been able to discover the role Bates played in the shooting: Mr G. shot Cargill before he fired into the toilet at Greer and immediately following that Bates shot Coyle. Farrell was shot dead when he rushed towards the Gents'. Others were shot as all the gunmen opened fire on customers huddled at the end of the bar. Mr G. was responsible for shooting Emerson as he lay on the ground.

Recent research into statements taken from witnesses suffering from trauma illustrates the difficulty police faced in trying to piece together the precise details of what actually took place. Their task was made even more difficult in this instance by the fact that the gunmen were hooded. Each witness has a vivid recollection of what they saw, but often their evidence proves to be only a fragment of the action.

Murphy had exhibited a lack of concern about the presence of Protestants when he attacked the lorry carrying workmen. Then, as on this occasion, no action was taken against the gang for killing members of their own community. Perhaps the UVF leadership did not move against them because three members of the leadership were directly involved in the planning of the operation.

A tragic dimension to the loss of innocent life that evening was Bates's remark that the 40oz bottle of vodka was the fee for carrying out the slaying. The conflict, it would seem, had caused human life to be thus devalued.

While Murphy remained in prison waiting for his trial to begin the Butchers maintained a low profile. The Chlorane Bar killing had been the result of a murder deal, one of the few, between the Brown Bear and the Windsor Bar units, and Bates had been involved in the deal. Moore and McAllister were aware of this. For whatever reason, they now decided to undertake a killing independent of Mr A. and Mr B.

After 10.00P.M. on 1 August Moore and McAllister set out in a borrowed black taxi in search of a Catholic victim. Moore chose the Cliftonville Road as their hunting ground. They drove from the Shankill to the Oldpark Road and along Manor Street to the Cliftonville Road. The same route had been taken by Moore and Murphy when they killed Ted McQuaid. On this occasion McAllister sat in the rear of the vehicle with a hatchet concealed inside his coat. Moore, as usual, had the task of searching for lone prey.

As Moore and McAllister were making their way towards the Cliftonville Road, forty-nine-year-old Cornelius Neeson was leaving a bingo club in North Queen Street, where he worked as a bingo caller. Earlier that night he had kissed his wife goodbye as he left their home in Clifton Crescent. His wife remembers he was in a

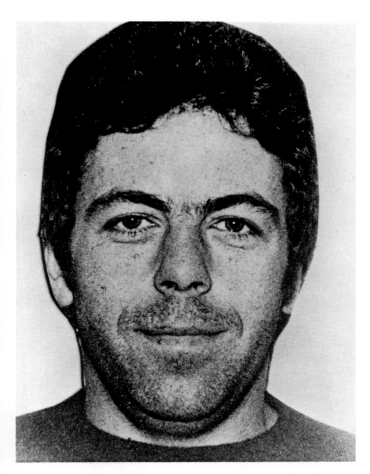

Hugh Leonard Thompson Murphy who formed the 'Shankill Butcher' gang and was later described by journalists as Mr X or The Master Butcher. To his friends he was known as Lenny.

Eight of the men whom Murphy chose as his gang members. The photographs were taken within prison shortly after the 'Butchers' were arrested. The top row of Moore and Bates contains those men who were most prominent in Murphy's reign of terror.

WAUGH NORMAN
MURDER 26·5·77
DOB - 10·1·52·

McCLAY ARTHUR
MURDER 27·5·77
DOB 12·10·53

McILWAINE EDWARD
ATT MURDER 15·6·77
DOB - 15·6·5?

BELL DAVID JOHN
MURDER 26·5·77
DOB - 4·12·53

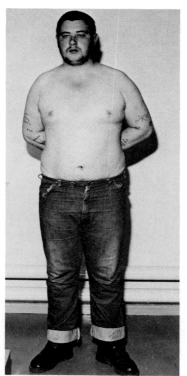

Left: 'Big Sam' McAllister was an appropriate nickname by which this leading member of the 'Butchers' was widely known. He was six foot in height and weighed over 16 stone. He used his huge frame to intimidate those around him but particularly those innocents whom he dragged off the streets of Belfast.

Below: The photograph of James 'Tonto' Watt is published in this book for the first time. He was the UVF explosives expert who made the device which killed a ten-year-old boy.

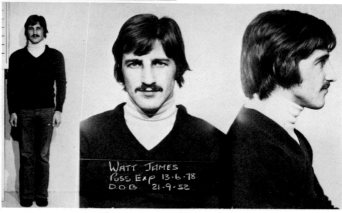

The Windsor Bar on Belfast's Shankill Road which was the meeting place for Murphy's rivals within the UVF but was also the place where murders were planned and often executed.

The bullet-riddled lorry which Murphy mistakenly believed was being used to ferry Catholic workmen through the Shankill area. While Murphy was firing at the lorry his gun jammed and he grabbed a weapon from an accomplice and continued firing.

Right: One of those killed in the attack was a 51-year-old Protestant, Archibald Hanna.

The knife marks on the hands of Gerard McLaverty were the tell-tale signs which eventually led detectives to a thorough investigation of McLaverty's abduction by the Butchers and proved crucial in their capture.

Below: The funeral of a 54-year-old part-time UDR Sgt., Tommy Cochrane, who was kidnapped and murdered by the Provisional IRA.

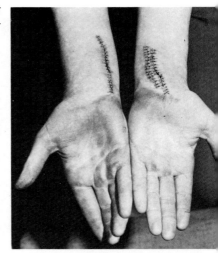

The bullet-riddled car in which Lenny Murphy met his death at the hands of a Provisional IRA hit squad.

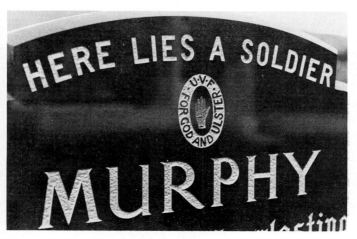

The mass murderer's headstone in Carmoney Cemetery on the outskirts of Belfast. Several hundred yards from Murphy's grave, in the same cemetery, lies the remains of one of the Butchers' victims – Stephen McCann, who had a premonition that he would be buried in Carmoney.

Right: Jimmy Nesbitt, head of C Division Murder Squad and, alongside him, one of his most trusted staff, Det. Sgt. Cecil Chambers.

Above: Det. Inspector John Fitzsimmons who is now retired from the RUC. He was Jimmy Nesbitt's counterpart in C Division with responsibility for 'ordinary' crime but he provided valuable assistance to Nesbitt's Murder Squad.

Right: Nesbitt, seen here with his family at Buckingham Palace in 1980 when he was awarded the MBE in recognition of his courage and success in combating terrorism.

happy mood. As he returned home along the Cliftonville Road he cannot have been aware of the danger of the dark streets.

Moore spotted him as he reached the Manor Street junction with the Cliftonville Road. McAllister was alerted that a victim had been found, and as Moore stopped the taxi he leaped out and struck Neeson over the head with the hatchet and then hit him repeatedly. Moore joined him, leaving the taxi's engine running. While McAllister continued to rain blows on the defenceless Neeson, Moore kicked him viciously about the head, face and upper body. Thinking that they had killed him, they ran back to the taxi and travelled down Manor Street and eventually to the Shankill Road. A passing motorist noticed McAllister running to the taxi, but drove on. He then changed his mind and returned to the corner of Manor Street to find Neeson bleeding to death on the pavement. An ambulance was summoned but Neeson died several hours later in the Mater Hospital. The motorist was able to give an accurate description of McAllister to the police but it did not lead to an identification. Like the McQuaid murder, the Neeson killing took place in D Division and was not associated with the Butchers until some of them were caught.

McAllister, when finally caught, made a statement to police which contained fascinating parallels with those made by Bates in respect of other crimes. Certain words and phrases were used deliberately to create an impression that the crime had been an accident and the death of the victim had never been intended. I contend, and will seek to demonstrate later, that Murphy, McAllister and Bates were so well versed in the law that they knew how to avoid making an admission of premeditated killing. In other words, they knew how to make statements which could lead to charges of manslaughter as opposed to murder and how such statements could lead to plea bargaining at the outset of a trial. I have italicized several phrases in McAllister's statement below which illustrate this:

I was out in a car with another fellow who I don't wish to
say. We drove down Manor Street towards the Cliftonville
Road. We were *looking for a* Taig *for a kicking*. There was
a hatchet in the car and I took it with me and got out of
the car. As this man walked past me on his own, I hit him
over the back of the head with the *wooden part of the hatchet*.
I hit him about twice when he was down. The other fellow
with me came over but didn't hit him. We then ran to the
car and drove away. We knew he was a *Taig* because he
was walking up there. It was only meant to *give him a
digging*. He was *not meant to be killed*. I don't wish to name
the other fellow. I think drink was the biggest cause of
this.

Again the killer has made an effort to suggest that the
killing was unintentional. McAllister was lying when he
stated he hit Neeson with only the handle of the hatchet.
He also seeks to maintain Moore's anonymity and to blame
the incident on alcohol consumption. In fact, neither
Moore nor McAllister were drunk on that occasion.

When Moore was caught and questioned about the
killing of Neeson he denied all knowledge of it but under
intense interrogation finally admitted that he had driven
the car for 'those who did the job'. His first statement in
relation to the killing of Neeson is an attempt to attribute
the killing to a person whose name he does not wish to
divulge:

We had a bit of a chat and decided to go out and get a
Taig and give him a bit of a digging. It was decided I
would go and get a black taxi and drive us to do the job.
I went to someone I know and asked him for the lend of
his black taxi. I didn't tell him what it was for. The other
fellows were with me when I got the taxi. They got in and
I drove to the Crumlin Road and finally to Manor Street.
It had been said that if someone was got walking on the
Cliftonville Road he would be a *Taig*. We saw a man
walking up the Cliftonville Road. He was on his own and
was just dandering along. There was no one else about.
The other two fellows got out of the taxi and whaled into

him, knocked him down and got stuck into him. They
kicked the lights out of him. They kicked him for a couple
of minutes. I swung the car round on the Cliftonville Road
and faced back up Manor Street, the way I had come.
The two fellows got back into the taxi and I drove to the
Lawnbrook Club. The next morning I heard on the news
on the wireless that the man we had done had been found
at the corner of Manor Street and that he had died in the
Mater Hospital. There was no guns or anything on this
job. It was just a digging.

Moore was giving up so much information at this stage
that time was needed to evaluate it and, allied to that,
Nesbitt was also preoccupied with constant briefings with
the police interrogators. Thus, it was not until 23 May
1977, four days after the above statement was made, that
he extracted the truth from Moore. The interrogations of
Moore and McAllister are discussed later in this book but
it is worth looking at this stage at the second statement
made by Moore. It offers an insight into Moore's devious-
ness and how, even when he admits his guilt, he is still
cunning enough to suggest that the motivation was as
described in his first statement:

I just want to clear up a mistake about the murder of
Neeson. It happened just much as I said except that there
were just two of us, me and Sam. I made a mistake when
I said there were two other fellows with me. I didn't sit
in the motor the way I said. I got out and gave the man a
digging too. Sam hit him with the hatchet. I just kicked
him. When Sam hit him over the head with the hatchet,
he knocked him to the ground. When the man was lying
there, Sam hit him about two or three times and kicked
him and gave him a doing.

The use of the expression 'gave him a digging' or gave
him a 'doing' or 'kicking' has to be measured against the
actual injuries inflicted on victims. In the case of Neeson,
the State Pathologist's findings were as follows:

There was a large area of bruising and abrasion centred

on the left cheek bone associated with depressed fractures
of the subjacent cheek bone and adjacent orbital margin
and puncture of the left eyeball. The left side of the upper
lip was bruised and the lower lip was lacerated, abraded
and bruised. The outer surface of the left ear was abraded
and just above the ear there was a horizontal laceration of
the scalp. Another laceration was situated above the right
temple. Internally there was fracturing of the skull in the
region of the left temple and eye and a fissured fracture
crossed the skull base to the region of the right ear. The
fractures were associated with laceration and bruising of
the left side of the brain. Blood from the fracture had
trickled down the back of the nose into the air passages
and lungs. Other injuries on the body were an abrasion at
the back of the left shoulder, lacerations of the first seg-
ment of the left middle finger with a fracture of the adjacent bone and a fracture of the left lower leg.

The pathologist concluded that all the blows were delivered with considerable severity from the hatchet, and from
fists and feet.

For several months after the killing of Neeson the Butcher gang was inoperative. During drinking sessions in the
Lawnbrook and the Brown Bear much of the conversation
focused on the dilemma facing their leader in prison.
Lenny Murphy, for his part, maintained his 'not guilty'
plea to the day of the trial. On the second day of the case
a deal was struck between the Crown Prosecutor and
Murphy's lawyers. Much to the dismay of Nesbitt and
Fitzsimmons, it was apparent that the case against Murphy
on two charges of attempted murder was based on what
the lawyers regarded as circumstantial evidence. From the
Crown point of view there were several considerations:
the prospect of a lengthy and costly murder trial, after
which Murphy could possibly walk free. This, in turn,
could create the risk that he might also beat the charge of
possession of a firearm and ammunition with intent. The
Crown was offered a plea bargain by Murphy's lawyers to
the effect that if the two attempted murder charges against

their client were dropped, he would plead guilty to the firearms offence. Agreement was reached between both sets of Crown Counsel and Murphy pleaded guilty to possessing a firearm and ammunition with intent. He was sentenced to twelve years' imprisonment. The prospect of incarceration was of little concern to Murphy. He told associates that he was content to be away from the prying eyes of the Tennent Street RUC murder squad. He was sufficiently well versed in such matters to know that in reality he would only serve six of the twelve-year sentence because of the fifty per cent remission rule on sentences in Northern Ireland. The fifty per cent remission rule was introduced solely in Northern Ireland in the mid-seventies with the phasing-out of Special Category Status which was a special provision for prisoners who claimed paramilitary allegiance. The phasing-out of this provision coincided with the completion of new expensive, purpose-built H-Blocks at the Maze Prison thus making the earlier detention of prisoners in RAF Huts unnecessary. The remission rule ended special category status for new prisoners but not for those serving inmates previously designated as Special Category Status prisoners.

The police had hoped for Murphy's conviction on charges of attempted murder for which he would have received a life sentence. Had this been so, the fifty per cent remission rule would not have applied.

Overall the plea bargain suited both sides. From the point of view of the Crown, the attempted murder case would have involved a long fought case demanding much public expenditure, police resources (since many police witnesses would have been required), and pressure on a Court system already overburdened with terrorist cases. In offering Murphy's lawyers an opportunity for their client to plead guilty to the firearms offence, a great deal of effort was avoided, taking into account the fact that a lengthy case might see Murphy beat the attempted murder charge, whereas the plea bargain ensured that he was taken out of circulation, albeit for only six years. Viewed by Murphy's Defence Counsel there was equally a risk that if their client was obliged to fight the attempted murder charge there was the possibility that he could be convicted. Defence Counsel was aware that the Crown case was not as strong as Crown lawyers would have hoped and in those circumstances the Defence sensed that the Crown would accept the opportunity to have the matter resolved quickly without incurring huge public costs. Murphy would have been consulted by his lawyers and been acquainted with the risk that a lengthy hearing could lead to a guilty verdict, but that a plea to the lesser charge would remove that possibility. In this type of issue there is a gamble for the Defence and it is likely in this case that Murphy, who witnessed many trials in Crumlin Road Courthouse, was unwilling to test the Crown case in a trial. To Murphy six years of a twelve-year sentence was preferable to being found guilty of the firearms offence, and a lengthy sentence in the event of being found guilty of the much more serious charge of attempted murder. Additionally, six years in prison was nothing to hardened criminals such as Murphy. He knew that inside prison he would be treated with respect, if not like a hero, and he would be away from the prying eyes of Nesbitt and his team. Leaving his wife did not seem to matter. His womanizing had ensured that they were not romantically inseparable and home was not a place where he spent a great deal of time when he was a free man.

Murphy was content with his lot. Out of reach of the police for six years, he could continue, with Mr A.'s assistance, to control the Brown Bear unit and give orders for further killings from his prison cell.

10
Orders from Prison

Once Murphy was locked away in the Maze Prison (formerly Long Kesh) he felt able to put into action a plan which would not only satisfy his craving for violence but would fool Nesbitt into believing that he was not, in fact, the cut-throat murderer.

Within a week of his confinement Murphy received a visit from Mr A. and told him that the cut-throat murders were to continue in order to throw the police off his track and allay any suspicions they might have about his associates. Mr A. conveyed the message to Moore and the others. Willing though he was to be the point of contact for the unit, he was determined to maintain a low profile and simply supply the weaponry. He was a loner who took only calculated risks and was not prepared to play an active role which could eventually expose him to police scrutiny. When Murphy was personally running the unit Mr A. was always present to provide advice, but rarely did he become physically involved in a killing. He was, however, an accomplice to murder at the time of the beating and shooting of Shaw, and during the lorry killings he sat in the car and watched.

Mr A. told Moore that Lenny's orders stipulated Moore should run the unit in his absence but would be assisted, if necessary, by Mr A. Weapons would be provided by Mr A., who would act as go-between for Lenny and the volunteers. Murphy's choice of Moore as 'leader' of the unit was both ideal and understandable. He worshipped and feared Murphy, possessed a good knowledge of the sectarian geography of the city and had been well tutored

171

by Lenny in the art of killing. Some people have suggested that Moore was easily led by Murphy and there is some truth in that assertion, but this is to neglect certain facets of Moore's character which made him an ideal surrogate. He hated all Catholics and, like Murphy, was a ruthless individual. Unlike Bates and McAllister, he was not known as a brash thug but was recognized as cool and thoughtful. Murphy, better than anyone, knew that Moore possessed the qualities of a killer. Murphy had taught him cunning and how to operate in a tactically random fashion, avoiding any pattern of action which might be detected by the police. Moore later argued that he continued the campaign of killing because he feared Murphy and because of the presence of Mr A. and Mr B. who were always lurking in the background prepared to follow Lenny's orders. There is no evidence to support this claim. Moore, like Murphy, enjoyed killing and he was surrounded by people who were willing to carry out his orders.

While Moore, Bates and McAllister planned their next move, Jimmy Nesbitt and his team were convinced they had the cut-throat killer behind bars. Their only concern was that he would be back on the streets in six years, but this was a matter to be faced in the future, or so they thought.

Friday 29 October was a miserable day in Belfast, cold and showery. It was an important day for two young lovers who, with the way of the young, appeared equally unconcerned about the increasing violence in their city or the inclement weather marking the onset of winter. Early that morning twenty-one-year-old Stephen McCann dressed and ate his breakfast at his home in Victoria Gardens off the Cavehill Road in the north of the city. His thoughts were centred on the meeting later that morning with his seventeen-year-old girlfriend, Frances Tohill. They planned to spend the day together. Stephen was a student

and had left school before completing his 'A' levels but
had now returned to studying. His return to school was
in many ways a consequence of meeting Frances, who was
studying for her 'A' levels at Fortwilliam Grammar School.
Stephen had always harboured an ambition to attend university, but had waited longer than most to begin to realize
his dream. There was, however, a rebellious side to his
nature and his commitment to study was not always as
serious as it might have been. As a result, for several years
he worked in his father's carpet shop in Belfast city centre
and then resumed his studies at St Patrick's School which
was the only school in Belfast prepared to accept mature
students for 'A' level studies. He enjoyed being a student
and hoped that if he were successful in finding a university
place it would enable him to leave Northern Ireland. His
real love in life, apart from his girlfriend, was writing songs
and playing a twelve-string guitar. On occasions he would
take his guitar into St Patrick's Secondary School on the
Antrim Road and play some of his songs for fellow students during breaks between lectures. He enjoyed being
regarded, within his own family, as the 'black sheep'
because of his nonconformist approach to life. In a family
of four brothers and four sisters, Stephen was the third-
born, and his unorthodox behaviour, by family standards,
was tolerated by his parents. His family was lower middle-
class and regarded as respectable and hardworking. His
father was finding running the family business difficult
after suffering a heart attack. His mother was quiet and
devoted to her family and, it seemed, reserved a special
affection for Stephen. He, for his part, attended school
only when it suited him and often remained at home
writing songs and playing his favourite records. Among
those which he played at full volume on the stereo in his
bedroom were songs by Gallagher and Lyle and Kris
Kristofferson. One song which he played constantly in
October 1976 was Kristofferson's 'Me and Bobby

McGee'. The lyrics reflected his own, often morbid, preoccupation with freedom and self-image.

Frances was from a middle-class family and lived in a large detached house in the Somerton district of Belfast's upper Antrim Road. Her father was a general practitioner, well known in North Belfast. She was deeply in love with Stephen McCann but believed that her affection was not reciprocated. She felt that Stephen was always dreaming of travel and leaving Northern Ireland. During the year she had known him their relationship had gone through stormy periods when they would separate for short intervals and Frances believed that during these separations Stephen would see other girls. However, on Friday 29 October 1976 they were together again and enjoying each other's company.

Frances had first met Stephen in the students' union bar at Queen's University. She was with friends and Stephen, by chance, was seated beside her. He joined her group and became the life and soul of the gathering that evening. 'He was always like that. What appealed to me were those big green eyes of his which were so full of life,' says Frances. From that night in the bar they became boyfriend and girlfriend and Frances soon began to observe a darker side to Stephen's character. He constantly talked about the violence in Northern Ireland and particularly in Belfast. When he sank into a dark mood, she says, he talked of people 'being out to get him' and of people who 'were going to shoot him'. During the week of the 29th Frances noticed that Stephen played his records for her but did not produce his beloved guitar. In fact, for reasons which have never been known, he had placed an advertisement that week in the *Belfast Telegraph* and sold the guitar on Thursday the 28th. Frances only learned of the sale of the guitar when she called at his home on the morning of the 29th and was told by Stephen that he had sold the guitar because he needed money.

Looking back, Frances still finds this puzzling because the guitar had been so precious to Stephen.

While Frances and Stephen were waiting for a bus on the Cavehill Road that Friday morning, Stephen was unaware that one of his school lecturers had finally lost patience with him and had delivered an angry tirade about his absence. The lecturer had asked Stephen's school-friends to convey to him that if he did not appear the following Monday he would be thrown out of school. No one was ever able to pass this message to him.

Frances and Stephen spent the morning wandering round Belfast city centre shops, laughing and joking about their lives and their hopes. Frances remembers running hand in hand along a pavement in the main thoroughfare, Royal Avenue, when their attention was drawn to a jeweller's shop. 'We both stopped and turned to each other and at the same time said: "Let's get engaged now." We had just enough money for lunch and that bought us a hamburger each,' says Frances.

In the afternoon Stephen produced money from a wallet, more than enough for several dozen hamburgers. It was probably the money from the sale of his guitar, and with it he bought himself a jacket. Frances, however, remains convinced that it was not the proceeds from the sale of the guitar, though I have been told by a friend that Stephen did intend to buy clothes that day because of a party scheduled for the Friday night and a Hallowe'en function the following day. Frances recalls questioning him a second time about the guitar and being told by Stephen that she 'talked too much'.

Late in the afternoon they both returned to Stephen's house where they played his favourite records and ate a light tea. At 7.00P.M. they made their way across Belfast to one of their regular haunts, Queen's students' union bar, where they met many of their friends, including Stephen's youngest sister and her boyfriend. Stephen was never one to drink much and that evening he sat for most

175

of the time sipping one pint of lager, but he entertained those round him with his sharp wit and conversation. However, Frances says he left the bar at one stage and returned a short time later in quite a different mood. 'He walked into the bar and sat down beside me and said, "They're gonna get me". He wasn't drunk and I did not know who he was referring to and so I just put it down to other comments of a similar nature which he had made in my company in the past.'

What Frances Tohill did not appreciate at the time was the extent of Stephen McCann's preoccupation with the violence taking place around him. His writing is revelatory and shows the intensity of his feelings and his secret fears, which at times seemed to border on paranoia. The song below was written at this time:

Chorus:
What price peace, will it cost us all our lives?
And when there's no one left to die,
Will peace come then?
What price peace? Is it coming, is it gone?
Have we had our share or is it still to come?

Verse 1:
It seems that because peace is very rare, the price is soaring
We can't afford to live in friendship but in hatred of this thing men call war;
Children come unnoticed among sounds of death and vengeance.

Chorus: What price peace . . .

Verse 2:
If the people who are fighting would consider for a moment
How their fathers fought before them in wars long ago
Then they would discover that these people had a cause to fight for
Seeing in the dark a spark of light to show there wasn't far to go.

Chorus: What price peace . . .

Verse 3:
But these brave men are long since dead, their memories now
Are only crude excuses which are drawn on gable walls to
signify their creed or race;
The cruel men today can't see a spark to show the way
To make a daytime of this nightmare of suffering and bravery
of innocent and dead.

Before the students' union bar closed, Stephen met friends
who told him they were having a party in a house in
Jerusalem Street, less than half a mile from the university.
They offered to let him spend the night there to avoid
having to travel across the city to his home. Stephen did
not take up the offer because seventeen-year-old Frances
was required by her parents to be home shortly after
midnight. Nevertheless, he and Frances decided to go to
the party and spend an hour there before setting out for
home. They arrived in Jerusalem Street after midnight and
eventually left the party at 2.00 A.M. Considering Stephen's
appreciation of the dangers abroad at this time, it is difficult to fathom why he took the risk of walking home. He
was not drunk and must have been aware of the chance
he was taking. Frances Tohill was later to regret that she
had been with him that night and says that if she had not
been there, Stephen would probably have spent the night
at the party with his friends.

Unfortunately, neither Stephen nor Frances had enough
cash to take a taxi ride to their respective homes. They
were left with a choice of two routes home, and both
placed them in equal jeopardy. Firstly, they were obliged
to walk into Belfast city centre. From there they could
either walk up Donegall Street towards Carlisle Circus
and the Antrim Road to the neighbourhood where Murphy
had kidnapped three cut-throat victims, or they could
travel by way of Millfield where the two women had been
killed in Casey's wine store. Anyone taking the latter route

would undoubtedly have been presumed to be Catholic because of the proximity to the Falls Road. Stephen McCann and Frances Tohill walked towards Millfield.

As they walked into Millfield they faced Unity Flats, 150 yards away. Stephen walked with his left arm around Frances's shoulder and she with her right hand buried deep in the pocket of his jacket. Frances recalls that they chatted about the party and the Hallowe'en function to be held in the students' union the following night. Neither mentioned to the other the lateness of the hour, or the fact that they were the only people in the vicinity. Millfield is today as it was then. There are no houses and it is a drab and lonely place, particularly after dark. It has two side streets which lead into the Shankill area and two that lead into Smithfield shopping precinct. Frances recalls:

As we walked past the corner of Brown Street we were both aware of men standing on the corner with Millfield. We did not look at them directly and simply walked on. Something was shouted after us but I did not hear the exact words. We both turned to look round and at that moment Stephen was dragged from me. One man grabbed me from behind with his hand held across my mouth. I will never forget the feeling. I inclined my head so that I was looking into his eyes. I will never forget those eyes. It was a look of evil. I thought to myself, 'Should I pretend to faint?' I decided it was the best thing and slumped to the ground. My attacker said, 'Don't move, don't scream.' It all happened so quickly. I was terrified and confused. I did not know what to think. Stephen made no noise. I didn't hear him scream or shout. I lay on the ground. I heard nothing, not the sound of a car or the attackers escaping. After a few minutes I got to my feet and ran in the direction of home. On the Antrim Road I screamed at passing cars in the hope that someone would stop and help me but all the drivers ignored me. I ran to a friend's house in Lincoln Avenue and hammered incessantly on the door. When the door was opened I just shouted and shouted, 'They've taken Stephen'.

The four men who abducted Stephen McCann were Moore, McAllister, William Townsley and Artie McClay. They had spent most of Friday night in the Lawnbrook Social Club drinking and planning a murder. They left the club in Moore's new, beige-coloured Cortina Mark 2, drove down the Shankill Road, turned into Millfield and then right into Brown Street where they parked the car out of sight of the main thoroughfare. Townsley remained in the car while the others walked to the junction of Brown Street with Millfield and waited for a victim to appear. It was almost 2.30 A.M. when Moore saw the lovers walking towards them. He told McAllister and McClay to wait until they passed Brown Street. He said he would apprehend the girl and McClay and McAllister should drag the boy to the waiting car. He added that two victims would be too much to deal with and that 'the boy would do'.

Frances Tohill's recollection of events differs from Moore's. He later admitted that he forced her to the pavement and told her that if she moved he would shoot her boyfriend. Stephen McCann did not resist as he was dragged to the waiting car. Moore released his grip on Frances and ran to the Cortina. He eased himself into the driving seat and Townsley sat alongside him. Stephen McCann was bundled into the rear of the car and placed between McClay and McAllister. Moore made for Brookmount Street but on the way McAllister and McClay questioned McCann about his religion and beat him. He neither screamed nor protested; he just admitted he was a Catholic.

At Brookmount Street Moore stopped the car and left the others while he went to a house in the neighbourhood. Meanwhile, McCann was subjected to an horrific beating by the others. Moore's journey on foot took him to Mr A.'s house where he collected a butchery knife and a .22 pistol. Mr A., the go-between, insisted that the method of killing be throat-cutting, but at Moore's request he provided him with a pistol. The reason Moore asked for a gun was because he was not sure that he could carry out Lenny's order for a further 'cut-throat job'.

When Moore returned to the car he handed the knife to McAllister who taunted Stephen McCann with it and ran it across each side of his neck several times, leaving long superficial cuts in the shape of symmetrical rings. Moore drove to Glencairn almost to the spot close to the community centre where Murphy killed Quinn, then Moore, McClay and Townsley dragged their victim from the car and marched him behind the community building. Moore ordered Stephen McCann to sit down but McCann knelt down with his head slightly bowed. At this point Moore shot him once through the top of the head with the .22 pistol, sending him sprawling sideways to the ground. Moore was handed the butchery knife by McClay and knelt down beside the body of Stephen McCann, and in view of the others, cut his throat back to the spine. When Moore had completed this gruesome act, he returned to his car with the others, still armed with the pistol and the bloody knife. He drove to Mr A.'s house, reported what he had done and returned the gun and the knife. He then drove his accomplices to their respective homes.

By the time police were informed about the abduction of Stephen McCann he was undoubtedly dead. They were first alerted about the kidnapping at 3.10A.M. when Frances Tohill and her friend drove towards North Queen Street Police Station and flagged down a passing RUC patrol. The patrol circulated details of the incident to all police radios. This alerted personnel in Tennent Street and their record shows that at 3.25A.M. Constable Alexander Rainey went to the Community Centre at Glencairn and found the body of Stephen McCann. When I at first read the documentation which indicated that a constable was able to go directly to the exact spot of the murder based on brief information about a kidnapping in D Division, I was somewhat puzzled. Jimmy Nesbitt explains that, together with information on a kidnapping, a report had been made to Tennent Street that a shot had been heard in the Glencairn area after 3.00A.M.

At 3.45A.M. the Deputy Police Surgeon arrived on the murder scene to find the body 'kneeling on the ground and rotated to the right'. The head was lying backwards almost severed from the body. The position of the body revealed an added sadistic dimension to this particular murder. When Stephen McCann was shot, he would have sprawled sideways. Moore's evidence supports this as does that of the forensic department. The body had, in fact, been rearranged before Moore and the others left the scene. When later Constable Andrew Flemming arrived on the scene he prepared a report, supported by other police witnesses and photographs, stating that the body 'was lying on its back with the legs bent back underneath; the head was lying back and the hands were drawn upwards to the chest'. Moore in other words had arranged the body so as to present as grotesque a sight as possible, with the throat wounds immediately visible to police arriving at the scene.

The pathologist's report concluded that death was due principally to the bullet wound to the head. The major wounds to the throat were not made by one single action, as Moore was later to claim in a statement to police. There were other injuries to the body which were consistent with a beating, including a laceration to the back of the scalp which could have been caused by a wheel brace or by the butt of the .22 pistol.

As the story unfolded later that morning Nesbitt suddenly realized that his belief that Murphy was the cut-throat killer was now in question; and he began to feel that Murphy could not have committed the other unsolved cut-throat killings.

The killing of Stephen McCann had a profound effect on all the men in C Division's Murder Squad. When I was researching this book I found that one detective still had in his possession copies of 'What Price Peace?', to-

gether with another Stephen McCann lyric which had
been given to him by a member of the McCann family
some time after the murder. Jimmy Nesbitt, when he spoke
to me of the killing, was also deeply moved, almost to the
point of tears: 'It struck all of us who were married that
it could have been one of our kids. I also felt impotent to
stop this but I was more determined than ever. I don't
think any of us forgot that particular killing. It was not
that it was worse than the others. It was simply that innocence had been wiped away in one ghastly moment.'

Nesbitt admits that once again he found himself in the
position of having no clues. It did not occur to him that
Murphy's associates might be responsible. His feeling was
that if Murphy was not the culprit, as he had originally
suspected, then there was no justification for believing it
was the work of those under Murphy's control. It is difficult to see how Moore or the others could have entered
police reckoning as there is no evidence to suggest that
Nesbitt and his men were aware of Murphy's operations,
or the people in his unit. This will be borne out by the
evidence the murder squad acquired during later interrogations of some of the butchers. In fact on 30 October,
with a third cut-throat victim on their files, detectives in
C Division were no further on than when Murphy began
his reign of terror.

In October Nesbitt was faced with six other murders in
his patch and a multitude of on-going investigations. The
figure for 1976 show a total of forty-seven murders in the
Division, thirty-eight detections and forty-eight persons
charged. Nesbitt puts it this way: 'We faced a massive task
dealing with killings by all the paramilitaries and with no
assistance from the public. We never allowed ourselves to
get depressed about the workload. In respect of the cut-
throat killings we knew that we needed a lucky break.'

A difficult aspect of the Butcher murders was the task
carried out by Nesbitt and his men of breaking the news
to the families of the victims whilst trying to protect them

from the awful facts of the crimes. Stephen McCann's
father, who later died from a heart attack, was spared the
details. Roy Turner met the father several times, together
with one of Stephen's brothers, but always hid from them
the details of the last minutes of the boy's life.

Frances Tohill has lived with the tragedy constantly on
her mind. When I interviewed her for the purposes of this
book she still displayed all the emotion of someone who
may never be able to recover from a terrible loss. She
married six years after the tragedy and gave birth to a baby
boy but her husband died within three months of their
marriage. She says there are still little details which constantly remind her of Stephen:

I remember the moment we were leaving the students'
union. Stephen saw his young sister and her boyfriend.
He turned to the boyfriend and said, 'Make sure you take
care of my wee sister.' Looking back, we might not have
stayed together because he was restless but I loved him
and I still do. I told my husband all about Stephen and
he was very understanding. I had nightmares every night
for one year afterwards about the walking through Millfield
and the evil eyes of the man who held me. For a long
time afterwards I was suspicious of strangers when I was
walking outdoors. I know we should not have walked
through Millfield but I suppose it was a case of believing
that it happened to other people and it would not happen
to us. It was silly. I did not know the area and at the time
I was more frightened of a parked car for fear it might
contain a bomb. Also in my thoughts is Stephen's feeling
that someone was going to kill him. I never understood it.
At his funeral a member of his family turned to me and
asked, 'Why did you do it?' I took this to mean that I was
responsible for him walking me home that evening. I felt
very guilty because he might have remained at the party
if he had not been obliged to take me home. I remember
walking towards Millfield and knowing that if only we had
the money we would have taken a taxi. I will never forget
reaching the Millfield junction with Stephen. The traffic

lights turned green and he said, 'The lights are turning green just for us.'

When I asked Frances how she felt when she saw the killers in the dock of Crumlin Road courthouse two years later, she replied: 'I wondered how they could have killed so many. I asked myself what drives someone to kill someone like Stephen?'

We need to look at the statement which Moore later made to Jimmy Nesbitt to find part of the answer to Frances Tohill's question. It will be noted that McClay is referred to as McKay in the statement. This seems to have been due either to the fact that McClay was not on police files, or that the interviewing detectives misheard Moore's pronunciation of McClay as 'McKay'.

I want to tell you the whole story. I want to get it off my chest. It was Lenny Murphy who first got me involved in killings. One of the ones I did was the wee lad we picked up in Millfield and dumped him in Glencairn. I was drinking that night in one of the clubs, I think it was the Lawnbrook. I was along with Sam McAllister, John Townsley and Artie McKay. I know Artie well and I think his second name is McKay. He used to live in Winchester Street and he now lives in Antrim town. After the club finished the four of us had a chat and decided to go out and get a *Taig*. My motor was outside. At that time I had a beige Mark 2 Cortina. Mr A. owns it now. The four of us got into my car and I drove down the Shankill and turned into Millfield. I turned into the first street on my right, Brown Street beside the car park. I parked the car a few yards up in Brown Street from Millfield. Artie and Sam and me got out of the motor. John Townsley stayed in the motor a while, Artie, Sam and me stood against the wall at the corner of Brown Street. We seen a fellow and a girl walking along Millfield towards the Shankill. That's why we stopped there. We were standing at the corner a couple of minutes when the fellow and girl reached us. The fellow was on the outside and the girl was walking on the inside taking his arm. They were on the same side

of the street as me. We waited until they walked past and
when they were about ten or twenty yards up the street
we ran after them. I grabbed hold of the girl and pushed
her onto the ground. I knelt beside her and held her down.
Sam and Artie grabbed hold of the fellow and pulled him
round the corner and put him in the motor. I let the girl
go and ran back round and got into the motor. I drove up
Brown Street, along Townsend Street and up the Shankill.
The fellow was between Artie and Sam in the back seat
and while I was driving along they hit him a couple of
times. He wasn't unconscious but he wasn't shouting or
anything. I drove to Brookmount Street and went to Mr
A.'s house which is – . I told him we had a *Taig* in the
motor and he gave me a .22 pistol and a knife to do him
with. I drove up into Glencairn. I drove up Forthriver
Road and turned at the car park where Morrissey was
found facing the community centre. Me and Artie and
John Townsley took the fellow out of the motor and walked
him across to the back of the community centre. I told the
fellow to sit down. He sat down. I shot him once in the
head just at the top. When I shot him he fell sideways on
the ground. When he was lying on the ground I cut his
throat. It was a butcher's knife I had, sharp as a lance and
it just slits his throat right open. We left him lying there.
Sam had stayed in the motor and he drove it over beside
us. I got into the driver's seat and drove back to Mr A.'s
house and gave him the gun and knife. I dropped the
other three off and went home.

In this statement Moore again proves to be a master at
understating the degree of planning and thought which
had been put into the killing. The choice of Brown Street
had been deliberate because of its proximity to the Shankill
and because it afforded cover from the main thoroughfare.
It also enabled the gang to return to the Shankill without
coming under scrutiny from an Army observation post
situated in Unity Flats. The statement was made before
Moore admitted to other murders, and it is worth noting
how keen he was to blame Lenny Murphy for those crimes
committed prior to Stephen McCann's death. He

produced this statement after he was 'broken' under interrogation by Nesbitt and Fitzsimmons and, though this will be dealt with extensively later in this book, it should be said that at the time of making this confession Moore was still trying to deceive the police about his role in many other Butcher-related crimes. He neglects to reveal the exact details of the treatment meted out to Stephen McCann in the car on the journey to Mr A.'s house and subsequently to Glencairn. His evidence about the position of the body before he used the knife is correct but he does not relate how he knelt on the ground to hack at McCann's throat and how he rearranged the corpse before leaving the murder scene.

The statements of his accomplices provide fewer details of the events of that night and morning. Twenty-four-year-old Artie McClay lived in Antrim, twenty miles from Belfast. He had formerly been a resident of the Shankill Road and, despite the travel involved, returned there regularly to spend time with Moore and others. In his statement he begins by refusing to name the Lawnbrook Club and the men in his company on that night. He uses a familiar Butcher expression, namely that the motive for the trip to Millfield was to 'pick up a *Taig* and give him a bit of a hiding'. The tenor of the statement is similar to that of Bates's in that it deliberately attempts to dilute the motivation, and what eventually occurred. The frequent use of expressions such as 'a bit of a digging' and 'a bit of a kicking' was intentional and well rehearsed by all the gang. As I have pointed out, it was a means of seeking to suggest that murder was not on the agenda at the outset of each reconnoitre. Also, it could be interpreted as a means of personally distancing the killers from the horrific reality of their crimes. McClay states: 'It was agreed among us that we would grab the first fellow who came along and give him a beating'. He claims that he took McCann to Moore's car 'to talk to him' and that at Glencairn he believed that McCann was 'going to get a good beating'. He ends his statement without mentioning that he watched the killing and adds simply that the following day he heard the news and realized that McCann was dead. He also makes the assertion, repeated by some of the other Butchers when caught, that he took part in the murder because he feared reprisals if he refused.

At the time of Stephen McCann's murder, William John Townsley was sixteen years of age, the youngest of the Lenny Murphy gang. He was a hardened terrorist whose height and physique gave the impression of an older man. His statement begins with an admission that he was in the Lawnbrook with the others but he claims that they 'all got into Moore's car to go for a bit of a run'. His statement treats the episode in a manner which suggests he did not know what was happening. He admits to witnessing McCann being shot and goes on to describe the trip from Glencairn. He then changes tactic and says, as if having remembered a vital point, 'I forgot to mention that one of the men with me cut this man's throat with a knife.'

Townsley also reveals an interesting detail, not mentioned by Moore or the others, that two of the passengers in the car got out for a short time at Tennent Street while they made a phone call to the news desk of two morning newspapers to inform them of the killing. Such a call was indeed made, on behalf of an unknown grouping, to the *Irish News* and *Belfast News Letter*. His statement mentions Moore and McAllister. Mr A. is not mentioned and Arthur McClay is referred to only by his Christian name.

'Big Sam' McAllister gave police a terse statement about the crime and, like his associates, chose expressions intended to downgrade his role:

> We were drinking on the Road and we had a car. We decided to go for chips and we drove to Brown Square and Millfield. I can't remember whether we decided to get a *Taig* before we saw this fellow or after. I can't recall if we saw this fellow and girl while we were in the car but

anyway the fellow and girl were coming up Millfield towards North Street. We were standing at Brown Street and they walked past. One of the boys grabbed the girl and the other two grabbed him and we put him in the car. He was asked in the car what his religion was and he got a slap up the face. We drove straight to Glencairn to up facing the community centre. The other three took him out of the car. He was walked towards the community centre. I moved into the driving seat and moved the car over to the community centre. I heard a shot and the three of them came back and got into the car. I don't wish to name these three men. When I heard it on the news the next day I heard his name was McCann. When we took him to Glencairn we were taking him up to be shot. I'm sorry about it all. I suppose we had too much to drink.

McAllister maintained his silence *vis-à-vis* the naming of accomplices in other statements given to the police. He understood well the risks of reprisal, especially had he named Mr A. However, this was not his sole reason for keeping quiet. He was a hardened criminal and someone the police considered impossible to break under questioning. They did, however, achieve this to some extent but he remained impenetrable in the face of police demands for the names of his accomplices, and those of others in UVF units. He was also meticulous in his choice of words to describe McCann's ordeal and did not refer to the use of the knife during the car journey.

McAllister had remained in the car at Glencairn for two reasons: Moore had told him it was necessary for McClay and Townsley to experience the killing and thus become accomplices. He was 'blooding' them as Murphy had done with him. McAllister was also on standby should he be required to drive the car from the scene in the event of an Army or police patrol entering Forthriver.

The behaviour of Stephen McCann raises questions. He acted like someone bent on bringing about the realization of his own premonitions, like a fatalist who had encountered reality. Yet his death has an intense poignancy. After his murder one of his brothers recalled how he once travelled with Stephen on the Belfast-to-Liverpool ferry. It was a summer's evening and as they made their way along the Belfast shoreline, Stephen pointed to Carnmoney Cemetery on a hillside on the outskirts of the city and said, 'Someday I'm going be to buried there.' He was indeed buried in that cemetery, just as he predicted. In closing this account of Stephen's death, I shall quote some of his own words, written at the height of the Northern Ireland Troubles in August 1973, which are both revealing and nakedly poignant:

SKIES

In our dreams we know a man
Who knows what life and death are all about;
Because he's seen them he can feel them,
He has been them so he knows.

We all live just for a moment
But we know we die for ever more
And all our dreams come true.

The man we know so well has come to take us
And to claim us
And to bring us to the place where we belong
And where we should have been the day we were born.

But all my dreams are over now,
I've lost the man who gave me life
To use it or to abuse it,
I returned it to him broken
And discoloured with my sins since time began;
But he forgave me.

11

A Natural Successor

Five days before Christmas 1976, Sam McAllister decided
to round off his day with a visit to a UDA club in the
Shankill area. He had spent most of the evening visiting
popular bars and clubs which were the haunts of Moore
and Bates. After 10.00P.M. he took the unusual step of
visiting premises used only by members of the UDA.
McAllister was feeling belligerent; a trait exacerbated by
his abuse of alcohol. He drank for a long time on his own,
standing at the bar ordering pint after pint of lager. There
was little love lost between the UDA and UVF and, at
various times in the 1970s, they found themselves at loggerheads over the control of various areas. The UVF
viewed the UDA as an amateur organization, unac-
complished in the ways of terrorism. McAllister was
regarded by the UDA in the Shankill as a 'swaggering,
boastful thug'. Because of his connections with the UVF
they tolerated him. On the evening of 20 December
McAllister overstepped the mark by threatening other
drinkers. One man took exception to this behaviour and
confronted him. The man was twenty-two-year-old
Thomas Easton, a UDA volunteer from Glencairn Way.
Although smaller in stature than McAllister, he felt himself able to 'take on' the bigger man. When the two were
about to come to blows, senior members of the UDA who
were drinking with their wives intervened in the dispute.
It was quickly pointed out that McAllister had been the
instigator and that he should be asked to leave. McAllister
protested that if Easton felt he could 'sort him out' then
they should both go outside and resolve the matter. The

prospect of a lone brawl outside the club made Easton lose courage and he declined the offer. McAllister angrily left the club, hurling threats at Easton as he walked from the building, and once outside he decided not to go home but to wait for Easton to emerge at closing time.

Shortly after 1.00A.M. Easton left the club, alone, and was confronted by the massive bulk of Sam McAllister who told him: 'You can do your slabbering now.' Then McAllister hit the smaller man several times, knocking him to the ground. While Easton lay dazed, McAllister kicked him incessantly, then he picked up a breeze block and brought it down repeatedly on Easton's head. When he was certain that Easton was dead he picked up the body, dragged it into a nearby churchyard and went home.

McAllister attributed the killing to drunkenness but alcohol had not rendered him incapable of going to the rear of the club to arm himself with a breeze block. The UDA demanded that the UVF punish McAllister for killing one of their members. A kangaroo court was set up by the UVF at the beginning of January 1977 to determine how McAllister should be punished for the murder. McAllister was summoned to appear and when he did so he pleaded that he had been provoked by Easton outside the club premises and that the crime was committed in self-defence and could be attributed to the effects of too much alcohol. A decision to kneecap McAllister was taken by those who sat in judgement. McAllister's wife was expecting a child at the time and the shooting was deferred until after the birth. McAllister used the opportunity to extract a further concession for domestic reasons. He asked to be shot through the arms instead of the knees on the grounds that kneecapping would cripple him and render him incapable of helping his wife after the birth of the child. His request was acceded to and he was shot through the arms with a .22 pistol two months later. The wounds were minor and healed quickly. Had he been kneecapped his injuries would have been incomparably more serious.

There was no intervention from the Brown Bear team on McAllister's behalf when it was known that he was to be punished. One might speculate as to whether he would ever have had to face a kangaroo court if Lenny Murphy had been a free man. There was certainly no question of Mr A. making representations. His chosen role was to make Lenny's thoughts known to the Brown Bear unit and provide practical assistance for their implementation. Moore would not have had the courage nor the authority to stand up to the UVF leadership and it is likely that he was warned by Mr A. not to interfere. Mr A. preferred, as had Lenny, to keep a distance from the leadership to prevent the gang's activities becoming known.

However, this was not the only confrontation the Brown Bear unit had with the UDA, though after the killing of Easton and the reaction of the leadership, they learned a salutary lesson.

'I'm away down here, kid. I'll see you about.' These were the parting words of thirty-year-old James Curtis Banks Moorehead to a girlfriend as he left the Rumford Street Social Club on the Shankill Road at 10.00P.M. on 29 January 1977. He had spent several hours in the club drinking and dancing with a girl he had known for one year, seventeen-year-old Margaret Benson, who later told police that Moorehead was regularly seen in Shankill Road clubs. On the night in question he was drinking for part of the evening with friends. Moorehead was a leading staff officer in the Ulster Defence Association and was known to be a man who could look after himself in a difficult situation. Jim Craig, a leader of the UDA in West Belfast, remembers seeing Moorehead that evening and says that he was in 'good spirits'. Such a statement could be interpreted literally because Moorehead was slightly intoxicated when Craig left the Rumford Club before 10.00P.M. Moorehead was known locally as 'the nigger' because of his dark complexion. He always dressed in flamboyant style and on the night in question he was wearing a pin-stripe suit with matching waistcoat and shirt and dark boots with cowboy heels.

At 5.15A.M. on 31 January a lorry driver was examining the engine of his vehicle when he saw the body of a man lying nearby on wasteground close to Adela Street near Carlisle Circus. The first policeman to arrive on the scene was Sergeant Robert Trevor McFarland who remembers seeing the body of a well-built man, five feet seven inches in height, lying on his back, his shirt pulled out of his trousers, his stomach bare and his jacket missing. Sergeant McFarland examined the body for signs of life and found it was cold and rigid. There was no sign of a struggle but there were marks which showed that the body had been dragged for a distance of twelve feet. Fragments of skull were lying close to the body. The deceased displayed multiple injuries to the head and face, and the middle of the forefinger of his right hand was missing.

Moorehead had in fact been killed in the Shankill area and his body dumped in the district covered by D Division. Murphy and his gang often did this to bring investigation under the aegis of D Division and, because of the proximity of the body to the Nationalist New Lodge Road, dupe the Division into believing the killing to be the work of the Provisional IRA. No one, not even Jimmy Nesbitt, was to deduce this killing to be the work of the Butchers until some of them were finally apprehended. This method of dumping the body of a Protestant close to a Catholic area was a cunning ploy, though on this occasion there was a flaw.

The UDA carried out its own investigation and handed privately to detectives in C Division a list of men they believed might have murdered Moorehead. None of the Butchers was on the list though it confirmed that Moorehead had probably been killed by members of another Loyalist paramilitary organization, namely the UVF.

When Moorehead left the Rumford Street club on the night of 29 January he had gone in search of Jim Craig. The first place he visited was the Long Bar. Craig was not there but was drinking in the Bayardo Bar, also on the Shankill Road. Loyalist paramilitaries tend to frequent most of the bars and clubs in the Shankill district, though one or two are favoured mostly by either the UVF or UDA. Moorehead made his way to the Windsor Bar, knowing it to be a UVF haunt but not thinking that by going there he was placing himself in jeopardy. A quick glance round the Windsor Bar told him that Craig was not present, so he decided to use the toilet facilities before leaving.

Unknown to Moorehead there were three men drinking at the bar, commenting on his presence and taking a decision to kill him. The three were Bates, McAllister and Moore. Their on-the-spot decision to kill a man whom they did not know personally can only be attributed to blood lust. Bates's account of what later transpired illustrates the gang's propensity for sudden violence when under Moore's influence:

> I was in the Windsor Bar drinking and talking to a number of people in the bar. During the evening I was watching 'Match of the Day' on television with three or four other people. While we were watching the match a fellow walked into the bar and through to the toilets at the back. I didn't know him and nobody said anything to him. When he went out to the back, somebody said, 'There's your man, the nigger'. One fellow who was drinking in my company went out to the toilets after him. We then heard a commotion like there was a fight. I went out to the toilet and saw the fellow had Nigger in an armlock from the back. Nigger was struggling but couldn't free himself. Another fellow I was drinking with came into the toilet with me. The fellow who was holding Nigger told us to get some-

thing to hit him with and the fellow who was with me went into the bar and brought out a big spanner and a knife. He took these into the toilet and closed the door. I was told to stay on the outside and make sure no one went into the toilet. After about two minutes they opened the toilet door and I went in. I saw Nigger lying on the floor and there was blood everywhere. He was lying on his stomach with his head to the side. I was handed the big spanner and told to hit Nigger with it. I hit him one blow which I think hit him on the shoulder. Altogether the three of us hit him to make sure we were all in on it. We all came out of the toilet and closed the door leaving Nigger lying on the floor. I just knew he was dead at this time.

The man who entered the toilets and held Moorehead was Sam McAllister; because of his huge frame he was considered by Moore to be capable of restraining Nigger, who was known to be a strong fighter. Bates does not describe the conversation before they decided to kill Moorehead because it was brief and to the point. McAllister was simply told to apprehend the stranger. I believe that this sudden and violent reaction was precipitated by the presence of a man who presented a threat to Moore merely by reason of his physical appearance. Another possibility may have been the racist nickname 'Nigger' which made Moorehead less than human in the eyes of William Moore. Moorehead was not killed because he was a member of the UDA. In fact, his membership of the UDA would have guaranteed him immunity in all Loyalist clubs and bars. Bates, in his statement, tries to minimize his role in the murder but it is obvious from the pathologist's report that the injuries to Moorehead were extensive. There were eighteen lacerations to the scalp and a knife wound to the throat, which did not cause death. There were multiple wounds all over the trunk and limbs attributable to blows with feet and fists. A butcher's knife was not used by Moore on this occasion but instead the type of wooden-handled knife used to cut sandwiches in a bar. Death was due to blows to the skull, most of which penetrated deep into the brain.

McAllister and Moore were never charged with this killing. Silence on the subject of the murder was ensured by Moore, as had been the case when Murphy led the gang, by the insistence on all three members of the unit playing a part in the killing. When they left the toilet, they walked casually to the bar, their clothes spattered with blood, and ordered drinks. Ten minutes later Moore ordered the other drinkers on the premises to go home and the barman to lock up. Moore, Bates and McAllister continued to watch 'Match of the Day' and when it finished Moore suggested that they move the body and wash out the toilet. First, they removed Moorehead to the rear yard of the Windsor Bar and left the body uncovered. They then cleaned both the toilet and hallway through which they had dragged the body to the yard. They all went home with instructions from Moore to return to the Windsor the following day, Sunday, to dispose of the corpse. They did not take the trouble to establish whether Moorehead was actually dead but were content to assume that he was. The following morning they met up again and Bates learned – for the first time, he claims – that 'Nigger's' real name was Moorehead. The three spent that Sunday drinking in the Windsor Bar. Bates later described how they took turns to go out to the yard to make sure that 'Moorehead was still there'. I find this both strange and macabre. Rigor mortis had already set in, causing the right arm of the corpse to remain pointing upwards from the elbow. In the event, no one was likely to have moved the body, since the rear yard entrance was locked and no one in the bar had any reason to visit it. Just before midnight Moore and his two accomplices loaded the corpse into a car and proceeded to Adela Street to dump it so that the police would asssume it was an IRA murder of a Loyalist.

On 2 February Joseph Morrissey left his home on the Antrim Road to meet a friend in Belfast city centre. Morrissey, a fifty-two-year-old Catholic who lived alone, frequently drank in the bars and clubs of Nationalist areas though he had no personal interest in politics. Morrissey was unemployed and his drinking activities relieved the day-long boredom of his life. Around 2.30P.M. on 2 February Morrissey met his close friend Gerard O'Neill, whom he had known for thirty years, in Mooney's Bar in Corn Market. Mooney's was an attractive bar, frequented by people of various ages and social backgrounds. It had gained a reputation for selling the best Guinness in town and it offered tempting plates of fresh oysters. Lenny Murphy was known to have frequented Mooney's when he chose to play his man-about-town role. O'Neill and Morrissey were commencing a pub crawl, leaving Mooney's at around 3.30P.M. for the Cosmo Bar a little distance away in Lower North Street. At 6.00P.M. they proceeded to the Glenshesk Bar and from there to the National Club in Berry Street, where they remained listening to a band in the entertainment area of the club before returning to the club's main bar.

According to O'Neill, Morrissey and he left the National Club around twenty minutes after midnight. O'Neill recalls that Joe Morrissey was not drunk when they went their separate ways and during the day they had 'had no arguments with other people'. Two others had seen Morrissey and O'Neill that night in the National Club. Paul Calwell, who had been playing snooker there, remembers seeing them and confirms that Morrissey was 'not drunk by any means'. Calwell offers his own description of Morrissey. 'When I left Joe, he appeared to be in good health. He was wearing a blue-and-grey-striped pullover with a rectangular button area at the top. He wore gold-rimmed spectacles and a small silver-coloured ring with a stone in it.' Patrick Hatton also observed Morrissey in the National Club but considered that by mid-

night Morrissey was 'rightly', in other words quite drunk.
One can assume that as Morrissey had been drinking since
2.30P.M., and had not eaten that evening, he would have
been intoxicated, though not necessarily so drunk that his
physical behaviour or speech would have been erratic.

On leaving the National Club, Morrissey set off on foot
towards the Antrim Road where he lived. It was a journey
which took him along Belfast's main central thoroughfare,
Royal Avenue, past North Street and into Upper Donegall
Street, passing the spot where Rice had been abducted.

Three members of the 'Butcher' Gang – Moore,
McClay and McAllister – were also drinking that night in
the Lawnbrook, where many of their crimes were planned.
They were discussing the idea of killing a Catholic, a
course of action advocated by William Moore. At midnight
the three men left the Lawnbrook and climbed into
Moore's Cortina, with Moore at the wheel. They took the
route favoured by Murphy which led to the Upper Donegall Street/Upper Library Street area. Around 12.25A.M.
they were passing St Patrick's Chapel in Upper Donegall
Street when Moore saw a man walking along the pavement
in the direction of Carlisle Circus and the Antrim Road.
It was Joseph Morrissey. Moore stopped the car and told
McAllister and McClay to run across the road and inter-
cept Morrissey while he turned the car to bring it alongside
the victim. This manoeuvre was cut short by Moore who
'swung the car round' to bring it alongside the pavement.
McClay and McAllister had run towards Morrissey but
Morrissey stood his ground when he saw them. McClay
was armed with a hatchet. A fierce struggle ensued, during
which McClay hit his victim with the hatchet several times
until he felled him. As Moore's car reached the pavement
adjacent to them, Morrissey rose from the ground and
began struggling. McAllister and McClay dragged him
into the rear of the Cortina and as the car doors closed
McClay struck his victim again with the hatchet.

Moore drove the car into Royal Avenue, turning right

into North Street and from there to Peter's Hill and up the Shankill Road to Mr A.'s house. Moore went in and informed Mr A. that he had a Catholic in his car. Morrissey had not even been asked his religion, but Moore was convinced that he was a Catholic simply because of the area in which he had been walking. Moore told Mr A. that he had a butcher's knife in the car but that he needed a pistol. Mr A., however, said that he did not have a gun available and that Moore should rely on using the knife. When Moore returned to his car Morrissey was undergoing torture by McAllister and McClay, with McAllister cutting Morrissey with the knife while McClay held him down in the rear seat. It was the same technique as had been used on McCann, telling the victim that he was about to die while relatively superficial incisions were being made on his neck and face. The facial cuts were made in a transverse direction and this gruesome treatment continued until the car reached the car park opposite the community centre at Forthriver Road in the Glencairn Housing Estate. Morrissey was now 'quiet and making no noises', according to Moore.

In the car park Morrissey was dragged out of the Cortina and dropped on the ground. Moore took the knife from McAllister and set to work. As Moore finished cutting his victim's throat, McClay handed him the hatchet and Moore then attempted to sever the head from the body with several blows. Moore was demonstrating that he could now kill someone with a knife while the victim was still alive, thus proving himself the natural successor to Lenny Murphy.

The three killers drove back to Mr A.'s house and informed him of what they had done. Moore's clothes were soaked in Morrissey's blood and he borrowed a pair of trousers from Mr A. and washed his shoes. After leaving the hatchet and knife in the yard of Mr A.'s house, the killers made their way home in Moore's car. At 2.35A.M. Police Constable Alfred Mullen, an observer in a Police

Mobile Patrol in the Forthriver area, saw someone lying on the ground near the Community Centre. His torch lit up the mutilated body of Joseph Morrissey. By the time Detective Constable Samuel Wark arrived at the scene the blood from Morrissey's wounds had been washed away by heavy rain and had flowed into the stream running along Forthriver Road.

The autopsy report of the State Pathologist, Dr Thomas Marshall, provides a grim account of the brutalization of Joseph Morrissey. I gave serious thought to whether to reproduce the material in this report but decided that it was necessary in order to describe adequately the severity of the attack on Morrissey and the extent of his torture. Statements later made by the three killers fail to indicate the extent of the horror and suffering which they inflicted on an innocent man. The pathologist's report is as follows:

This man was healthy. There was no natural disease to accelerate death. The first rib had been fractured some time in the past and it had healed with some deformity.

He had sustained numerous blunt force injuries. There were eight separate lacerations scattered all over the scalp and another on the left side of the forehead. There were linear, V-shaped, cruciate and arcuate and they could have been caused by a hatchet. One of the wounds to the scalp, above the right side of the forehead, was associated with a subjacent fracture of the left side of the skull. Two more lacerations were situated under the right lower jaw and there were a further two lacerations on the left side of the neck, below the left angle of the jaw. These four lacerations were transverse and the two on the left were associated with fractures of the left side of the lower jaw with teeth torn out. These injuries could also have been caused by a hatchet. There were numerous injuries on the back of the left upper limb obviously sustained in an attempt to defend himself and some of these could have been caused by the blade of a sharp hatchet. There was a wound across the little finger side of the forearm as clean-cut as an incision but associated in its depths with a fracture of the ulna bone. Another incision-like wound across the base of the fore and middle fingers was associated with fractures of two finger bones and the crushing of a ring on the middle finger. There was also a bruised laceration on the back of the forefinger and two abrasions with some bruising on the back of the ring finger. Some bruises and abrasions scattered on the front of the left leg and slight abrasion on the front of the right leg were by comparison, trivial. They could have been caused in a fall or a scuffle.

The other injuries on the body were incisions of a type made by a sharp knife. There were seventeen incisions, some of them superficial but many long and deep, across the face mainly in a transverse direction. The forehead bone and the nasal cartilages were found incised in the depths of two of these. Another of the incisions opened up the mouth cavity. Across the front of the neck, just above the voice box, there was a gaping incision about seven inches long. It extended down to the spine and the cartoid artery and the jugular vein at each side of the neck was severed. The incision had been made by at least four cuts and something like a hatchet had also struck there because there was a crushed spinal vertebra in the depths of the wound. A short superficial incision lay above the inner end of the collar bone. On the left upper limb, along with the defence wounds already mentioned, there were some defence incisions. Four were situated on the back of the upper half of the forearm, another crossed the back of the hand and the bones in its depths were incised and there were four superficial incisions on the back of the ring finger.

The blunt head injuries were inflicted with a force of moderate degree. They could have stunned him but they would not have caused his death. The incisions on the face did not involve any vital structure but haemorrhage from them could have endangered life. The serious wound was that across the front of the neck. Haemorrhage from the severed arteries and veins would have caused rapid death and the blow which crossed the spinal vertebra would also have been fatal. The defence wounds on the left upper limb were not serious enough to have accelerated death.

When McAllister later admitted his involvement in the killing he began by saying that the three of them decided to 'go out and get a *Taig*' and he also added that he (McAllister) was 'half cut' when he left the Lawnbrook. He went on to describe his participation in the abduction and killing, but he made no mention of having the knife or torturing Morrissey in the car. He did not refer to Mr A.'s house and he pointed out to the police that he could not watch the throat-cutting. This is his statement:

> I think it was in Donegall Street. Me and one of the fellows got out and pushed him into the back of the car. He put up a bit of a fight. I don't remember where we drove but we finished up at the car park at Glencairn. Me and one of the fellows with me pulled him out of the car. I can't remember if he was unconscious or not. We took him behind the car and the other fellow with me stayed with him and I got back into the car. I knew he was going to get his throat cut but I couldn't watch him. We then drove away and split up. I was very drunk that night and it's hard to remember all the details. Drink was the cause of this as far as I was concerned.

McAllister sought to attribute all his violent actions to alcohol. Drink may have put him in the right frame of mind but it was not to blame for his actions. He also shows in this statement, as in others, that he was aware of the nature of the crime and how it would be perceived and treated on conviction. He studiously avoided mentioning names, and the major omission from the statement is the fact that the knife used by Moore and himself was returned to him by Mr A. for future use. By the time of the Morrissey killing McAllister was the keeper of the knives which had been used in all previous killings. Along with them he kept a cleaver and a sharpening tool. McAllister's prime object, even in confessions to the police, was to protect himself. Pride, and fear of Mr A. and the UVF leadership, did, however, oblige him to shield the other gang members. To the end, he wished to be seen as a tough individual, who could accept his own guilt because he had been caught but would never 'rat' on his associates.

McClay presents an interesting study because he came to prominence only with the emergence of the Butcher gang under Moore's tutelage. This twenty-four-year-old Antrim man did not possess the criminal record of many of the others and he did not come under police scrutiny until Moore and some of the gang were caught. McClay was regarded as shrewd, cunning and dangerous. In some respects he was similar in character to McAllister. He minimalized his participation in the torture and killing of Morrissey and set out to suggest that he was present almost as an observer. Like McAllister, he made the point that he did not wish to name names:

Me and two other fellows were drinking in a club in the Shankill Road. These two men I cannot name. They approached me and told me I was to go on a job with them and as I am a member of a certain organization I could not refuse. One of these men had a car and it was decided between us that we get out and lift a *Taig*. I got into the back seat of the car and the other two men got into the front. We drove down the Shankill Road and around the North Street area for a while and eventually finished up in Upper Donegall Street, just above the chapel. It was there we seen a man walking on his own. This man was walking up towards North Queen Street. Myself and one of the other men got out and walked over to him. I asked him where he was going and he started to slabber. He had taken a lot of drink. In the meantime the car had pulled up beside us. This man started struggling and me and the other man put him into the back seat. The other man, I think, got into the front seat and I got into the back seat beside the man we had captured. He fell down on the back seat when I got in beside him. We then drove down towards Royal Avenue and up North

Street and on up the Shankill. On our way up the Shankill we called at a house but I am not prepared to state where. After this we drove on up to Glencairn. The driver pulled into the car park off the Forthriver Road and stopped. The driver of our car got out and he opened the back door and ordered the man we had kidnapped out. This man was still conscious and was struggling quite a bit. He was again ordered out and he got out. I remained in the back seat with the door open. The driver took this man away a bit. It was dark, I could hear something falling and the next thing I saw was the driver returning to the car. He got back into the car and the three of us drove off back down to the Shankill where a short time after this I was left home. The next day I seen a few fellows and was told that there was another body found in Glencairn. I knew this was the one we had done. I was told to shut my mouth and say fuck all or else suffer the fucking consequences. It was after this I caught myself on and moved away as I was scared of getting more deeply involved.

McClay did move away from the Shankill area but remained a gang member. He was not, after Morrissey's death, party to any further crimes. This may have been due in part to the fact that he spent less time in the company of his fellow murderers, and much more near his home in Antrim, twenty miles from Belfast. The most disturbing part of his statement concerns the claim that Morrissey was still alive and conscious when he left the car in Glencairn.

McClay neglected to mention that Moore and McAllister forced Morrissey from the car but it was he who had been holding the hatchet and handed it to Moore at the scene of the murder. Morrissey was killed beside the car so it is feasible that McClay sat and watched Moore; McAllister certainly did. Moore did not, as McClay claimed, lead the victim off into the darkness.

When Moore confessed to this killing he spared no one, and named other gang members, but he did not, nevertheless, admit the full details, such as McAllister having tortured Morrissey in the car. In the case of Moore I believe his reason for not admitting the totality of the crime was to escape the horrific reality of his own actions. This is Moore's statement, in which McClay is again spelt 'McKay':

Big Sam, Artie and me were drinking in the Lawnbrook Social Club. It was discussed that we got out and get a *Taig*. It was about midnight when the three of us left the club. I drove away in my Cortina with Sam in the front and Artie in the back. We drove about the town for a while and after some time I drove up Donegall Street. As I drove up Upper Donegall Street, I saw a man on my right walking past the chapel. I stopped my car on the left-hand side going up. Big Sam and Artie got out and ran across to this man. I swung the car round in the street and stopped beside Big Sam and Artie. They were struggling with this man as I stopped beside them. I reached over and opened the back door nearest to them. Big Sam and Artie put him into the back seat and they got into the back beside him. As I drove to the Shankill this man was struggling quite a bit and I remember Artie hitting him with a hatchet and telling him to keep quiet. I knew to drive to – [Mr A.'s house] at – for a gun to shoot this man. I turned left into – and then to – where I pulled up outside [Mr A.'s] house. I got out and went to the door and [Mr A.] opened it. I asked him for a gun and he told me he had not got one. I then got back into the car and drove on up to Glencairn. I pulled my car into the car park opposite the community centre on Forthriver Road. I got out and went to the boot of my car and got a butcher's knife out of the boot. Me and Sam pulled this man out of the back seat. He was quiet and making no noises. As he was pulled out of the car he fell to the ground. I reached down and cut his throat with the butcher's knife. Artie had the hatchet in the back seat and somehow I managed to get hold of it and hit him once or twice with it. Big Sam and me and Artie got back into the car and we went back to [Mr A.'s] house. The three of us went in and I had to get the loan of a shirt and a pair of trousers from [Mr A.] as I was covered in blood. The hatchet and knife were left in [Mr A.'s] back yard. After changing I drove Sam and Artie back to Sam's house and I went home.

In his statement Moore does not shield Mr A. Instead, he seeks to blame him for having encouraged him to commit the crime. During subsequent confessions this willing and seasoned killer attempted to paint a picture of himself as a pawn in the hands of Murphy and Mr A. and to shift the blame from himself onto them. He does, however, spare McAllister, his close associate for many years, by omitting to mention the torture or the fact that 'Big Sam' used the knife in the car before they reached Glencairn. He further tries to give the impression that Morrissey's final demise came about suddenly. He does this by the use of the words: 'I reached down and cut his throat' and 'somehow I got hold of the hatchet'. Contrary to McClay's statement, Moore says that Morrissey was quiet and 'making no noises' when he was pulled from the car. Here again, Moore avoids facing the reality of what actually took place and the fact that the unfortunate Morrissey was conscious of what was happening to him. Moore's description of the incident, compared against evidence from the autopsy, can reasonably be deduced to be an attempt to deny the central details of the killing.

The murder of Morrissey provided no further clues for the murder squad of Tennent Street Station. Nesbitt and his squad were preoccupied by other killings taking place at the time. Ten days before the Morrissey murder, Loyalist paramilitaries killed two men in a car and set the vehicle alight. One of the dead was a Catholic and the other a Protestant.

Again, within a week of the Morrissey murder, Nesbitt and his team were required to investigate the killing of another Catholic in the Cliftonville Road area, a crime which they attributed to the UDA. Thus, in terms of the actual cut-throat murders, the RUC were simply adding to their increasing file of basic information and hoping that the break in the Butcher case, which they constantly discussed, would soon come about. But Moore himself was taking some precautions. After the McCann killing he sold his car to Mr A. believing that it could attract too much attention. The car used in the Morrissey killing was also a Cortina but this time yellow and bearing the registration number DOI 9651.

Towards the end of February the Tennent Street detectives were busy with quite different murder enquiries. This time it was not the Butchers but the Provisional IRA, and investigations centred on the shooting of John Lee, a Catholic, who had been killed because he had formerly been in the 1st Parachute Regiment. Lee had returned to Belfast to live in the Ardoyne area with his wife who came from that area. The 1st Parachute Regiment had been responsible for the shooting of thirteen unarmed civilians in the Bogside area of Londonderry on 30 January 1972, an event which became known as 'Bloody Sunday'. The involvement of his regiment was sufficient for the IRA to condemn Lee to death.

Some three weeks later another married man, Daniel Carville, was shot in front of his son while driving along Cambrai Street, which runs between the Shankill and Crumlin Roads. Daniel Carville had slowed his vehicle because of a ramp on the road when two youths walked towards the car and shot him dead. Carville was unknown to his killers, who were members of the UDA, but they must have known he was a Catholic merely because he was seen leaving a Nationalist district. The two men who murdered Daniel Carville were Kenneth McClinton and Samuel 'Hacksaw' McGaw. One month later McClinton murdered a Protestant bus driver who had driven his vehicle against the express threats of Loyalist paramilitaries, issued when Loyalists were protesting in a political strike orchestrated by the Reverend Ian Paisley. Paisley had been attempting to re-create the Workers' Strike of 1974 which had brought Northern Ireland to a standstill and which also overthrew the Power-Sharing Executive which had been formed between Unionist and Nationalist parties at Stormont.

The bus driver, Harold Bradshaw, had been driving along the Crumlin Road when he was waved down by McClinton and his accomplice. McClinton boarded the bus and shot Bradshaw through the head at point-blank range. After he was arrested he offered the police this extraordinary parallel: 'It was just like that shooting which they have shown on television, the famous one where a South Vietnamese army officer shoots this member of the Viet Cong on a street in Saigon. The blood spurted out of his head. Shooting the bus driver was just like that. I could see it all in colour. It was just like I saw it in that television report . . . it was just like you would see it in a film.'

McClinton was ultimately given two life sentences with the recommendation that he serve no less than twenty-five years. In prison he became a born-again Christian and was later to write about his conversion in one of the local newspapers. The letter was read by the widow of a police inspector who had been shot by the IRA and she wrote to McClinton in prison. This correspondence brought about a friendship between the widow and McClinton and at one stage they pledged they would marry and that she would wait for his release. McClinton's conversion was a phenomenon which affected a significant number of Loyalist prisoners. Some of these prisoners experienced a genuine conversion while others claimed to have been converted in an effort to appear reformed and thus influence the Life Review Board, or assist in their appeal against their sentence. And in some cases too, such conversion was a temporary means of absolving the feeling of personal guilt on arrival in prison. I shall discuss this conversion phenomenon later in relation to one of the Butchers.

By the end of March it was again time for the Shankill Butchers to make their mark on events in Northern Ireland. Once more it was an example of Murphy issuing orders from his prison cell. These were conveyed to Mr A. or Mr B. on their visits with him. Murphy revelled in the fact that, while in prison, he was not without the power to effect events in the outside world and, at the same time, to undermine any police suspicions that he was the cut-throat murderer. One has to understand the criminal mind of Murphy as Nesbitt did to understand how he received pleasure from being cunning and from believing he was constantly deceiving the police. In his mind was the knowledge that, before he was sent to prison on the firearms charge, Nesbitt and Fitzsimmons had made it clear that they believed he was the mastermind behind the cut-throat killings and other terrorist incidents; and yet such crimes were still occurring while he was closeted in prison. Early in March Moore had been given a pistol by Mr A. It was the 9mm Walther which had been used by Lenny Murphy in the killing of Ted McQuaid. Mr A. selected another member of the unit, twenty-four-year-old unemployed labourer, Davy Bell, to accompany Moore on a journey in Moore's Cortina along the Falls Road in West Belfast. The objective was for Moore to demonstrate his daring in penetrating the heart of IRA territory on a killing mission. Such incursions by Loyalist paramilitaries had occurred on a few occasions during the troubles. On this occasion Moore and Bell travelled up and down a one-mile stretch of the Falls Road several times, before abandoning their mission because they could not find an easy target for abduction. Moore was unwilling to risk firing from his car, given the obvious danger that he might not be able to escape from the area. Yet his intention was undoubtedly to use the tried and tested technique of kidnapping a lone individual, preferably one under the influence of drink. This incident is a further illustration of the number of times when the Butchers toured areas of Belfast in search of victims. Jimmy Nesbitt agrees that the random nature of the Butcher killings may be explained by the fact that, although they travelled frequently in search of victims they were on occasions thwarted by the presence of the Security Forces or by the fact that a suitable victim was not readily available. I traced one man who had a narrow escape at about this time, an ex-soldier who was walking up the Cliftonville Road after midnight with his wife and her elderly parents. He saw a passing car, containing several men, stop on the brow of a hill mid-way along the Cliftonville Road. His soldier's training and his awareness of the realities of Belfast made him take evasive action. The car made a U-turn on the road and then drove slowly in his direction. My source describes what happened:

My Army training taught me never to stay in the one place for too long so I moved my wife and the others into the garden of an adjacent house and told them to lie down and make no noise. I heard the car stop outside the house where we had been and saw the two men enter the garden, one of them with a spanner in his hand. I am over six feet but I know I would have been presented with a difficult situation even if I had been alone. The fact that I was accompanied by my wife and her elderly parents made life even more difficult for me at that moment. Luckily for all of us, a bedroom light was switched on in the house facing the garden where we had previously been considering hiding. Presumably this happened because of the noise being made by the two men. They fled when the bedroom light lit up the area they were searching. I was lucky because I would have been the one they would have snatched and had I stayed in that first garden, I might not be alive today. I phoned the police and told them about the incident but I was never contacted again. When I eventually saw the photos of Bates, McAllister and Moore in the paper, I recognized them as the men who followed us.

A middle-aged Protestant who lives off the Cliftonville Road was almost a victim of the Butchers. He was battered and left for dead close to the spot where Neeson was killed. This man was not able to describe his assailants to the police at the time and suffered brain damage as a result of the attack, but I was informed that Moore and McAllister were the culprits.

On 29 March then, Moore decided once again to initiate three members of his gang in a cut-throat murder. He chose Davy Bell, who had made the unsuccessful tour of the Falls Road with him, twenty-five-year-old Norman Waugh and 'Winkie'. The nickname 'Winkie' is the only evidence to connect the fourth member of the gang. Despite exhaustive enquiries the police have never been able to trace him and Jimmy Nesbitt has told me that this nickname is very common within the Protestant communities of north and west Belfast. Moore, Bell and Waugh refused to name him during questioning though Moore went as far as revealing the nickname.

On the evening in question, Moore and his three associates changed their drinking venue and headed for Tigers Bay, a small Protestant enclave off Duncairn Gardens in North Belfast. The money needed for their pleasure was either Unemployment Benefit or the proceeds of extortion. Moore was in the position of being able to claim such benefit, and was also able to use his car illegally as a taxi on the Shankill Road whenever it suited him. The Butcher gang was always flush with money, like many of the people in similar paramilitary organizations. Where wives existed, they were given a basic amount of money to run the household while the bulk of earnings, legal and illegal, was spent in the clubs and pubs by the men. When they arrived in the club a pool match was in progress, and the four Butchers watched the games and drank a considerable amount of alcohol. They had made an earlier decision that the time had come 'to kill another *Taig*'. Moore suggested they should leave the club after midnight, it being

the most expedient time in which to operate. The Tigers
Bay area is within fifty yards of the Nationalist New Lodge
Road district and, because of communal street rioting
between the two neighbourhoods throughout the early
seventies, both areas were partitioned by a corrugated
fence which is locally called a 'peace-line'.

However, the New Lodge Road offers clear access to
North Queen Street and Upper Donegall Street where
many of the Butcher victims were abducted. Moore knew
that part of the New Lodge Road was accessible through
two streets which lead from Duncairn Gardens: Spamount
Street and Edlingham Street. His wide knowledge of the
area and the use of the two side streets presented him
with the opportunity to enter a Catholic area with the least
risk possible. He was able to draw up a plan of action for
a quick getaway in his car, which would be driven in the
direction of the safe Protestant area of Tigers Bay in the
event of unforeseen hindrances.

After leaving the club, Moore drove his three
accomplices up Duncairn Gardens to the Antrim Road
and entered the New Lodge Road, turning immediately
into Spamount and Edlingham Street. He repeated this
exercise several times without attracting undue attention.

At 1.00A.M. Moore, with Norman Waugh alongside him
in the front passenger seat, saw 'a boy' making unsteady
progress along the pavement in Spamount Street. He
informed the others and told them he would pull the car
alongside the pavement. He instructed Waugh and Bell to
abduct the solitary figure, which they did.

The unfortunate person was forty-three-year-old
Francis Cassidy, a single man who lived at Victoria Gardens off the Cavehill Road, close to the home of Stephen
McCann's family. Cassidy had become unemployed following an accident while working at the Belfast Docks.
When Moore spotted him he was on his way home from
his sister's house on the New Lodge Road. She remembers how they spent the evening together:

At 3.00P.M. on 29 March my brother came to my house, stayed for about ten minutes and then left for Lynch's Bar. At 8.00P.M. he returned and watched television until 9.30P.M. and then asked me to go to the Carela and play bingo. Eventually I agreed to accompany him. I followed him to the bingo hall and when I arrived at 10.00P.M. he was on his own. We played bingo and had a few drinks until 12.05 on 30 March. We walked back to my house and I went to a Chinese restaurant on the Antrim Road to buy a curry for Francis. At 12.40A.M. Francis and I left my home and I walked him to the junction of Edlingham Street and the New Lodge Road. I returned home and went to bed. It would have taken him about five minutes or more to walk to his house but as he was drunk it would probably have taken him longer. When he left me he was in his usual good health and spirits. He was wearing a navy anorak, striped shirt, fawn jeans and brown slip-on shoes.

Waugh and Bell approached Francis Cassidy from behind and gave him a severe beating with their fists, kicked him and then dragged him to the waiting car. Cassidy, who was struggling, was pushed onto the back seat between Waugh and 'Winkie'. Moore drove off towards the Cliftonville Road, turned into Manor Street and made for the Shankill Road via the Oldpark and Crumlin Roads.

Moore's route, once on the Shankill Road, was pre-arranged. Mr A. had been briefed about the gang's intentions the previous day, and Moore now headed for his home. On arrival the manner of killing was discussed and Mr A. stipulated it should be a 'cut-throat job'. As before, Moore requested a gun; Mr A. had anticipated his needs and had one at the ready. Moore returned to the car where Cassidy was being subjected to a fierce beating in the rear of the vehicle.

It is necessary at this point to examine the statement later made by Moore about the events which occurred after he had left Mr A.'s house, because, at the time of making this particular confession, he had already admitted

213

his involvement in the other cut-throat murders. He displayed a certain reticence about this crime, and I believe I can offer an explanation for his disinclination to admit to the full details. His statement is set out below:

> About the end of March I was at a pool match in Tiger's Bar with Norman Waugh, Davy Bell and a fellow named Winkie. We took a fair bit of drink during the night and at 12.30 we left the pool place and headed off in my car towards the New Lodge Road. We drove in and around there and at one of the side streets, Spamount Street or Edlingham Street, I saw a guy walking along the footpath. When we saw this boy we knew he must be a *Taig* so we decided to pick him up and do him. I pulled the car up down the street from him and Davy and Waugh got out and gave him a digging and pulled him into the car. Big Norman, Davy and Winkie got in as well and I drove to – Street. I stopped the car in – Street and went into [Mr A.'s house]. I spoke to [Mr A.] and told him I had got a *Taig* and I wanted a gun. I asked him for a knife too. He went and got me the knife and the gun and I went back to the car and drove to Highfern Gardens. Big Norman got out of the car, pulled yer man out and I went and shot him. I was going to cut his throat but I could not do it. I then shot him again and got back into the car and drove off leaving yer man on the pavement. I drove the car back to [Mr A.'s] house and gave him the gun and knife and told him I had killed yer man. Winkie, Norman and Davy got out of the car and I went back home. The next morning I heard on the news that yer man was dead. There was a bit of blood in the car so I washed it out the next morning. I should say the bit about giving the knife to [Mr A.] is wrong and that I threw it away that night but I cannot remember where.

At 2.05A.M. on 30 March, Peter McCallion had been in bed with his wife in the front upstairs bedroom of their home in Highfern Gardens, when he heard the shots which had been fired by Moore. He also heard a car door closing and a car being driven away at speed. He went to the window, looked out and saw 'something lying on the street close to a grass verge'. He says that he knew the Army or police would arrive and he waited for them to do so. I can only conclude that he was too frightened to investigate the 'something' lying in the street and this was also his reason for not phoning the security forces. However, another resident of the neighbourhood was returning home at approximately 2.00 A.M. and his evidence is crucial to an understanding of Moore's statement. The witnesses name is Robert Oliver and this is his testimony:

> I was returning home and was driving my own car when I turned into Highfern Gardens from Highland Parade. I saw from the headlights of my car what appeared to be a body lying on the footpath sixty yards from my house. As I drove closer I saw it was a body. I thought at first that it was a drunk so I drove my car closer. I didn't get out of the car but screwed down the driver's window and took a look at him. I could see a lot of blood around his face and on the pavement. He was a man in his thirties and was lying with his head towards the grass and his feet out on the road. I thought then that he was dead so I turned the car and came back to my home and phoned the police from a telephone kiosk outside my house. I waited at the kiosk for the police to arrive. While I was waiting I noticed a yellow Cortina Mk 3 drive down Highland Parade and turn left into Highfern Gardens. I lost sight of it then. I don't know how many people were in it.

Robert Oliver was close to the body and did not notice that the victim's throat had been cut and yet it was apparent to policemen who began to arrive on the scene from 2.15 A.M. onwards that the victim's throat was evenly slashed. Oliver also says he saw a yellow Cortina and the description he gave of it tallied exactly with Moore's car.

Moore, in his statement, says that he was unable to carry out the throat-cutting but we know this to be untrue. His statement raises the question of when he actually committed the act of cutting the victim's throat. Waugh and Bell make no mention in their statements of the use of a knife and yet they did witness Moore shooting Cassidy. I questioned Jimmy Nesbitt about this matter and, in particular, why it was that in his confession Moore failed to admit that he had used the knife to cut Cassidy's throat in the same manner as he had used it on McCann and Morrissey. Nesbitt's explanation is that the two detectives who took the statement after Moore's interrogation were not intimate with the details of the case and did not recognize the omission. I cannot accept this explanation though I know of no reason why it should have been offered. The statement was taken by a detective sergeant and a detective constable who would have been fully briefed, as it would have been vital to establish the full facts of the killing for the purposes of preferring a murder charge at a later date.

In his statement Moore gives the name and address of Mr A. but, again, for legal reasons this information cannot be included here. At the end of the statement he corrects himself about the return of the knife to Mr A. It is my belief that Moore, under orders from Mr A., returned quickly to the scene of the killing and cut Cassidy's throat before disposing of the knife. The journey from Edlingham Street to Mr A.'s house would have taken less than ten minutes and from there to Highfern Gardens was also a short distance. The shooting of Cassidy took place quickly and the car was driven away at speed. Moore admits that the rest of the gang that night dispersed outside Mr A.'s house, whereas Moore entered the house.

There is further corroborating evidence to support my contention and it comes from the police interview notes on Moore's interrogation. When Detective Sergeant John Scott put it to Moore that he believed he was the man who had cut Cassidy's throat Moore replied, 'On that night I loaned my Cortina to persons I cannot name. They wanted it for a job and I heard later that they shot a *Taig*.'

After Detective Sergeant Scott put this question Jimmy

Nesbitt and John Fitzsimmons took over and extracted from Moore a confession which they placed in their interview notes: 'I might as well tell you about the boy Cassidy. I was supposed to cut his throat but I hadn't the heart to do it.'

John Scott interviewed Moore on the Cassidy killing once again and Moore said that he had cut the throats of McCann, Morrissey and Cassidy to 'take the suspicion off Lenny Murphy'. 'It was that bastard Murphy led me into all this and I had to carry on to take the pressure off him,' he told Scott. Six days later in an informal admission Moore came up with the following description: 'I closed my eyes and put the knife in his throat. I didn't cut his throat but just pushed the knife into it.'

During further questioning Moore reveals that Murphy had continued to lead the gang from inside prison and his orders for the continuance of cut-throat murders were conveyed through Mr A. The position and power of Mr A. is made credible by the initial statement made by Moore and the statements of the others who also admit to the shooting of Cassidy. Thus, from such a position of strength, it is feasible that Mr A. did, in fact, order Moore to return, alone, to commit the throat-cutting. The fact that Waugh's and Bell's statements are no more revealing than that of Moore on the subject would lead one to speculate that Moore carried out the act at a time when they were not present.

Moore chose Highfern Gardens rather than Glencairn on the orders of Mr A. who, at this stage, believed that Glencairn might be under police surveillance and in any case Highfern Gardens was a shorter distance to travel. Moore's admission about the use of the knife was made before his formal statement was taken but even at that stage he chose to ignore the throat-cutting and was anxious to correct the version of what he did with the knife. In his confessions about the killing of Morrissey and McCann he showed no such wish to deny the manner in which

217

they had been carried out. Moore's confusion *vis-à-vis* the killing of Cassidy arose from the fact that he had returned quickly and alone to carry out the act. It was a calculated risk but the streets were empty, as confirmed by Robert Oliver, who saw nothing but the travelling yellow Cortina. The police at the time attributed no special significance to Oliver's observation of the yellow Cortina and, when I speculated on the subject, they dismissed my version of possible events.

Whatever the truth, Cassidy was killed by Moore and the autopsy report reads much the same as the pathologist's evidence in the other murders.

Moore referred to Cassidy as 'the boy' and I can only assume that this was because he was unable to discern his age after the first savage beating in Edlingham Street which must have distorted his features. Perhaps also the fact that Cassidy was dressed in 'trendy' clothes caused Moore to believe they had picked up a boy. A similar mistake was made with Quinn; after they had severely battered his diminutive body and covered him with his own blood they were unable to judge whether they had a man or a boy in their possession.

The statements made by Waugh and Bell after their capture exhibit a degree of collusion between them. They were not arrested until after Moore and therefore had time to prepare for being questioned by the police. It has been put to me by a journalist who followed these events closely that, within twenty-four hours of Moore's confession the UVF knew he was 'singing'. I have found no evidence to support this, though I do believe that once Moore and several others were arrested it became apparent to those still on the streets that the time had arrived to prepare for the unthinkable. Waugh and Bell were no exception.

In his statement Bell did not name any of the participants in the killing and, as with most of the other statements made by the gang, he sought to underplay his role:

I met three mates in the bar on the Limestone Road and after 11.00p.m. we got into a fella's car and drove off past Artillery Flats. We then did a U-turn and went back up a hill. Somebody staggered in front of the car and the car stopped. I got out of the car and went over to this man and asked him to move. He wouldn't move so I just banged him. I picked him up and just flung him into the front seat of the car. The car was then driven to Highfern Gardens and I threw him out of the car and he just banged his head on the pavement. The driver had got out of the car also and I was standing beside the man lying on the ground and heard shots. We all got back into the car and dropped off.

Bell circled the central issue throughout his confession, ignoring the brutality and representing his participation as peripheral. Like Moore, Bates and McAllister he relied on terrorist terminology, using phrases such as 'banged him', and sought to suggest that Cassidy presented himself to them by walking in front of the car. It was a further example of the technique whereby the culprit renders a diluted account of events, thus distancing himself from the reality. The matter-of-factness, the brevity of the statement and the feigned lack of knowledge of place names was designed to obscure the fact that the crime was premeditated.

Waugh indulged in the same game by telling the police that Cassidy was abducted as though by chance. 'We were on our way home and were cutting through a side street when I heard someone say: "There's a *Taig*. Go and get him,"' he told John Scott. He went on to claim that he thought the man was going to be subjected to 'a bit of a doing'. Here Waugh was seeking to give the impression that he was unaware that the man he was kidnapping would be killed.

Waugh named his accomplices but did not identify Winkie nor name the street on which Mr A. lived: 'Moore said: "Throw him out there." I threw him out of the car and got back in. I didn't want to look and then I heard a shot. Moore got back into the car and drove towards town, dropping me off at the corner of Battenberg Street. During the journey up the Shankill the man got a bit of a beating. I was told to hit him so I gave him a couple of thumps.'

These admissions by Waugh do not properly reflect the truth of events when examined against the autopsy report, which shows that Cassidy was beaten unconscious in the car and left with multiple wounds. The choice by Moore and Mr A. of Waugh, Bell and the unidentified Winkie for this operation illustrates the tactics used by the Brown Bear unit: members were deliberately made to participate in a killing to tie them irrevocably to the organization.

The killing of Cassidy offered no further clues to C Division in their investigation of the cut-throat murders. There was no additional evidence to assist them and no significance was placed on Robert Oliver's evidence about a yellow Mk 3 Ford Cortina. Should the police have considered this evidence to have been significant? Jimmy Nesbitt says that they believed the murderers would have been far away by the time the yellow Cortina was seen, and he relied on the evidence of McCallion who said the car sped away after the shooting. This would seem to support Nesbitt's view and, at that time, he would have had no reason to suspect that the murderers would return so quickly to the scene of the crime. All of this presupposes that it was, in fact, Moore's car, a fact about which we may never know the truth. Retrospectively, one can speculate that if a search had been made for a yellow Mk 3 Cortina owned by a Loyalist paramilitary, it might well have led to Moore being on a list of suspects. The police, after all, had had their suspicions about Moore when his taxi was forensically tested.

12
The Bombing Mission

A dimension to terrorism which was never contemplated by the Butchers under Lenny Murphy's leadership was the use of bombs. The Provisionals initiated the tactic of using car bombs, particularly in the early seventies, against civilian targets. Explosives had been used in the UVF campaign of the mid-sixties but in a manner which did not endanger life. However, the gradual emergence of the Provisional IRA saw the use of explosives against both 'economic targets' and the civilian population. The Provisionals have consistently argued that their bombing campaign from 1972 onwards has been directed against 'economic' targets. These are defined as buildings or centres of 'oppression'. The falsity of such a claim is exposed by the history of violence in Northern Ireland. A leading member of the Workers' Party of Ireland, who was an internee in the Maze Prison (then known as Long Kesh) in 1971, explains the strategy of using explosives: 'I remember being in the Kesh with Gerry Adams. He was young but was regarded as the contemporary symbol of a freedom fighter. He became the Provo theoretician and was so well respected that it was Adams who was released by the Brits when Harold Wilson wanted to deal. While I was there Adams advocated the use of explosives as a means of stepping up the IRA campaign. He talked of using explosives in built-up areas. I interpreted that to mean the car bombs which later wrecked Belfast and caused untold casualties in 1972 and 1973.'

This statement was made by a member of a party with a Republican past but which has now chosen to exchange

221

its history and rhetoric in favour of a socialist ideal which includes condemnation of the Provos. The truth contained in his testimony is that the IRA did seek to develop a strategy which involved the use of explosives and subsequently, whether they care to recognize it or not, brought about mass murder. They refined their tactics to the point where British security forces admitted they were unable at times to deal with their sophisticated methods in the new manufacture of bombs. They were, with their international contacts and history of violence, adept at developing a strategy using modern technology and creating bombs without the basic ingredients such as gelignite or plastic explosives. They initiated methods of mixing fertilizers in the absence of a supply of other basic raw materials. Bombs were placed in areas populated by civilians and, after deaths had been counted, the Provisionals claimed they had issued warnings which had been ignored by police. They developed the means of destroying the economic heart of Northern Ireland, convinced that though civilian casualties would occur they were unimportant in terms of the overall object of demoralizing a population and its government.

The UVF and UDA sought to imitate the Provo strategy but they were latecomers to this contemporary form of terrorist warfare and they did not possess the expertise which the more professional IRA terrorists had cultivated. They had neither knowledge of, nor access to, explosives. There was no desire on their part to bomb the 'heart' out of Ulster and for this reason they never set out to acquire the same sophisticated knowledge. Nevertheless, they were interested in the murder of Catholics on a large scale. Their chosen method, amateur in comparison, was the manufacture of bombs using small quantities of explosives, or the conversion of gas cylinders into bombs which they placed outside Catholic pubs or clubs. In the mid-seventies the UVF had but one bomb maker, whose skills did not measure up to those within the IRA. This man was

James 'Tonto' Watt, a fitter by trade from Benview Park in North Belfast. He was in great demand in 1976 – and was, therefore, not always available to units such as the Brown Bear team. The procedure at this time was that the UVF would sanction the use of an explosive device and Watt would be called in to put it together. He joined the UVF in 1973 because, in his words, 'the IRA was blowing up my city'. 'It was the right thing to do at the time,' he later told detectives.

Lenny Murphy never chose to use the services of 'Tonto' Watt because this would have required sanction from the West Belfast leadership of the UVF, thus depriving him of his independence. However, at the beginning of April 1977 Mr A. devised a plan to use explosives which he thought would appeal to the UVF leadership. He discussed the matter with Moore and it was agreed that Mr A., on the grounds of seniority within the UVF hierarchy, should approach the UVF Brigade Staff with the project. The idea was that the Brown Bear team would undertake the planning and execution of the bombing but that they would require the services of Watt.

Mr A. and Moore were certain the plan would meet with the Brigade Staff's approval since it involved the bombing of Republicans in the heart of the Falls area of West Belfast. Although the activities of the Brown Bear team did not always have the blessing of the UVF, the prospect of bringing about the deaths of large numbers of Republicans and serving members of the IRA was bound to be attractive to UVF leaders.

Easter Sunday, 10 April, was the day for the annual celebration by Republicans throughout Ireland of the Easter 1916 Rising in Dublin. Traditionally Easter Sunday is when Republicans stage a large demonstration which includes a march to Milltown Cemetery in West Belfast to the Republican Plot, where speeches are read in Irish. Some marchers dress in what has become the IRA uniform of dark clothes, berets and sunglasses. People of all ages participate in the march along a three-mile stretch of the Falls Road, which is always lined with spectators. Until 1969 there was one traditional march through West Belfast on Easter Sunday. With the advent of the split in the Republican Movement, the residents of the Falls Road found themselves offered two marches: by those who saw themselves as the traditional IRA (the grouping which has since become the Workers' Party), and by those who believed themselves to have inherited the Pearse tradition of blood sacrifice, the Provisional IRA.

By 1977 the routine of the separate marches was well established. The Workers' Party traditionally marched to the cemetery in advance of the Provisionals. This was not simply a convenient arrangement but one which reflected the tensions between them which had resulted in bitter feuding and the deaths of members of each organization.

Mr A. recognized that the Easter Sunday celebrations in West Belfast afforded the ultimate opportunity to accommodate Lenny Murphy's ambition to kill a large number of Catholics. The fact that the planned killing would occur during a parade in celebration of Republicanism would be certain justification for murder. This rationale was, however, flawed. To believe that everyone present at a Republican commemoration parade was in fact a Republican failed to take into account that the parades are watched every year by spectators; by people who happen to live in the Falls area, as well as those who actively support the IRA or Sinn Fein. Mr A. held a blinkered view of his society; he shared the endemic prejudice which labels people because of where they live, where they go to church or whether they watch a parade. It would be true to say that many of these who watch such parades would vote for Provisional Sinn Fein but others would be present with their children out of a sense of tradition, or simply to watch the spectacle. A corollary would be to believe that every person watching an Orange procession was either a member of a Loyalist organization or a passive supporter of Loyalist violence.

The Provisionals themselves have, in recent times, exhibited an acceptance of this equation; for example, their belief that all those present on Remembrance Day at the cenotaph in the town of Enniskillen were, in their terms, part of the 'British war machine' and could therefore be arbitrarily and summarily dispensed with. The absurdity of such views has led to much of the terrible violence in Northern Ireland. It was Voltaire who suggested that any man who gives himself to absurdity is capable of mass murder.

The Loyalist perception of Easter Commemoration Parades is analagous with IRA thinking in many aspects. Loyalists believe anyone at such a parade is part of the IRA war machine and it is inconceivable to them that there might be present those who are not members of the IRA or Sinn Fein.

Against this backdrop, Mr A. told Moore that he could convince the UVF leadership that Easter Sunday was the time to strike at the IRA. His plan was that members of the Brown Bear unit would conduct reconnaissance missions the week before the parades and decide on the most strategic point at which to place a bomb. The bomb which would be small so as to avoid detection would be positioned the night before the parades and set with a timer to explode when the parades were under way. Mr A. was convinced his plan could be achieved but he would need the services of the UVF's bomb maker, James 'Tonto' Watt.

On 4 April Mr A. made his approach to the UVF Brigade Staff, put his plan before them and asked for the assistance of Watt. He was given the go-ahead after assurances had been sought that he would bring about the mass murder of members of the IRA only. Mr A. called a meeting of the Brown Bear unit and selected a team to carry out his plan. He chose Benny 'Pretty Boy' Edwards,

Waugh, and two other people who cannot be named because they have never been charged before the Courts. They have not been the subject of any incident previously dealt with in this book and will be referred to as Mr K. and Mr L.

Between 4 and 6 April Mr A. discussed his plans with Mr B. and 'Tonto' Watt. This was the first example of Mr A. taking over the complete planning of an operation. He chose to involve Mr B. and to exclude William Moore. Moore was the secret cutting edge of the private war being conducted from Lenny Murphy's prison cell and for this reason Mr A. believed he should be excluded from an operation which had been sanctioned by the leadership.

Mr A. and Mr B. between them had an extensive knowledge of Belfast already but they carried out research through newspaper files and by talking to older people in the UVF, and learned about the organization of Easter Sunday parades. They arrived at the conclusion that Beechmount Avenue was one of the main routes from which Republicans marched onto the Falls Road and therefore it was there that a bomb should be planted.

Edwards and Waugh were sent on reconnaissance missions into the Falls area to identify an exact spot where the bomb could be placed without attracting attention, since it would be planted and primed on the night prior to the parade. The reconnoitre failed and they returned unable to provide satisfactory information for Watt, who insisted on having precise details. They made a second journey and again returned unsure how the bomb should be planted or which type of device was required. Within twenty-four hours they made another trip but this time they took 'Tonto' Watt with them. At Beechmount he asked that the car be halted while he studied a security barrier which had been erected by local people to prevent sectarian incursions into their area. It consisted, as do many such barriers in Belfast, of a number of metal beer kegs through which had been driven a metal pole and the beer kegs filled with cement. The security forces often used these devices to limit IRA access to certain streets in the event of a car chase.

'Tonto' Watt had discovered the ideal disguise for his bomb. He instantly told Mr A. that he could construct a bomb and place it in a beer keg which, when laid alongside those in the security barrier, would not arouse suspicion. The three UVF men returned to the Shankill; Mr A. and Mr B. to put the final touches to their plan, and Watt to make the bomb, which Mr A. told him he needed on Saturday night. A further meeting was held on Friday 8 April at which Mr A. and Mr B. told Leckey, one of the original members of the Murphy gang, Waugh and the others that they believed the best time to leave the bomb in Beechmount was in the early hours of Easter Sunday morning. Those who would be 'up and about' later that morning would be preoccupied with going to church services and, afterwards, crowds gathering for the parade would be caught up in the excitement and therefore not likely to notice an extra beer keg sitting alongside a security barrier.

Waugh and the other accomplices were instructed to be at Mr A.'s home by midnight when the final details would be conveyed to them. Mr A. instructed that the bombing team would travel to Beechmount in two vehicles, the first to lead the way and to alert the second if a security road-block lay ahead, the second to transport the bomb. Mr A. boasted to the team that this would be the greatest blow ever struck against the Provisionals. For the first time the imminent operation bore the hallmarks of something which was being well planned with the presence of a second vehicle which would be used in a scouting role. In previous operations where a victim was picked up only one vehicle was required. In this instance the gang saw themselves as attempting a more daring plan which involved thorough preparation; a plan which would take them outside of their own territory and would involve greater risk.

By Saturday lunchtime Mr A. and Mr B. informed Watt that they had 'earmarked' a van for hijacking for the purposes of carrying the bomb and it would be driven to his house to collect the device in the early hours of Easter Sunday. The first vehicle was to be a car which, in the event of being stopped by the Army or police, would show up on a computer as 'clean'. Mr A. had in mind a car belonging to a UVF contact who lived near him. The man was approached and agreed to collude with the gang; in the event of his car being stopped by police he was to allege that it had been stolen.

At midnight on Saturday Mr A. told Mr B. to drive the hijacked van to collect the bomb. Shortly after midnight Waugh, Leckey, Mr K. and Mr L. arrived at Mr A.'s house. They were given drinks, and discussion about the bombing was deferred until 2.00A.M. when Mr B. arrived with the bomb, which was primed to explode at 2.00P.M. the following day. Mr B. consulted Mr A. concerning the instructions from the bomb maker and told him that since the bomb in the beer keg was primed, one of the team would have to sit in the rear of the car and hold it steady on the journey to Beechmount. Mr A. outlined to the team that Mr B. would travel in the lead car with Leckey at the wheel and, should a hitch arise, the lead vehicle would make a detour which would be repeated by the van. Mr B. was the man who knew the route and exact spot where the bomb was to be placed and he reassured the others that there was nothing to worry about since the route they were taking had been carefully mapped out. Mr A., the director of operations, once again was not to be party to the action. This was a classic example of the manner in which he manipulated members of the Murphy gang while acting as go-between and remaining at a distance from the actuality of operations.

Edwards, without prompting, offered to drive the van

and this was agreed but with the stipulation by Mr A. that Waugh should sit alongside him. Mr K. and Mr L. were given the task of remaining in the rear of the van to ensure that the bomb remained steady. Watt's instructions were that the bomb was composed of sticks of gelignite in an unstable condition and care was imperative when the van was traversing road ramps.

Mr A. watched from his house as the van drove towards the Shankill and turned in the direction of Glencairn. Leckey was instructed to keep his vehicle at a sixty-yard distance from the van. He was directed by Mr B. towards Ainsworth Avenue on the Shankill, which led directly to the Springfield Road, a distance of half a mile from Beech-mount Avenue. At this point Leckey began to panic but was reassured by Mr B. who pointed out that the bomb was in the van and not the car in which they were travelling. Mr B. guided the car into the Beechmount district and on to Beechmount Avenue where he produced a pistol and again told Leckey that they had nothing to worry them. He told Leckey to stop the car, at which stage the van came to a halt. Waugh and the others carefully unloaded the bomb and positioned it alongside the other beer kegs which formed the security barrier. Then Mr B. instructed Leckey to lead the way in his car and they drove back to the Springfield and into the Shankill. Leckey drove the car to the home of the man who had loaned it for the operation and he dropped the keys through the letterbox. Together with Mr B. he returned to Mr A.'s house where the others arrived a short time later. They all celebrated the success of their mission by drinking for several hours. During the drinking session Leckey was the butt of the rest of the gang's derision on account of his nervousness.

After lunch that day the bomb exploded not, as planned, while the Provisionals were marching but during the march organized by the Official Republican Movement (now the Workers' Party). Watt had set the timer on the bomb on the instructions of Mr A. who had mistaken the starting time of the Provisionals demonstration. A ten-year-old boy, Kevin McMenamin, was killed and many people injured.

No group claimed responsibility for the atrocity, with the result that the Official Republican sources pointed the finger at the Provisionals. The Provisionals denied involvement and attributed the bombing to Loyalist para-militaries but without specific reference to the UVF. A journalist, Jim Cusack, who dealt with the story the following day suggested that the RUC knew the UVF or UDA were the perpetrators but were unwilling to make this information public because it suited their purposes to have the Provisionals and the Official IRA in conflict. Relations between the two Republican groups came close to breaking point until talks between them clearly established that the bombing had, in fact, been carried out by Loyalists. The RUC reacted to Cusack's claim by replying that they did not publicize their suspicions for fear of heightening sectarian tension, especially during the Easter period which was widely recognized as a time of community strife and suspicion.

Two months after the bombing 'Tonto' Watt was caught and admitted to making the bomb: 'On the Monday, I heard about an explosion in the Beechmount area and I knew this was the bomb I made. I didn't know that it was going to kill any kids but I always had it in my head that it was going to kill somebody. When I heard about the kid I felt sick and I am sorry it happened. I didn't know the man who collected it to plant it.'

Watt knew well the devastation his bomb would create and the risk to civilians of all ages, as do the Provisionals when they plant bombs in city centres or in built-up housing areas.

Ten days after the Easter Sunday killing Watt provided another bomb for a UVF unit. It exploded at a funeral in the Ardoyne area, killing two civilians. On 2 May another bomb manufactured by him killed Corporal John Geddis

230

of the Ulster Defence Regiment. He was passing a filling station on the Crumlin Road which had been instructed to close by the UVF and the UDA. The filling station owner had disobeyed the edict, and the punishment for his courage was a bomb, which exploded as Corporal Geddis drove past the premises.

Watt was later given nine separate life sentences but did not receive a recommended sentence. His lawyers asked for each murder charge against him to be presented separately at court hearings, with the result that he was sentenced on each charge individually. Had he pleaded guilty to nine murders during one judicial sitting, the likelihood is that he would have received a recommendation of at least twenty-five years. The fact that no recommended sentence was decreed means that his case will come up for review with the prospect that Watt may serve a great deal less than twenty-five years.

When Leckey finally agreed to confess to the murder of Kevin McMenamin, he made a statement in which he said that in the early hours of Easter Sunday he returned home with his wife from a club and was approached by Edwards, who requested him to drive a car. They drove up the Shankill and into Ainsworth Avenue, where he stopped the car and a van passed them. He made no mention of Beechmount or of the fact that the van contained a bomb, and he named no one else but Edwards. Six hours after making this statement he told police he wished to tell the 'whole truth' and then named all those involved, with the exception of Mr K. to whom he attributed initials only, and Mr A. and Mr B. to whom he made no reference.

Waugh made a statement about the same time as Leckey but was unwilling to name accomplices and expressed no regret over the killing of the boy. 'It was the Provisionals we were after,' he told detectives. He admitted to assisting others in unloading the bomb from the van and placing it alongside other beer kegs which formed the security barrier in Beechmount Avenue.

Edwards also later confessed to his part in the bombing mission but refused to name his associates or express regret about the death of the ten-year-old.

Mr A., Mr B., Mr K. and Mr L. were never charged in connection with this crime.

13

The Ultimate Witness

By the beginning of May 1977 Jimmy Nesbitt and his team were no closer to catching the Butchers than they had been at the commencement of the cut-throat killings. The Press continued to publish speculative stories about them. The *Irish News* carried a story claiming that the residents of the Glencairn area, where most of the bodies had been dumped, had asked for greater police and Army security. The newspaper said it was informed by the RUC that the 'mad butcher' was believed to be a resident of Glencairn. The same newspaper carried a report that a well-known priest, Father Denis Faul from Dungannon in County Tyrone, had received information from sources in Belfast that the 'knife-man was known to operate in the Carlisle Circus area, was aged about fifty, and wore a surgical collar'.

It was also the *Irish News* which in February 1977 reported the following:

> Father Faul said he was disappointed to note in the reports of a Security Review at Stormont that no reference was made to the barbaric murder of Mr Joseph Morrissey or to the psychopath murderer operating in the Shankill/ Glencairn areas of the city. The public would have been reassured, he said, if the Security Committee was taking these gruesome murders of Catholics seriously. He asked if Consultant Psychologists had been asked to provide a mental identikit picture and whether the records of known psychopaths, with a tendency to use knives, had been checked out.

This report also contained claims by Father Faul, a man

well-known in the Province for making statements to the media about what he sees as injustices, that bloodstains found where the victims lay would be vital evidence. A police spokesman replied to the *Irish News* report by saying that no dramatic developments were expected immediately but detectives were confident that they would eventually find 'a pointer to the killer and his accomplices'.

The reaction of the police and the comments of Father Faul, some of which were naïve but understandable, represented a situation which, by May 1977, showed no signs of change. In the office of C Division murder squad, Nesbitt and those men close to him, such as Fitzsimmons, Chambers, Reid and Scott, believed they had covered all the groundwork necessary for the much-needed breakthrough in the case.

Nesbitt expresses his feelings about this period as follows: 'You have to understand that we needed a break. We were just waiting for our luck to change. All we needed was one clue. Imagine that above my office was a large balloon filled with lots of information but none of it is vital until I can find the device to prick the balloon. Oh, I knew once I found that device, literally a piece of evidence, I would be able to burst that balloon and everything needed for a successful resolve to the cut-throat killings would be there at our disposal. People forget that, when you are not able to catch criminals, you acquaint yourself with every scrap of detail available, even though it may not have significance at the time, so that when the lucky break comes along you are prepared.'

At 4.30A.M. on 11 May Jimmy Nesbitt was in bed at home when he was awakened by a telephone call from the duty inspector in Tennent Street station. He remembers the context of that call, which was to have considerable bearing on his professional life: 'The duty inspector told me that there was a serious assault in an alleyway off Emerson Street on the Shankill Road and the victim, who was found unconscious, had been taken to the Royal Victoria Hospital.'

Nesbitt admits that he did not see any significance in this communication at the time because such assaults were commonplace in the Shankill area: 'It was a way of life in that district but the reason why I was phoned was because I requested that every serious assault be referred to me because of the Butcher killings. However, I must be honest and say that call at the time was not terribly meaningful. I did, however, ask for two detectives, not from the murder squad, to spend part of their night-duty hours by making their way to the Royal Victoria Hospital to check it out as a matter of routine.'

When Nesbitt arrived in the station a few hours later he was informed that the two detectives had been refused admission to talk with the assault victim because he had been placed in intensive care. They had, however, established the identity of the victim as twenty-year-old Gerard McLaverty. Nesbitt admits that at this stage he did not link the assault with his Butcher investigations. On 16 May he dispatched two other detective constables, Turner and Coulter, to the Royal Victoria Hospital on behalf of CID (not the murder squad) to investigate the 'serious angle' to the McLaverty case; 'serious angle' referred simply to the gravity of the crime rather than any added significance. Retrospectively one might have expected Jimmy Nesbitt to be alerted by the fact that McLaverty was a Catholic but on the other hand past experience of Butcher attacks confirmed that victims were never left alive.

Detective Constables Turner and Coulter were eventually given access to McLaverty, who was released from intensive care and permitted to speak with them. Immediately upon their return to the station they informed Nesbitt that McLaverty had knife wounds to both wrists. Nesbitt recalls that moment vividly: 'As soon as they told me he had been slashed, my thoughts were that here was some-

thing sinister. Bells began to ring in my head. I summoned
John Scott and briefed him on the fact that there was
something more to this one and, knowing his experience,
I directed him to accompany Turner and Coulter to the
hospital to interview Gerard McLaverty.'

John Scott returned to Nesbitt's office within an hour
with McLaverty's account of how four men, posing as
Tennent Street detectives, kidnapped him at gunpoint on
the Cliftonville Road and drove him to the Shankill area.

Nesbitt says: 'I knew we were onto something. I contacted the hospital and asked if McLaverty was well
enough to be released and was told he could be signed
out the following day, 17 May. On the morning of that
day I instructed Roy Turner and his colleague to collect
McLaverty and bring him to me. When he arrived I made
him feel at ease and talked to him at length about his
experience. When he had finished telling me his story, I
went into my boss and said, "We've got the big one".'

During McLaverty's session with Nesbitt he told his
story, which he later put into a written statement:

> On 10 May I was living alone in a flat in Belfast. I left
> the flat at 6.30P.M. and went to a friend's house on the
> Antrim Road. I stayed there until approximately 11.30P.M.
> when I left accompanied by two girls and I walked with
> them to the junction of Cliftonpark Avenue and the Clif-
> tonville Road. The girls turned up Cliftonpark Avenue
> and I turned down the Cliftonville Road towards the
> Antrim Road. As I walked past the Belfast Royal Academy
> I saw a yellow Cortina car. It was parked on the opposite
> side of the road with its lights out. It was facing up the
> Cliftonville Road. I could see two men in the front of this
> car and at the same time two men walked towards me on
> the same footpath on which I was standing. I had seen
> this car draw up while I was walking and had seen these
> two men get out. I then saw them cross the road and walk
> towards me. I was the only person on the street at the
> time. I would describe one of these men as large and fat.
> The two men stopped me and the large, fat man told me

they were from the CID Tennent Street. They then asked
me for my identification. I showed my diary with my name
on it to the fat man. I then felt the fat man put a gun in
my back. He ordered me to go to the yellow Cortina across
the road. As I was getting into the back of the car I could
see the gun in his hand. I got into the back seat of the car
and the fat man got in also and sat on my right. The other
man got into the car and sat on my left. There were
already two men in the car. I said to the fat man, 'I've
done nothing to be picked up'. He said: 'We are taking
you to Tennent Street to check you out and then we will
drive you home again.' He then put the gun in his inside
jacket pocket. None of the others spoke. The car did a
U-turn on the Cliftonville Road, drove down the Antrim
Road to Carlisle Circus, up the Crumlin Road to Cambrai
Street and along Cambrai Street to the Shankill Road.
The car then turned left into a street off the Shankill Road
and stopped on the right-hand side of that street. No one
spoke to me during the journey. I was stopped at the side
door of a building which fronted onto the Shankill Road.
The man sitting on my left got out of the car and I saw
him opening this side door with a key. It appeared to me
to be a steel- or metal-covered door because it rattled
when it opened. While this was going on the fat man told
me that I would be going into the building and would be
kept there to get more details. We all got out of the car.
The two men in front of the car took one of my arms each
and marched me into the building. The fat man came
behind. When I got into the room, the fat man said:
'You're staying here.' I saw a dining room chair and two
electric heaters in the room. They made me sit on the
chair. There was what looked like a shop counter in the
room. The fat man said: 'We're gonna check up on you
and we won't be back till the morning.' They did not go
out. The fat man and the car driver went behind the
counter and came back with sticks. The stick that the fat
man had had a nail driven through the end of it. They
both started beating me around the head with the sticks.
I put up my hands to protect my eyes. I was afraid of the
nail in the fat man's stick piercing my eyes. The fat man

said: 'Get your fuckin' hands down or we'll give you more.'
I started to squeal with fear and pain and they stopped
beating me. They had a teapot and a kettle and the driver
of the car went and made some tea. The fat man asked
me if I wanted tea and I refused. I said: 'I want to go
home'. The fat man said: 'You are not going home. There
is no way you are getting out of this.' They all sat and
drank their tea. I was sitting in the corner and they were
all sitting watching me. When they had finished their tea,
they put their cups away and came back to me. The driver
punched me on the side of the face and eye with his fist.
I was knocked onto the floor and he took his heel and
drove it into the side of my face. They set me down on
the chair again and the driver of the car took the lace out
of his right boot. He gave it to the fat man and then they
held my hands behind my back. The fat man held me and
tied the lace loosely round my neck. Throughout this the
other men did not touch me but they stayed at one of the
two doors in the room. When the lace had been tied
loosely round my neck, the other two men left and locked
the door from the outside. The fat man and the car driver
had broken open the other door before the first two left.
When I was alone with the fat man and the car driver they
took me out of this open door into an entry. The yellow
Cortina was in the street at the end of that entry. At this
time the fat man had a large clasp knife. The driver
tightened the lace around my neck and the fat man started
slashing at my clothes with the knife. With the tightening
of the lace around my neck I lost consciousness. When I
regained consciousness I was lying in the entry. There
was a crowd of people around me and I was taken by
ambulance to the Royal Victoria Hospital. Both my wrists
were severely slashed and my neck was sore and swollen.
I would describe the fat man as being twenty-four-years
old, tall and fat. He was wearing a black leather jacket
and black trousers. I think he was wearing a jumper. At
one time I saw his right arm and he seemed to have a scar
inside opposite his elbow. I would describe the driver as
being about twenty-five to twenty-six years old, tall, of
medium build and longish hair. He was wearing a brown

leather jacket and blue trousers. It was the fat man and
the car driver who attacked me. I would describe one of
the other two men as small, of light build and about
twenty-two years old. He was wearing a white jacket.

Nesbitt recognized that McLaverty was exhausted after
giving his account of events and thought it would be unfair
and unwise to attempt to extract any further revelations
from him at that point. It could be argued that he should
have shown McLaverty photographs of known terrorists
but Nesbitt believes that such a course of action would
have been foolish and says: 'At that stage I knew firstly
that he was tired. I felt that he needed a rest since his
injuries were only six days old. There was no question,
anyway, of showing him photographs because the investigation was at too early a stage for that procedure. I knew
from experience that producing photos for identification
at a primary stage can later damage positive identification
evidence. I was thinking: "This guy can identify these men
if we can catch them. If I show him photos and he later
identified them, it could be argued that the identification
was based on his seeing the photos." I knew what I wanted
and there was no way I was going to jeopardize the potential that McLaverty presented to me.'

McLaverty for his part asked Nesbitt if he could leave
the station and return home for a rest but Nesbitt told
him that his safety was of paramount importance. Further,
he could not be permitted to return to the Antrim Road
area because his attackers had possession of his diary and
therefore his address, and would by this time know that
he was still alive and a potential witness against them.
Nesbitt also pointed out that it would be impossible to
give him ideal security in the Antrim Road area because
it would expose policemen to attacks from the IRA. McLaverty suggested going to his mother's home in – (a town
in County Antrim which I prefer not to name to preserve
Mrs McLaverty's privacy and because Gerard McLaverty

may still be a marked man). McLaverty assured Nesbitt that his mother and other members of the family had only recently moved to the town and were not known to other residents in their neighbourhood. Nesbitt agreed to this alternative because he felt that McLaverty required the comfort and security of his family after such a terrible ordeal. Police in the town were contacted and said that they were unaware that the McLaverty family had moved into the area. This satisfied Nesbitt who ordered an armed guard to be placed discreetly round the house and surrounding neighbourhood as an added protection.

By now Nesbitt felt he was 'getting closer to something big' though he would not have defined McLaverty's evidence as leading directly to the cut-throat murderers. He felt there were clues which could possibly lead him in that direction.

The following morning he instructed Detective Constables Turner and Coulter to collect McLaverty from his mother's house and drive him to the precise point on the Cliftonville Road where he was abducted. They encouraged him to retrace the route taken by the Cortina and, if possible, to lead them to the building where he had been held. McLaverty, with the events of the night of 10–11 May etched on his mind, was eventually able to guide them to a disused doctor's surgery at the corner of Emerson Street on the Shankill Road. The satisfied detectives returned to Tennent Street with their charge and informed Nesbitt that McLaverty had been able to show them the route taken by his attackers and the very building in which he had been beaten. Nesbitt reacted with the speed and professionalism of a detective of many years experience. 'I know what we'll do,' he told Turner and Coulter, 'we'll take full advantage of the massive identification parade on the Shankill Road and, if McLaverty is as good as he says he is, then we should have results.'

Turner and Coulter looked at Nesbitt, not understanding the full significance of what he was saying. Nesbitt explained: 'Look, there are lots of people on the Shankill Road at the moment, many of them members of the UDA and UVF. That is our identification parade. Take an unmarked car, put Gerard in it, but put a hat on him and dark glasses as a disguise, and do a tour of the Road.'

Nesbitt's thinking was simple but clever. At that time the Province was experiencing its second general strike, the first having occurred in 1974. This second strike, though it failed after two weeks, resulted in the mobilization of Loyalist paramilitaries at a time most expedient for Nesbitt's purposes. On 18 May the Shankill Road was full of members of the UDA and UVF, many of them simply standing at street corners.

As Turner and Coulter drove McLaverty down the Shankill Road he indicated that two men walking along the pavement were the 'fat man' and another of the gang described in his account to Nesbitt. Turner knew he had to be sure and drove the car past a second time to allow more certain identification. McLaverty had no doubts. Turner and Coulter would have liked more than anything at that moment just to stop the car and apprehend the two men, whom they knew to be Samuel McAllister and Benny Edwards. However, Nesbitt had warned them to observe but not to act. This was shrewd advice because to have attempted to arrest the two suspects, with paramilitaries out on the street, would have put McLaverty's life in mortal danger. Instead, they returned in haste to the station to inform Nesbitt. Nesbitt says that at that moment he knew he had made the breakthrough to the Butchers. When he first mentioned this to me I was puzzled about why the identification of two men should bring him to such a conclusion. He replied that during that day he had dwelt on McLaverty's story and, by the time Turner and Coulter returned from the Shankill, he had accepted that the facts of the case pointed to the Butchers. He went immediately to the office of his Divisional Commander and told him that he believed he now 'had the link' which would lead him to the cut-throat gang. He outlined the McLaverty case and the identification of the two men and requested that an arrest and search operation take place the following morning. He also decided to include William Moore in the arrest operation because, he says, of McLaverty's mention of a yellow Cortina. If Moore was known to Nesbitt's murder squad, as this decision implies, it prompts the question why the sighting of a yellow Cortina on the night of the Cassidy killing was not investigated. I have commented on this earlier and given reasons for the lead not having been followed up. Now it seems the police knew that Moore owned a yellow Cortina. I believe there was more to the decision to arrest Moore than the fact that he owned a Cortina. He was, in fact, a prime suspect in relation to serious crimes other than the Butcher murders. At the very least, he would have been known as an associate of McAllister and Edwards. I can only assume that his arrest came about as a result of the previous interview when his taxi was tested after the Rice murder. Presumably all such information would be on file, together with details of the Cortina which replaced the taxi. These details would have permitted positive identification of the Cortina mentioned by McLaverty. Nesbitt has not commented on my analysis of what led to the arrest other than to reiterate that he was arrested because he owned a yellow Cortina. It is interesting to note, however, that Nesbitt also told me that his murder squad 'knew a lot about everybody'.

The simple explanation may, in fact, be that Moore was known to drive frequently around the Shankill area in his car and in this way had come to the notice of the police. However, I do believe that Nesbitt and his team had long harboured suspicions about Moore and his associates, but to convert such suspicions into hard evidence had been too difficult.

Whatever the truth of this matter, Nesbitt decided to

act quickly. He picked three parties of men, made up of detectives and uniformed staff, and briefed them on the search operation he had in mind. He told them that the homes of McAllister, Moore and Edwards were their targets and the three were to be arrested. The operation was scheduled for 5.15A.M., a time when Moore and his associates would least expect such an operation and when there would be no paramilitaries on the streets to impede their arrest.

McLaverty was kept for his own safety in Tennent Street Station that night. Nesbitt believed he was closing in on his targets, and his precious witness had to be prevented from placing himself at risk at this critical stage.

At 5.15A.M. three separate parties of detectives and uniformed officers left Tennent Street, each one under instruction to search the respective houses for knives. When an arrest party arrived at Edwards's house they found he was not at home and his wife explained that they had had a marital dispute the previous evening because of 'Benny's womanizing' and he had stormed out of the house. The premises were searched but nothing found and a communication was issued to all patrols to arrest him on sight.

Moore was at home and was arrested under Section 12 of the Prevention of Terrorism Act 1976, which gives police the right to hold a suspect for questioning for seven days. The house was searched, much to the surprise and consternation of Moore's elderly mother, and Moore was arrested and taken to Tennent Street. He feigned surprise at his arrest and protested that he was an innocent man who was being wrongly 'lifted'.

Detective Constable Matt Russell of the murder squad was given the task of leading a search and arrest party to McAllister's home at 23 Lawnbrook Street. McAllister and his wife were in bed when police arrived and he complained strongly that the search was an intrusion into his privacy but added that he had nothing to hide. Matt

Russell was not convinced by McAllister and, with the assistance of Detective Constable George Mason, he searched the marital bedroom. To his astonishment, he found a butcher's knife sticking out of the floorboards beside the bed. Detective Constable Mason found another such knife under the bed. In a cupboard in the kitchen, Matt Russell found two butcher's knives and a butcher's steel for sharpening the knives. McAllister was arrested and Russell hastened back to Tennent Street to present the knives to Jimmy Nesbitt.

Nesbitt says that when Russell entered his office he told him that he could not believe his luck at finding the knives. He added that when McAllister was asked why he had the knives in his possession he had replied that they were for his protection in the event of the IRA attacking him in his own home.

Nesbitt was triumphant but told his men not to think too far ahead because the primary objective was to obtain a breakthrough on the McLaverty case, after which, he felt sure, other things would fall into place. He ordered an immediate examination by a forensic team of the disused doctor's surgery where McLaverty had been held captive.

At the next stage of the proceedings Nesbitt displayed a characteristic which had helped make him one of the most popular and respected detectives in the Station. He asked for Roy Turner, and other men who were not in the murder squad but had provided valuable assistance, to be made available to him for the remainder of the investigation. This opportunity to experience 'a slice of the action', as Turner put it, was welcomed with enthusiasm by all. Roy Turner was given the task of finding Moore's Cortina, which was not at his home but in the keeping of an associate. Turner collected it and took it to the Department of Industrial and Forensic Science for examination.

The knives were conveyed to the same department and all the exhibits were tested for blood by Richard McClean, a member of the forensic science staff. His tests on Moore's car produced the following evidence: 'I found no blood on the inside surface of this car. On the rubber mat lining of the boot and on the rubber seal of the boot I found evidence of blood staining. There was widespread blood staining on the rubber mat taken from the boot. This blood and blood on the rubber seal of the boot gave reactions consistent with it being sheep blood. [No explanation was ever sought for the unusual presence of sheep's blood in the car and I was unable to discover the reason for the find.] There was nothing of apparent significance from any of the items in the car, except for fibres found in the car which matched those taken from a boiler suit worn by Gerard McLaverty.'

McClean also examined the knives, which ranged in size from six inches to ten inches and bore the marks of having been well honed and used in the butchery trade. The sharpener showed signs of heavy use. No blood traces were found on any of these items.

Nesbitt was not unduly concerned with these results. He was occupied at this stage with selecting men to carry out the interrogations of McAllister and Moore, which were scheduled to begin that afternoon. Nesbitt stressed to the men assigned the task that they were to proceed only on the McLaverty assault. He briefed the interrogating officers in the following manner: 'McAllister is well known to me and previous interviews with him have proved exceedingly difficult because there was never evidence. He is a tough nut to crack but we know we have something in our favour and that is the clear identification by McLaverty. Be confident but take it slowly. Concentrate on the McLaverty business and, in Moore's case, on the fact that his car was used in the abduction.'

Moore and McAllister were taken across Belfast to Castlereagh Holding Centre where most terrorist suspects are questioned. The building is custom-built with scores of interrogation rooms. Here, Nesbitt would have the assistance of officers from the Regional Crime Squad who were skilled in interrogation techniques, though Nesbitt wanted his own men to make the initial breakthrough which would unravel the cut-throat murders.

A concern of Nesbitt's at this time was the safety of Gerard McLaverty. The arrests of Moore and McAllister, according to him, would have 'hit the streets' by breakfast time, thus making McLaverty a target for UVF circles. Nesbitt discussed this with McLaverty but the young man seemed unable to recognize the dangers and exhibited no sense of self-preservation. He was no longer in police custody and was free to leave Tennent Street Station at any time. Nesbitt says: 'I was concerned to make proper arrangements for his safekeeping but this proved difficult because of his behaviour. I could not restrain him but only offer guidance and sound advice, which he ignored. In the days that followed he slipped away and wandered the streets of Belfast. The moment when I panicked was when I received a call that he was in a bar in the Loyalist area of Sandy Row near Belfast city centre discussing his ordeal with people unknown to him. Luckily, someone in the bar had the sense to phone the RUC, and subsequently myself. He could have been blown away and we would have had no witness and been left with a statement which had not even been registered with the court. I decided that the only way to protect him was to remove him from the jurisdiction of Northern Ireland to the Irish Republic. I made enquiries, we supplied him with a sum of money and placed him in an institution run by a religious order in Dublin. Even after that, he telephoned me on a number of occasions, having returned to Belfast. Each time this happened, I sent Coulter and Turner to pick him up and drive him to the border and put him safely on a train to Dublin. I always selected those two detectives because they were the first guys to meet him.'

Because of his concern about McLaverty, Nesbitt used unorthodox means to circumvent the complexities of the legal system – a necessary step at the time. Although not normal practice, he took McLaverty to a remand court and converted his statement into a deposition, which was the only way to preserve his evidence in the event of the young man being murdered. The deposition did not differ markedly from his initial statement but there were several interesting details which emerged in his second telling of the story. In the first account he had said he was at a friend's house on the evening of 10 May. In the deposition he revealed that he had in fact spent the whole evening in the Simon Community on the Antrim Road. McLaverty, who was unemployed at the time, was a frequent visitor to this charitable centre, where he was often provided with food or given small sums of money. Another detail which he had omitted from the statement was the fact that while being held and beaten in the disused surgery he was questioned about membership of the IRA and whether he knew of anyone involved with the Provisionals.

McAllister's interrogation began at exactly 3.15 P.M. on 19 May. The following is an account of how the interview progressed, taken from notes made at the time by Detective Constable Raymond Coulter:

> On 19 May at 3.15 P.M., accompanied by Detective Sergeant Stockdale and Detective Constable Turner, I saw Samuel McAllister in the Police Office at Castlereagh. Detective Sergeant Stockdale identified us to McAllister and fingerprinted him and Detective Constable Turner completed crime forms. Detective Sergeant Stockdale informed McAllister that we were making enquiries into the attempted murder of a Gerard McLaverty on the night of 10–11 May and cautioned him. McAllister replied: 'I was at home in bed with my wife and if you ask her she will tell you.' We then informed McAllister that on 11 May this person, McLaverty, was picked up on the Cliftonville Road, badly beaten and left for dead. We informed McAllister that on 18 May at approximately 10.10 A.M. he was one of a group of men who were seen outside the Stadium Cinema on the Shankill Road and that he had

been positively identified as one of the men who took
part in this attempted murder. McAllister told us that
McLaverty was wrong and he was nowhere near it. He
was asked by Constable Turner if he had scars on either
arm. McAllister pulled up a sweater he was wearing and
showed us a scar which was on the inside and outside of
his left elbow. He stated that these scars were caused by
gunshot wounds. We called for a photograph to be taken
of these scars and continued to question McAllister
strenuously about this incident but he equally strenuously
denied being involved in it. He maintained throughout
the interview that he was at home. At 5.45P.M. Detective
Sergeant Stockdale left the room and Detective Constable
Turner and I continued the interview. McAllister still
denied being involved and told us that he was at home
with his wife that night and the reason why he was so sure
of that was that he had stopped going out at night because
he had been the subject of a punishment shooting and he
was scared that something more serious might happen to
him. The interview terminated at 6.30P.M. and McAllister
was returned to his cell.

Meanwhile, Nesbitt and Fitzsimmons were about to concentrate their efforts on Moore. This duo of interrogators
shared a wealth of experience in dealing with terrorists
and Moore was undoubtedly aware of the formidable
opponents he was about to face. Nesbitt led the questioning with constant interjections by John Fitzsimmons. They
harassed, cajoled and convinced Moore they had a store
of evidence and that he would be well advised to admit to
his part in the abduction of McLaverty. Nesbitt told him
they had McAllister in custody, that he had been identified
and that he was 'grassing' on the others. Unlike McAllister, Moore was not resilient, and Nesbitt knew this. Both
detectives told him he would go down on the attempted
murder charge but if he admitted that he had driven the
car which McLaverty clearly identified as belonging to
him, he might be able to plead to a lesser charge. Within

an hour Moore admitted that he had been one of the four
men involved in the kidnapping, and he made a statement:

> Four of us went out last Tuesday night. We were in my
> yellow Cortina car. We went to the town of Holywood in
> County Down and visited nearly every pub in it. We left
> Holywood about twelve midnight when the bars shut and
> headed back to Belfast. On the way home somebody said:
> 'Come on and we'll knock the bollocks out of a *Taig*.' We
> drove onto the Cliftonville Road. We saw this fellow come
> down the Cliftonville Road on his own. He was on the
> opposite side of the road from us over by the school. Two
> of the boys got out of the car and went over to him. We
> did a U-turn on the road and drove over beside him. I
> was driving and two of the others got out and went over
> and spoke to him. I don't know what they said to him but
> he just got in. There was no fight or anything. We drove
> off and one of the boys said: 'Take him to the wee place
> at the corner of Emerson Street.' I drove there and we
> took him in. We gave him a digging. I had a stick and I
> hit him with it. We then took him out the side door into
> Emerson Street, down Riga Street and up Carnan Street
> into an entry. We took him to the corner of the entry and
> knocked his bollocks in. I had a knife. I hit him with it in
> the wee place in Emerson Street. I think I hit him with it
> on the back of the hand. It was a penknife and I didn't
> cut or slash him. I remember I didn't.

Nesbitt knew, of course that Moore had cut both McLaverty's wrists before he left the alleyway in Carnan Street.
Had a butcher's knife been available in place of the penknife, Moore would have cut his throat. Nesbitt was now
almost certain he had the cut-throat murderer sitting
before him.

Moore completed his statement at 10.05P.M. and Nesbitt immediately asked him if he had ever worked as a
butcher, to which Moore replied: 'I worked at Woodvale
Meats and one of the butchers there showed me how to
do the job and let me help him'. When asked if he had
ever kept butchery knives in his home Moore replied that

he had not. Nesbitt and Fitzsimmons continued to probe this issue but without ever alluding to the cut-throat killings. Of the interview, Nesbitt says: 'We let him know we were on to him but there was no question of us confronting him with the major crimes for a while. We wanted him to ponder on his situation and the fact that we might just have hidden evidence to connect him with other things. This was our way of making him sweat it out.'

When Nesbitt left the interview room he summoned two of his most experienced men, Detective Sergeants Cecil Chambers and John Scott, to instruct them in the methods of interrogation to be used on McAllister. In two four-hour sessions they followed Nesbitt's advice and extracted this statement:

Me and two other fellows went to Holywood for a drink. We left the bar after closing time and the three of us had a fair amount of alcohol. We were looking for a chippy. We ended up on the Cliftonville Road. We were coming up the Cliftonville Road from the Antrim Road when we seen this man walking down the Cliftonville Road on the right hand side. He looked like a Provy and we turned round and came down behind him. We asked him if he would come with us and he got into the car voluntarily. We took him into the Shankill and took him into a place at the bottom of Emerson Street and the Shankill Road. We took him inside. We just questioned him about arms dumps belonging to the Provisionals or any other Republican Movements. I know it wasn't right questioning him about anything but it was only that we had too much alcohol on us at the time. During the questioning, I hit him a smack up the ears and asked him if he was involved with the provisionals. He replied, 'Yes.' I had a bit of wood in my hand and it is possible that I may have struck him with it at some stage. During this time I went out and made tea. He was still being questioned by two other fellows. When the tea was ready, they stopped questioning him. We kept him on a chair in the room for about an hour and a half. I want to state that in that room there was no guns and two other fellows with the man started to walk up Emerson Street. One of the fellows with me took the shoelace out of his boots. We turned left into Riga Street and into Carnan Street. While this was all happening, at no time did I have a knife. One of the others might have had a knife. It would only have been a short-blade knife. I stood at Paris Street for about three minutes. The other two fellows came back to me and told me that the other boy had got a bit of a digging. We all split up and I walked home.

As soon as Nesbitt saw this statement he was struck by McAllister's reference to the size of the knife blade. The obvious inference to be drawn was that on other occasions larger knives had been used.

Nesbitt was highly satisfied to have McAllister's confession and he felt he had him on the spot. However, he realized that McAllister appreciated the significance of the McLaverty identification and that to get him to admit to any further crime would be exceedingly difficult. His statement demonstrated his artifice. He had named none of his accomplices, diminished his role in the attempted murder and tried to blacken McLaverty by claiming that he was a member of the Provisional IRA.

In police interview notes of the McAllister interrogation, John Scott recorded him as claiming that McLaverty admitted knowledge of where the Provisionals kept explosives. It was also recorded that he said Moore used the knife. However, neither detail was included in the actual statement by McAllister.

It should be stated categorically that Gerard McLaverty was never involved with any Republican grouping. He was a young man of low intelligence who may well have admitted to anything under torture. I feel that those who dealt with him had no understanding of his behaviour following the violent attack upon him. Such behaviour may well have been attributable to trauma; recent studies have shown that victims of hijackings behave irrationally during and after the event and often identify with their captors as a means of self-preservation. This could explain, perhaps, McLaverty's visit to a bar in the Loyalist enclave of Sandy Row only a short time after his horrifying ordeal.

With statements extracted from Moore and McAllister, Nesbitt knew he had the opening he needed and Moore was the one most likely to crack first. He was also aware of the statistic that ninety-five per cent of all criminal cases in the United Kingdom were solved by methods of interrogation. He returned to the room where Moore was held, told Fitzsimmons about McAllister's confession and stated that the time had arrived when it should be put to Moore that he was the cut-throat murderer. The two detectives recapitulated the details of the McLaverty case for Moore's benefit and then Nesbitt told him: 'If you look closely at all of that, there can be little doubt that you are the Butcher we are looking for.' Moore began to panic, and the signs were only too familiar to the two detectives. Nesbitt says he recognized that Moore's agitation was being caused by the litany of other crimes as yet unmentioned and his desperate attempts to keep his interrogators at bay by supplying a confession on the McLaverty kidnapping.

Nesbitt adds, 'I thought Moore was saying to himself: "I've given them McLaverty and that will make them go away", but we wouldn't go away. The next thing he gives us Shaw and admits that he drove the car carrying Shaw's body. We watched Moore make this admission and, again, knowing the criminal mind we knew that he was looking at Fitzy and myself thinking: "That'll get them off my back". I knew we had the bastard and there was a lot more to come. We pressurized him. We gave him no room for manoeuvre so he confesses that he drove the car on the night of the McQuaid shooting. You see, he was only giving us the stuff where he was not the central actor, and God we knew it. Finally, by 11.35P.M. he tells us that he also drove the car the night that Neeson was killed but denied he was involved in the killing. I began to realize that we were dealing with someone very big and not just cut-throat killings . . . something very big. I returned him to his cell to sweat it out. I was convinced that he had a lot more on his mind and he would have all night to worry about it because he knew the two of us were going to hound him to the very end.'

On 20 May Detectives McGahan, McCaw, Boyd, Ogilvie and Turner were assigned the task of 'softening up' Moore. They interviewed him, two detectives always present, in three sessions throughout the day, beginning at 10.15A.M. and ending at 10.15P.M. They tried to encourage him to admit to the cut-throat murders but Moore refused to comment, with the exception of two remarks: that he had only heard of the murders on television and that any man who would have committed them 'would have to be mad'.

The following morning at 10.00A.M. Coulter, Turner and Stockdale met Moore once again in Castlereagh Holding Centre and told him they believed him to be responsible for the cut-throat killings. Moore replied: 'I had nothing to do with them. It was the UDA in the lower Shankill who committed those murders.' The interview ended at 11.15A.M. The questioning was resumed with Detective Constable John McCawl and Detective Sergeant Jim Reid present. What transpired is contained within John McCawl's notes as follows:

> I introduced Detective Sergeant Reid to Moore and reminded him that he was still under caution. We put it to him that he was involved in the cut-throat murders. He denied this but I said I could tell from his attitude that he still had something on his mind. He said that he had nothing on his mind and that he had told us everything. Detective Sergeant Reid asked him if he could account for his movements on the dates of the murders. He said he couldn't remember any of them or where he was. We continued interviewing him and putting it to him that he

was involved in these murders and that his attitude convinced us that he was involved. He continued to deny it but became more hesitant in his denials. At 12.25P.M. Detective Sergeant Scott came into the room. He introduced himself and told Moore he was also investigating the cut-throat murders. Detective Sergeant Reid left at 12.30P.M. We continued the interview until 1.30P.M. On the way back to the cell, he stopped Detective Sergeant Scott in the yard and said, 'Wait, I want to see you.' Detective Sergeant Scott asked him why and he replied that he could help us. He said: 'I know about the cut-throatings.' Detective Sergeant Scott reminded him that he was still under caution and we took him back to the interview room. He said: 'I don't know what to do, I'm scared. I want time to think this thing over.' I told him he could have time to think it over. He said: 'I'm scared. I don't know what to do. Will you two see me again?' Detective Sergeant Scott told him to think it over and we would see him after tea. He agreed to do this and we returned him to his cell. At 7.35P.M. Detective Sergeant Scott asked him if he'd had plenty of time to think during the afternoon. He said he had. I asked him what he was going to tell us about the throat-cut murders. He said he had been involved in them all. Detective Sergeant Scott asked him if he had done any of the throat slashings himself. He said: 'Murphy done the first three and I done the rest.' He added: 'It was on Murphy's instructions when he was in gaol to take suspicion off Murphy.' He broke down and cried and said: 'It was that bastard Murphy led me into all this. My head's away with it.' He asked us did we think he was wise. Detective Sergeant Scott asked if he could give us details of each murder and he said: 'Go ahead and ask and I'll tell you.'

This session ended at 8.30P.M. by which time Moore had named most of his accomplices in the cut-throat killings, most of the members of the UVF Brigade Staff and the manner in which the victims had been killed. Nesbitt was informed immediately and made his way to Castlereagh with all the files available on killings in the Shankill area at the time of the Butcher murders. He also issued orders that those mentioned by Moore as his accomplices be arrested. Scott and McCawl were in the interview room with Moore when Nesbitt arrived at 8.30P.M. to undertake the harrowing job of recording the details of Moore's involvement in the Butcher murders.

That evening while Moore was being interviewed, McAllister was also being questioned in a room less than twenty yards away. The policeman in charge of McAllister was the experienced murder squad detective from C Division, Jim Reid. His notes contain this entry:

> At 7.30P.M. I had a general conversation with McAllister regarding his movements on the nights of the murders involving the knife slashing. He denied being involved in any of these murders and I put it to him that I could not believe him and that no other reasonable man could believe him when they knew that knives had been found in his house and also that the victim of a knife attack could identify him as one of the men who had beaten him up. He continued to deny that he was involved in any of these murders and stated: 'What can I say to convince you?' At this stage McAllister said he wanted to speak with Billy Moore. I asked him how he knew that Billy Moore was here and he replied: 'I can hear him next door.' He added: 'If I can speak with him, I will tell you all. I swear by my child's life that if I can speak with him I will clear it all up for you.' He again stated that if he could speak to Moore he would clear up his part in the cut-throat murders, and he began to cry.

McAllister persisted with his request that if he were allowed to see Moore they could 'clear it up together'. While McAllister continued to cry, Jim Reid contacted Scott, Fitzsimmons and Nesbitt and told them of McAllister's request. Nesbitt detected McAllister's ploy. 'I knew', says Nesbitt, 'that McAllister was thinking that if he could see Moore and know that Moore had not confessed then McAllister would keep his trap shut.'

The events which followed are not recorded on official police files because they represented an unorthodox practice but they are evidence of Nesbitt's determination. He told Fitzsimmons to drag the crying McAllister from his interview room and give him a quick look at the broken Moore who was, by now, revealing all the details of the murders. McAllister was bundled into the doorway of the room containing Moore and told in front of Moore that his accomplice had confessed. Then he was summarily returned to his cell. The glimpse of Moore was enough to convince McAllister that he had been exposed by Moore's testimony.

John Scott recalls how shocked he was when he saw 'Big Sam crying like a baby'. 'I never thought that McAllister, hard as he was, would break down like that', he says. During the remainder of the interview McAllister agreed to make statements about his role in the murders but insisted he would not name anyone else.

Armed with Moore's and McAllister's statements Nesbitt issued instructions for Bates and Townsley to be arrested and this was done at 6.00A.M. on 23 May. Nesbitt believed Townsley, a juvenile, might prove less formidable in interrogation than his elders.

'Townsley you would think would have been easy but he was tough and stubborn', says Nesbitt. Townsley did make a series of confessions in the presence of Cecil Chambers and Detective Constable Tom Starrett. Nesbitt decided to send for Townsley's father at the time of the interview.

Nesbitt kept the following notes on the Townsley episode:

At 9.10P.M. I saw the accused, William Townsley, in an interview room at Castlereagh RUC Station in the presence of Detective Sergeant Cecil Chambers. The accused's father had come to the station by arrangement and I showed Mr Townsley senior into the office. He sat beside the accused and said to him: 'Did you confess?'

FINGER PRINTS OF A CONVICTED PRISONER					

Form F.P. 2/2

This Form is not to be pinned.

N.I.C.R.O. No ... **64/1180**

'R'　　　　MALE

Name **MURPHY. HUGH. ALMRS. TOWNSLEY**

Aliases ....

Prison ....　　Classification No. ... I R ⁴₅

Prison Reg. No. .... 　　 11 0.....

RIGHT HAND

1.—Right Thumb	2—R. Fore Finger	3.—R. Middle Finger.	4—R. Ring Finger.	5.—R. Little Finger.
O	15	15	17	14
(FOLD) W	/	\		(FOLD)

The accused replied: 'Yes I did but Moore and Big Sam are here and they made theirs first.' The accused and his father had a conversation during which they discussed how Townsley senior was going to convey all the details to the accused's mother. I asked the accused to tell his father whether it was true, the statement he made, and he replied that it was so. I asked Townsley senior if he would witness the statement which had been made by his son and he agreed to do so and signed it.

Nesbitt had got what he wanted. When I put it to Jimmy Nesbitt that his handling of the Townsley interrogation might be questioned he was adamant that it was the right thing to do because of the nature of the crimes and the people with whom Townsley associated. 'I knew he was another one who had to be taken out of circulation. For his age he was hard, a confirmed terrorist,' adds Nesbitt.

By 25 May McClay, Bates, Waugh and Bell were also in custody. After constant interrogation they all made statements implicating themselves and other members of the Brown Bear team. None of these statements provided the extensive information given by Moore, which included references to the participation of Mr A. and Lenny Murphy. The others determinedly avoided naming accomplices, in particular Mr A. and Mr B. Meanwhile, Edwards and McIlwaine were on the run, in the certain knowledge that warrants had been issued for their arrest. Edwards was discovered hiding in a flat in the Woodvale area on 13 June and McIlwaine was detained on the same day. Nesbitt contends that McIlwaine was dismissed from the Ulster Defence Regiment before his arrest but my belief is that the dismissal came about as a result of a communication from the police that he would shortly be questioned about serious crimes.

Mr A. disappeared from the Shankill area after the initial arrests and was not located until July. After two days of police interrogation he was released. In the autumn of 1977 Mr B. was also questioned but was released after two days in custody. Nesbitt says there were no means by which they could have been encouraged to admit their guilt.

On 1 June, at Moore's request, Nesbitt visited him in Crumlin Road Prison, where he was being held on remand, and was told by Moore that there had been an operation which he had forgotten to mention: the attack on the lorry transporting workmen in Cambrai Street.

During the weeks following Moore's arrest, charges were preferred against most of the gang. In each case Moore replied 'guilty' and his accomplices 'nothing to say'.

John Scott feels it is debatable whether the murder squad would have apprehended the Butchers without McLaverty's identification of McAllister and Edwards. There were further fears at the time that, after charges had been preferred, McLaverty might prove to be a poor witness in court.

Of Moore and his confession which provided the breakthrough, Scott says: 'I think it was a relief for Moore to get it all off his chest. He had a big barrier to cross before he admitted to the cut-throat jobs. He wanted clear. He wanted out and finally he behaved in a manner which implied that he was ashamed of what he had done. I think he was more concerned about his mother because she was dying of cancer and was disgusted by her son's actions, and Willie Moore knew that. He was rock bottom when we were interviewing him, until he admitted all the crimes.'

He says the following about McClay: 'McClay was the last one to be interviewed and it took us three days to break him. He had never before been interrogated but we knew he had received tuition in anti-interrogation techniques while he was on the run.'

Detective Inspector John Fitzsimmons has a lasting impression of McAllister during the days of interrogation which, he says, is revealing about the way in which McAllister viewed himself and, more particularly, Moore. He expresses it in the following: 'I remember going into the room to confront "Big Sam" with the fact that his leader [Moore] had said that Sam used a hatchet on Neeson. McAllister was forced to admit it and that annoyed him. Afterwards, in conversation with me, he returned to the question of his relationship with Moore and said: "Billy Moore's a fuckin' nutcase." In my mind this was his way of retaliating by implying that Moore was the man who was sufficiently crazy to be responsible for the cut-throat murders.'

With the Butcher gang in prison, Nesbitt now turned his mind to a matter which constantly exercised his thoughts: how to make Lenny Murphy accountable for the murders he had committed. He also wanted Mr A. and Mr B. brought to justice and he figured that the only means of achieving this would be to encourage one or two of the Butchers already in custody to make formal statements implicating these three leading terrorists. He proceeded with his plan to obtain accomplice evidence by having secret consultations in Crumlin Road Prison with both Moore and Bates. I have been unable to discover whether Nesbitt took the decision to follow such a course of action with the authority of his Divisional Commander and the advice of the Office of the Director of Public Prosecutions. His meetings were designed to persuade Moore and Bates to put in writing their knowledge of the roles played by Murphy, Mr A. and Mr B. Each visit necessitated sealing off part of the prison building and placing prison staff known for their trustworthiness in charge of the interview area. A prison officer who was serving in Crumlin Road Prison at that time told me that only two or three officers were chosen for the task and no one else was allowed near the interview room. Nesbitt is reluctant to confirm that this was the case because it is an indication of how the police viewed the loyalties of some of the prison staff.

Murphy was capable of murdering an accomplice in prison and in view of the fact that Major Mullen believed at the time that some of his staff in Crumlin Road Prison may have colluded with Murphy on that occasion, it is natural to assume that Nesbitt and the Prison Authorities were apprehensive about the type of person selected for the aforementioned task. In sealing off the prison for the exercise, CID and the Prison Administration attempted to ensure that any suggestion that Moore and Bates were cooperating with the police was information to which only a few would be privy. There were staff within the Prison who were known for their political loyalties and others who were likely to be vulnerable to Loyalist paramilitary pressure. The Prison Administration chose prison officers who were unquestionably men of integrity to assist Nesbitt who eventually persuaded both Moore and Bates to agree to his plan. He says no deal was done and he intended the statements to be presented to the Director of Public Prosecutions for a case against the three ringleaders. Moore and Bates both gave statements containing the evidence required by Nesbitt, who is adamant that no incentive was offered. However, soon afterwards, both the accused were moved into a wing of the prison which housed 'ordinary' criminals. If, as Nesbitt claims, there was no incentive offered and their removal to another wing containing different category prisoners was not reward for their compliance, the question is raised as to why they risked their lives by acceding to Nesbitt's request. The risk would have been a very real one, inasmuch as they were about to begin life sentences in a prison where they would encounter Murphy, who had already killed a fellow prisoner, and where they would be in the company of other paramilitaries who would regard them as informers and traitors. It is possible that Nesbitt suggested, particularly to Moore, that the statements made in Castlereagh compromised leading members of the UVF and as a consequence his life would be placed in danger throughout his long term in custody but, if he cooperated with the police, they could arrange for him to remain in Crumlin Road in the company of common criminals. Crumlin Road Prison offered the opportunity to be free from the pressure of fellow members of paramilitary organizations and in particular the UVF. At this time Murphy was in the H Block of the Maze Prison outside Belfast where the presence of fellow members of the UVF ensured that there was a degree of discipline required and where Moore and Bates would be at risk if it was suspected that they had assisted the RUC. In the company of common criminals in Crumlin Road their safety could be guaranteed and they could escape the influence of the UVF. Murphy demonstrated in the early seventies that he preferred Crumlin Road Prison because it possessed a relaxed atmosphere and was less regimented than the Maze Prison but perhaps the most salient reason why life in Crumlin Road would have appeared attractive at this time to Moore and Bates was that it contained fewer prisoners and it would prove easier to maintain a separation from convicted terrorists who could harm them if Murphy or the UVF leadership so ordered. So was such an offer made to them?

Nesbitt denies that this happened and says simply that they agreed to co-operate after much persuasion. I personally believe that, on the contrary, an incentive was offered. Moore was only too aware that if the UVF leadership, and more particularly Lenny, Mr A. and Mr B. learned of the nature of the statements made in Castlereagh, he would be placed on a hit list before the case began. Bates must have had similar fears.

I remain puzzled about Nesbitt's reasoning in relation to this matter. When I spoke to him about it, he told me that he extracted the additional confessions to help the Director of Public Prosecutions prepare a case against the ringleaders. The solicitor who represented Moore and Bates says he never saw the statements which were made within the prison and his clients were never offered a deal. There was no supergrass system in operation in 1977 and I am inclined to believe that at any rate there would have been no judicial or political will to sanction an immunity deal for two men who admitted being mass murderers. However, I am convinced from informants I have contacted that a different type of deal was offered, to the effect that Moore and Bates would be allowed to serve their sentences in Crumlin Road Prison and not the Maze Prison so that they would be out of the reach of Murphy and other members of the UVF. Moore and Bates were on a UVF hit list from the moment they made their initial statements in Castlereagh and they knew that. For legal reasons I cannot reveal how the UVF knew the precise characters of both men's statements but I have been informed that the UVF leadership were aware of the content of Moore's statement within forty-eight hours of it being made. Moore knew that and took a certain course of action, which once again I am not allowed to divulge, for legal reasons. This course of action was a signal to Nesbitt that the mass murderer felt that he was under threat and was vulnerable to the suggestion that he should cooperate. Likewise Bates followed Moore's lead and took a decision which affected the manner in which his case was handled legally. I also believe it is possible that the DPP's Office discussed with Nesbitt the prospect of bringing Moore and Bates before the court in advance of other members of the Butcher gang so that they could be sentenced and would therefore be free to give evidence for the Crown against the ringleaders. If this was, indeed, the intention of the Crown then it was a course strewn with considerable difficulty, since the evidence of convicted mass murderers, namely Moore and Bates, would have made for a weak case against Murphy, Mr A. and Mr B.

Nesbitt claims that he presented the additional statements to the Director of Public Prosecutions but did not receive a reply for eighteen months, by which time Moore and Bates had retracted their confessions. One is obliged to ask whether the DPP decided it was not worth proceeding on the evidence of accomplices or whether Moore and Bates were left for too long to languish in prison contemplating whether they would ever be safe if they gave evidence against Murphy. Whatever the explanation for this train of events, there is no question that Nesbitt was consumed with a desire to bring the ringleaders to justice. The statements made by Moore and Bates are reproduced here in full, because their contents prove Nesbitt's conviction that he had a case against Murphy, Mr A. and Mr B. These statements were never made public or used in any proceedings. For legal reasons certain names are deleted.

1 July
Robert William Bates aged twenty-eight years.

I have known Lenny Murphy for the past ten years. Around about July 1975 after I got out of prison, I started to run about with him then. At this time I was already a member of the UVF and was transferred to the Brown

Bear team. Lenny Murphy who lives in Brookmount Street was the commander of my unit. He had overall charge of the unit I belonged to. There were about fourteen or fifteen men in this unit. Occasionally over a period, the unit had meetings in the Brown Bear Bar and the Lawnbrook Club and Lenny Murphy always took charge of these meetings. On occasions I saw him carrying a .9mm short pistol and he had overall charge of the weapons and ammunition which belonged to the unit. Around November 1975 there was a feud taking place which began over the shooting of Stewart Robinson who was a member of the Windsor Bar team. Robinson was only to be kneecapped along with Ned Bell and Roger McCrea for tying up an old woman and robbing her. Instead, Robinson was killed and this started the whole thing. As a result of this Archie Waller, a member of my team, was shot dead in Downing Street. After this I saw Lenny Murphy. He had gone completely mad after hearing of the death of Waller. I had to help to hold him as he was getting out of control. A meeting was held in the Lawnbrook and the whole team was ordered to be there. There must have been twenty men in the hall. During the meeting, Lenny Murphy said that Roy Stewart, Dessie Balmer and Noel Shaw were to be killed before six o'clock that day because they had killed Waller. After the meeting, I went round to my mother's for dinner and I went back to the club at 2.00P.M. or 2.30P.M. When I went in I saw that Shaw was there. He was sitting in a chair. His face was covered in blood and there was men guarding him. I heard Lenny Murphy questioning Shaw about the death of Waller. There was still about twenty people in the club. Murphy went into a store in the club and came out with a gun. It was the short .9mm that he often carried. He walked up to Shaw and said words to the effect that he was going to die. Lenny Murphy then fired five or six shots one after the other, into Shaw. There was an awful mess and blood everywhere. I was completely amazed at what happened but we all had to help to clean the club up. I was sick and I got out of the club as quickly as I could. I want to tell you about the night the old man Quinn was killed. It was Murphy's idea to lift this man who had been in Library Street. Murphy got out of the taxi and hit this man over the head with a wheelbrace and threw him in the back of the taxi. Lenny Murphy ordered us to go to the Lawnbrook Club. I thought he was going for a gun but when he got back into the taxi, he had a fairly big bread knife. Murphy kept hitting this man in the taxi and he ordered Billy Moore to drive to Glencairn and stop a short distance along For-thriver Way at some broken railings. I saw Murphy with this knife and I saw him trailing this man down the grass bank. Murphy was on his own with the man. I was back a wee bit when Murphy came back and said the man was dead. He brought the knife back with him. I want to tell you also regarding the shooting at the lorry in Cambrai Street. It was Lenny Murphy set the whole thing up. One morning before the actual shooting, I was there along with Lenny and Billy Moore when the whole thing was called off because of an Army patrol in the street. Murphy was in charge of the whole operation. At 6.30A.M. on the morning of the shooting I was picked up by Billy Moore. I was then taken to a house at – where [Mr A.] was already there. [Mr A.] had charge of the guns and had them ready in the front room of the house. Lenny Murphy then left to get a car to do the job and returned with a red car. Billy Moore, [Mr A.] and I waited in the house. [Mr A.] did lookout for the job. Lenny and I put the guns into the car and Billy Moore did the driving. Lenny Murphy had already explained that we were to shoot *Taigs* on a J. P. Corry's lorry. I had an MI carbine and Lenny had a Thompson machine gun. When the lorry arrived, Lenny was first out and opened fire. His gun jammed and he took my gun from me and kept firing at the vehicle. He gave me his gun. We both went back to the car. I remember the killing of a young fellow in an entry between Mayo Street and Esmond Street. This was also Lenny Murphy's idea. This man was picked up in Donegall Street. Lenny Murphy got out of the taxi and hit the man over the head. There were four of us on the job and we stopped at Lenny's house. He went into the house and came back with a knife. He ordered us to drive to Mayo Street. When we stopped in Mayo Street, Lenny Murphy trailed this man out of the taxi. [Mr C.] and me were along with him. Billy Moore went off to turn the taxi. Lenny Murphy trailed the man up the wee side entry off the main entry and leant over the man. I saw Lenny Murphy using the knife on the man's throat. The three of us got back into the taxi. Lenny brought the knife with him. All these killings I have mentioned were Lenny Murphy's idea. I have known him for a long time and I believe that he took a great delight in killing people. He is a ruthless man and when he gave instructions I had to obey them.

Bates's statement is flawed in terms of dates and times but these are minor inaccuracies compared to the manner in which his confession is designed to ignore the important role he played in the killing of Rice and Quinn. When he states that Lenny took the carbine from him because his own gun had jammed, he forgets to mention that he had already fired the carbine. He gives the impression that this was not so. He fails to mention the presence of the two women who were in the taxi the night Dominic Rice was murdered, or the fact that he was involved in the violence directed at Rice. The statement demonstrates how Bates was willing to lie about the part he himself played in each of the crimes he attributes to Murphy.

Moore gave the following statement to Nesbitt three days later:

I have known Lenny Murphy from school days. During the present Troubles, the first time I had anything to do with him was one Thursday night, I don't remember the date, when he took my taxi off me. I discovered immediately after this that he was a leading member of the UVF. From then on I became involved in the UVF. I was under the control of Lenny Murphy. He chaired all the meetings along with Mr A. After Archie Waller was shot he was furious and all the UVF members were informed to be at the meeting in the Lawnbrook Club. I heard him say that he wanted Dessie Balmer, Noel Shaw and Roy Stewart all shot as Stewartie had shot Waller. I was aware that this

was against Brigade Staff instructions and that Lenny was
taking this on in his own bat to have these people shot.
About twelve noon which was a Sunday, Lenny Murphy
was in charge of this meeting and [Mr A.] and [Mr B.]
were also there. There were about fifteen to twenty UVF
men there. Lenny did all the talking and he ordered me
and Bates to go down the road and pick up Noel Shaw.
We drove back with him to the Lawnbrook and took him
in. As he walked in the door he was given a good hiding
and he was kicked about and threw around. All of us hit
him and he was then sat on a chair. Lenny Murphy walked
up the bar and then walked back to Shaw. He said something to him which I couldn't make out. He pulled a .9mm
pistol and opened fire. He was only about five feet away
from Shaw. Shaw slumped forward and remained half
seated. He was an awful mess and there was blood all over
the place. Lenny Murphy told me to go and get a taxi. I
left and went to the Road and hijacked a taxi which was
coming down the Road. When I walked back into the club
I saw Shaw lying in a laundry basket. Lenny told me and
[Mr B.] to take the taxi and the body and dump them.
After abandoning the taxi we saw an Army patrol and ran
back to the club. Lenny was there and asked me what I
had done.

Moore's statement deals with a crime in which Moore is
not the central figure and it is noticeable that he, the man
who was later to imitate Murphy, was not asked by Nesbitt
to deal with Murphy's role in the first three cut-throat
murders. Presumably, this was to confine Moore's evidence in this statement to a crime in which he had played
a minor role.

Nesbitt, armed with the knowledge provided by these
two statements and the others made by the Butcher gang
in May, made arrangements to have Murphy transferred
from the Maze Prison to Castlereagh Holding Centre for
an interview on 22 July. Nesbitt was prepared to tell
Murphy that there was evidence to connect him with the
first three cut-throat murders, the killing of Shaw and the

two men on the lorry. John Fitzsimmons accompanied Nesbitt to Castlereagh and they both questioned Murphy about his movements at the time of these murders. Murphy laughed each time he was asked about a killing and when Nesbitt mentioned the first three cut-throat murders Murphy laughed loudly and said: 'Sure, you guys know I was busy at that time.' He also told the two detectives: 'If you're so convinced, prove it.'

Nesbitt and Fitzsimmons were unhappy about the arrangements for the interview, which was conducted in the presence of a prison officer. When the two detectives arrived at the room provided by the prison authorities they asked the prison warder to leave, but he refused to do so. Nesbitt considered the warder's behaviour irregular and believes it likely that he was under Murphy's control.

The two detectives left the prison convinced that the only way to bring Murphy to justice was to use the evidence given by Moore and Bates. Fitzsimmons has this to say about his meeting with Murphy: 'I remember the intense hatred he showed for Catholics. He said at one stage: "I hate the bastards. Even their cells are dirtier than ours." '

While most of the Butcher gang were in prison awaiting trial a crime came to light which, when I examined it, illustrated once again that police work was at times lax when it came to analysing the peripheral events surrounding the activities of the Butchers. On Easter Monday, the day after the murder of Kevin McMenamin, Moore and Townsley were drinking in the Brown Bear in the company of twenty-one-year-old James Potts, an unemployed labourer from Wigton Street in the Shankill area, and twenty-seven-year-old John Alexander Murphy, a brother of Lenny. From early afternoon until 9.00P.M. they paid a series of visits to various bars in the Shankill area. At 9.30P.M. the four were involved in a fracas which was witnessed by Lieutenant Alan Myles Startin:

I was in charge of a party of soldiers in the sanger [Army slang for a look-out post] at the junction of Upper Library Street with Peter's Hill. [*Author's note*: this sanger would have been almost inside the Unity Flats complex and would have overlooked Millfield where Stephen McCann had been killed, the junction of Gresham Street from where the killers at the Chlorane Bar emerged, and would have had a clear view of North Street and the section where it joins the Shankill Road.] At this time I heard a disturbance going on in Upper Library Street. I took a party of soldiers out of the sanger into Library Street to deal with the trouble. Two rival groups were stoning and verbally abusing one another. One of these groups, numbering six, retreated into Unity Place and the other group of four continued to shout abuse. I approached the group of four and told them to move away but they started shouting abuse at me. I eventually quietened them down and they moved into North Street. I know these persons now to be William Moore, John Townsley, John Alexander Murphy and James Potts.

The four men moved on some little distance but Lieutenant Startin, in the presence of other soldiers, arrested Moore and his associates at the junction of Upper North Street and Royal Avenue with the intention of handing them over to the RUC to be charged with stone-throwing. In the interim between Startin's initial observation and the actual arrest, a forty-nine-year-old pedestrian was seriously assaulted. In his statement Startin neglects to mention that he told the four Loyalists to 'move on' at the outset. One has to ask why he did not arrest them at that moment. The only explanation I can offer is that he was waiting for a Land Rover to arrive to transport them to North Queen Street police station. Had he arrested them outside Unity Flats, where all the tenants are Catholics, a more difficult scene could have ensued which might have resulted in the soldier having to protect the four men until the arrival of a military vehicle. When Lieutenant Startin eventually stopped these four men he was unaware they were deliberately making a detour back to their own area, the Shankill. Nor could he have known that in the intervening period between his first encounter with them and the actual arrest, they had had time to give vent to their mounting anger and frustration on an unfortunate pedestrian walking in the area. As Moore and the others passed Library Street they saw a middle-aged man walking towards Royal Avenue and they ran towards him. The pedestrian, Harold Underwood, said later that he was unaware of the presence of the four until they were assaulting him. Each of them punched and kicked him viciously and left him bleeding on the pavement. They quickly left the scene and headed for Royal Avenue to circle round and make their way back to the Shankill from a direction which, they believed, would not connect them with the crime. The fact that they had blood on their clothing caused them no consternation. Lieutenant Startin did not notice this when he arrested them but when they were taken directly to North Queen Street police station, Constables Shields and McGreevy spotted heavy blood-staining on the clothing of all four men.

These two constables were fully briefed on the attack on Underwood because they were responsible for finding him while patrolling Library Street and they had had an opportunity to question him briefly before he was taken by ambulance to the Mater Hospital. Underwood was able to tell them that all four men who attacked him were wearing denim jeans. He was lucky to survive such a vicious attack; his injuries required 130 stitches to his face and there were slight fractures to his skull and cheekbones. Unknown to his attackers, Underwood was a Protestant.

Constable McGreevy cautioned the four men in the station regarding the attack on Underwood but they denied knowledge of the incident, or of being in Library Street. Constable Shields recorded in the station log that items of clothing were 'seized' from the four by his colleague.

Joseph Orr of the Forensic Science Department of the

RUC examined clothing belonging to the four and found widespread blood-staining on Townsley's trousers, which matched a blood sample taken from Underwood. Similar tests on jeans belonging to Potts and Moore also proved positive in this respect. Later that night the four men were released after denying involvement in the crime and refusing to make statements.

On 18 June charges were preferred against the four and each of them replied, 'Nothing to say', despite Moore, Townsley and Potts having by then made statements to the effect that they had attacked Underwood. John Alexander Murphy did not make a statement and the following are replies given during an interview in January 1978:

Detective: Were you with William Moore, William Townsley and James Potts on 11 April 1977 in Union Street?

Murphy: I just want to say I was there. We went down the town and had a few drinks. We went past Unity Flats. A crowd of fellows came out and started hitting us with belts and bottles and we had to give it back to them. We went down to Union Street and we saw this fellow. We thought he was one of the Unity men and all ran up Union Street to get him. The next thing there was a fight and the whole lot started hitting and punching him. I don't want to say no more. That's the way it happened.

Detective: Did you know this man?

Murphy: No, I never saw him before.

Detective: Where did you go?

Murphy: We all went to North Street to get a bus home.

Detective: Did you know how badly Mr Underwood was injured?

Murphy: I don't know anything about it.

Detective: How do you explain the blood on your shoes?

Murphy: He fell on me. I don't want to say any more about it.

Detective: Had you much to drink?

Murphy: A brave lot.

After this interview, Murphy was arrested, charged and cautioned, to which he replied, 'Nothing to say.'

Potts told the police:

> I met three mates whom I do not wish to name in the
> Brown Bear on the Shankill Road. We had five or six
> pints of lager then went to the Royal Bar and the Silver
> Jubilee. I think I had quite a number of vodkas. We
> decided to go into town and took a black taxi down the
> Shankill to Unity flats where we all got off. We were going
> into town for more drink. At the Flats a number of youths
> threw bottles at us and attacked us. There was a short
> fight and the Army arrived. The Army told us to go down
> the Road into town. When we got to Union Street, one
> of my mates spotted this man at the junction of Union
> Street and Library Street. My mate told me that this was
> one of the men from the Flats. My mate ran towards this
> man and most of us followed. We caught up with the man
> in Library Street. We all got into him and kicked and
> punched him until he fell to the ground. As the man was
> going down, he caught me and put his arms round me. I
> took his arms away from me and started to walk off. I
> think I hit the man, whom I didn't know, two or three
> times. I am sorry for assaulting this man.

After he made this statement Potts was asked by Detective
Constable John Strain of the Regional Crime Squad if he
was involved in an illegal organization and he replied: 'I
have not been involved with any illegal acts apart from the
one I have mentioned. I was asked to join the UVF three
years ago but I declined.'

Moore and Townsley in their statements alleged that the
attack on Underwood had been provoked. They claimed to
recognize Underwood as one of the crowd which had
attacked them. This was pure fabrication.

If, as Potts claimed, they were going into town for more
alcohol, why did they take a taxi only as far as Unity Flats?
Had it been their intention to reach Royal Avenue, they
could easily have circumvented the notorious Unity Flats
flashpoint. It later became known that they were actually
on foot, walking towards an area they knew well: the side

streets off North Street, Library and Upper Library Street, Union Street and Upper Donegall Street. These were roads with which Moore especially was familiar because he had traversed them on previous victim-hunting sorties. A likely scenario would have been that they spotted a man they believed to be a *Taig*, and decided to attack him.

Concerning this incident, I was struck by the fact that the police in D Division had for a short time in custody two men who were later to become infamous. The police of C Division appear not to have taken much notice of the incident despite the fact that it occurred in an area defined by Nesbitt as under suspicion during the Butcher investigation. The matter may well have been regarded in much the same way as the assault on McLaverty was to begin with: that such incidents are commonplace in that part of Belfast. With hindsight it is easy to see a significance in the attack upon Underwood but, nevertheless, proper communication between D Division and C Division could have proved invaluable.

14

The Public Avenger?

Between May 1977 and February 1979 the Shankill Butcher gang appeared in court on numerous occasions, during which lengthy depositions were recorded. Three solicitors had the task of representing the accused men. One of those solicitors was a Catholic who was a former member of the Nationalist, Social Democratic and Labour Party. He acted for Moore, Bates, Waugh and Edwards only after they decided at an early stage to change their legal representation. I have examined documents which indicate that many of the accused men were advised by their lawyer to plead guilty to the most serious charges to avoid a recommendation by the trial Judge of severely long sentences. However, these accused rejected the advice on the basis that they never intended to cause serious death or injury and would therefore plead not guilty. Even on 25 January, the day set for the opening of the trial, some members of the gang were instructing their legal advisers to contest the charges. The trial began in Crumlin Road courthouse under Mr Justice O'Donnell, with the Crown case put forward by Mr Ronald Appleton QC, a lawyer of outstanding ability. He delivered a lengthy and scholarly outline of what was an extremely complex story. During the lunchtime recess that day legal consultations were held with some of the accused, and in some cases these took place in the presence of relatives. This resulted in several of the Butchers changing their plea to guilty.

McClay and Townsley decided to persevere with their pleas of not guilty. Those who changed their pleas were returned to prison on the instructions of Mr Justice

O'Donnell pending psychiatric reports being made available, after which they would be sentenced.

McClay claimed that the statements which he had made to the police were made under duress but this was dismissed by the Judge. Townsley, who was attempting to plead to a lesser charge than murder, was told by the Judge that he would not accept his plea. The case was heard before Mr Justice O'Donnell sitting alone without a jury, in accordance with Northern Ireland's Diplock Court procedure which has been designed to remove the jury system in terrorist cases to eliminate the risk of intimidation of juries following a history of such pressure from the beginning of the present conflict.

Jimmy Nesbitt remembers sitting in court while McClay took the witness stand to argue that the murder squad in C Division had used ill-treatment and threats to coerce him into making his statements of guilt. 'I was watching McClay,' says Nesbitt, 'and I looked closely at him in disbelief, wondering what other lie he was going to tell. Somehow my eyes strayed to a tattoo that he had on his hand, between his right thumb and forefinger. I focused on this and recognized the letters UVF. Now, here was McClay saying that he was an innocent man, unconnected with an illegal organization and with no political allegiance which would associate him with violence. I told the Crown lawyer what I had seen and, while McClay was being cross-examined and making these points again, our lawyer turned to him and said, "What is that on your hand?" I could see that McClay was dumbfounded. That really sickened him and was essentially the end of his case and his contention that he was unconnected with anyone.'

It wasn't until the morning of 18 February that eleven accused men stood in the dock before Mr Justice O'Donnell charged with nineteen murders. They were Moore, McAllister, Bates, Edwards, Townsley, Bell, McClay, Waugh, Leckey, Watt and McIlwaine. Ronald Appleton QC addressed the court and outlined the Crown case.

Hours later he was still on his feet describing how many of the victims had met their deaths.

Mr Justice O'Donnell began his summation and subsequent sentencing of the gang on the morning of 20 February. At 10.30A.M., in a courtroom stilled by silence, the Judge began by expressing his view of the case, describing it as a 'catalogue of horror'. He reserved special attention for the crimes committed by Moore and Bates, but firstly addressed Bates: 'You pleaded guilty to ten murders. While there is undoubtedly a distinction in those crimes between you and Moore, I cannot see any real distinction in the end result; that result being the deaths of ten innocent people.'

Then he turned to Moore, the man who pleaded guilty to the largest number of murders, and told him: 'You, Moore, pleaded guilty to eleven murders carried out in a manner so cruel and revolting as to be beyond the comprehension of any normal human being. I am satisfied that without you many of the murders would not have been committed.'

In a dramatic voice, the Judge then turned his attention to both of them and announced their sentence: 'I see no reason whatever, apart from terminal illness, why either of you should ever be released.'

Moore had begun his morning in court waving to friends and relatives in the public gallery and chatting with his lawyer. He was sporting a new moustache, was dressed in a white pullover and a black and white open-necked shirt. Bates, who had grown a beard while in prison, was dressed in a green and orange V-neck sweater over a dark-blue open-necked shirt. He remained silent while in the dock. Both of them listened intently and remained impassive while the Judge delivered his verdict on their crimes. Justice O'Donnell told the packed courtroom that even the most dispassionate recital of the facts was calculated to cause rage and indignation at the deaths meted out to so many innocent people. He took twenty minutes to deliver his sentences, which totalled 2,000 years imprisonment in concurrent sentences. He pointed out that he had resisted the temptation to cast himself in the role of the 'Public Avenger'. 'The facts speak for themselves and will remain for ever a lasting monument to blind sectarian bigotry,' he told the Court.

McAllister, McClay and Edwards were given life sentences with a recommendation that they serve no less than twenty years. Waugh was given two life sentences with a recommendation that he serve no less than eighteen years.

Watt, who was already serving eight life sentences, was given another one to run concurrently with the other sentences he received.

Bell was given a life sentence. Townsley, because he was a juvenile at the time of his crimes, was ordered to be detained at the pleasure of the Secretary of State for Northern Ireland.

Leckey and McIlwaine were the last to be sentenced. Leckey, who admitted the manslaughter of Kevin McMenamin (the young boy killed on the day of the Easter Parade) was given ten years. McIlwaine, who pleaded guilty to kidnapping and wounding McLaverty, was also sentenced to ten years imprisonment.

The Judge reserved praise for McLaverty and the courage he had shown.

One man whom the Judge was not in a legal position to mention by name was, of course, Lenny Murphy. The Crown Prosecutor did refer to him on several occasions as Mr X. and pointed out that, though he was not before the court, he had been the central figure in the Butcher killings. The court was not told that there were many more people who had not been brought to justice, and many other crimes apart from the nineteen for which the accused had received a total of forty-two life sentences: the largest number handed down in one sitting of a court in British legal history.

Mr Justice O'Donnell did not forget the role played by

Jimmy Nesbitt and his team. He praised their diligence and tenacity and said that 'the thanks of the whole community' should be accorded them.

As the accused were led from the dock Moore raised his right hand and waved to relatives. Bates hesitated as he was led away, tapped his right hand on the wooden rim of the dock and walked down the stairs to the corridor leading to Crumlin Road Prison.

The following morning all the national and local papers carried the story and some reserved their editorials for comment on the trial. The *Irish Times* printed this editorial which summed up the feelings of many people:

> Religious and racial fanaticism often goes no farther than wild words; it seems to be merely vulgar and offensive; but the scorn, a dilution of hatred, which the words carry, may be taken by the over-impressionable, the disordered, as a directive and a pardon in advance. Religious invective in the North is often covered with a veneer of earthy heartiness ... it is deadly just the same.
>
> How can men murder their fellow human beings because they are of a different religion or race? This question was raised on a horrendous scale when the full details of the Nazi extermination camps became known at the end of World War II.
>
> Yet it was to be demonstrated that Western civilisation is a thin layer in Western man, and whilst the list of crimes by the 'Shankill Butchers' is infinitesimal in comparison to the holocausts of Europe a generation ago, the principle seems to be the same; Catholics to men like these desperadoes were taken as a species marked out for extermination just as, to the German camp commanders, Poles and Jews filled the same roles.
>
> Once persuade an impressionable mind, starting with childhood, that his or her neighbours are inferior, in some basic respect ... in religious beliefs, in colour of skin or in some other allegedly racial respect ... and the way may be open, as it was to so many apparently normal Germans all those years ago, to treat people so labelled as less than normal in standards, and by progression less than human

and therefore to be exterminated. Professional men, doctors, chemists, lawyers were apparently no more immune to the virus than less privileged folk.

There have been other atrocities which have accounted for Northern lives in quite appalling fashion . . . burning alive in the La Mon restaurant for example . . . but there is something particularly chilling about the close quarters butchering which was involved in so many of the Shankill murders.

After the war as an SS Commandant was interviewed by a newspaper interviewer who asked how so many educated men in the SS could have done what they did. 'They were led astray by that man,' was the answer. Who initially, and who proximately, could have led these miserable murderers to do what they did?

The answer to the final question in the editorial became the focus of media speculation. The day after the trial, the *Newsletter* carried the headline: 'Butcher Boss to be Unmasked'. The story beneath claimed that the 'crack police squad which brought the Shankill Butcher gang to justice' was determined to unmask Mr X.

The Northern editor of the *Sunday World* newspaper in Ireland, Jim Campbell (who had taken a message from the killers when he was working for the *Sunday News*), was the most revealing in his treatment of the Mr X. story. He did not name Murphy but indicated why he was in prison and when he was likely to be released.

Most newspapers examined the police handling of the case and accorded to the RUC the same respect as was given to them by Mr Justice O'Donnell. The Northern editor of the *Irish Times*, David McKittrick, who now works for the *Independent*, was, however, more probing than some of his colleagues in his analysis of the police handling of the investigation. This is what he wrote on 21 February:

Some of Moore's team are still at large, and there are other teams, principally in the Shankill and Woodvale,

which retain the potential for similar violence. But a
number of factors have combined to persuade them to
remain inactive, and one of them has certainly been the
charging of their colleagues.

McKittrick also looked at the clues which he believed had
been available to the police, and added:

The Butchers could easily have provided unnecessary
clues by using the same taxi and car every time, and one
of them kept a selection of knives in his home. Another,
in a telephone call, said he was Captain Long, which
would immediately have brought to mind the Long Bar to
anyone with the barest background knowledge of the UVF.
Such names have often served as significant clues; the real
name of the original Captain Black of the Ulster Freedom
Fighters (the name used by the UDA from June 1973 to
claim responsibility for sectarian killings) was White.

Now that the trial is over one final question lingers . . .
could anything else have been done to prevent any of the
deaths, which were after all spread over eighteen months?
No one is suggesting that the detectives who led the investigation, Jimmy Nesbitt and Cecil Chambers, were in any
way lax but their Serious Crimes Squad, centred at Tennent Street, consisted of only ten detectives, supplemented
occasionally by others. There were hundreds of other
killings in Belfast and the rest of Northern Ireland over
this period, and the ten detectives had many other murders
to investigate. Enquiries which would be handled in
England by a Detective Chief Superintendent are often
handled here by a Detective Constable. Ten detectives
were handling these murders, while across the water hundreds of policemen may be put to investigate a single
killing. With such resources, the Major Long clue could
have been checked out, by surveillance on all those associated with the Long Bar. There are several hundred black
taxis but with more police available each could have been
checked out right from the first death. Witnesses heard
vehicles which sounded like a taxi engine. Bates was a
barman in the Long Bar and Moore owned a taxi and in
this way a connection might have been made. But in a city

which has had more murders than detectives, the niceties often go by the board. RUC manpower is scarce everywhere and the blanket coverage available in England is not available here. In this case the police took their chance well enough when it came; but with more men on the ground, they might not have had to rely on such a phenomenal stroke of fortune.

With the end of the trial, Jimmy Nesbitt was promoted to the rank of Detective Chief Inspector. Yet he remained obsessed with the Butcher gang and was as determined as ever to bring Murphy to justice. Nesbitt feared what could happen when Murphy was released from prison in 1982, and on the top of his desk remained the file with Lenny Murphy's name on it. 'I knew that this psycho was going to be back on the streets, and there was practically nothing we could do about it,' says Nesbitt. But his chances to deal with the Butcher who remained at large were at an end. He received further promotion to the rank of Superintendent and was awarded the MBE, then he was moved from Tennent Street to Police Headquarters. Subsequent to the sentencing of the convicted Butchers, Nesbitt was also advised by the Director of Public Prosecutions Office that earlier statements made by Moore and Bates would not be used in a case against Murphy. He was sorely disappointed, yet the DPP decision was understandable. Moore and Bates were now facing the grim reality of spending the rest of their natural lives in prison and they had nothing now to gain in testifying against the man described by newspapers as 'Mr X. the master Butcher'.

Nesbitt decided to visit Moore and Bates once more while they remained in Crumlin Road Prison. They were still held in cells separate from paramilitary prisoners, whereas their convicted associates were now serving their sentences in the Maze Prison. Nesbitt recalls: 'Bates said to me that he would not give evidence against Murphy because it was a matter for God and God would deal with

Murphy. Moore made the point forcefully that he was facing the rest of his life in prison and there was no purpose in him jeopardizing his own existence by testifying against Murphy. He said that no one could protect him.'

Moore's judgement was not unjustified. Some eight months later an assessment was made as to whether it was safe to transfer Moore and Bates to the Maze Prison. It was concluded that the threat to their lives had receded with their refusal to cooperate with the police.

Bates underwent a temporary change of personality with a 'conversion' to evangelism. Bates's wife sent Biblical tracts to Nesbitt via Tennent Street station and on one occasion Bates actually sent his wife to see Nesbitt. Nesbitt says of that visit: 'She told me that "Basher" said he would never wish his kids to follow in his footsteps and she handed me a tract from the Bible.'

In Moore's case a further shock was in store with the death of his mother. Moore's request for leave on compassionate grounds was denied.

Bates's prison conversion is part of a phenomenon common to a number of convicted Loyalist prisoners. It may well be the result of confinement with the attendant removal of social contacts. In Bates's case a further dimension was that confinement increased his suggestibility, as evidenced by the statement he made to Nesbitt. In short, in prison Bates was vulnerable and open to new emotional experiences. As part of the Butcher gang he had enjoyed some personal status, but detached from it he was insecure. In some cases 'conversion' has had its uses as a ploy to convince judges that a shortened sentence would be appropriate, and on occasion, judges have been impressed by claims of conversion. In Bates's case his commitment to God was short-lived. With his removal to the Maze Prison, he was once again returned to the group structure and in this context his violent personality re-emerged with a serious attack on a prison officer. He was brought before the prison visitors' board where he behaved truculently, pointing out that he was 'one of the Shankill Butchers' and there was nothing much the board could do to him. They accordingly denied Bates the normal prison privileges for twelve months, but his behaviour before the board was something more than an act of mere bravado. He tried to intimidate the board members. A person who met him in prison told me that he regarded Bates as a fatalist with a terrifying propensity for violence.

Ironically, one prisoner who learned a great deal about Bates in prison was a former IRA leader, Brendan Hughes. He had a cell which was close to one inhabited by Bates in one of the Maze H Blocks and they conversed frequently. This was not unusual because Loyalist and Republican prisoners were obliged to share accommodation in close proximity once Special Category Status for terrorist prisoners was phased out. Hughes had this to say of Bates: 'He talked a lot to me and was intrigued to know about Republicanism. I felt that suddenly here was a guy who had been involved in killing a lot of people and who had probably mouthed political slogans but never understood them. Like many Loyalist prisoners he had a loose tongue and talked about the crimes he had committed in a general sort of way, but to an extent where he named a lot of other people in the UVF who were not in prison. It was as a result of this type of exchange that the IRA built up a dossier on the activities of Loyalist paramilitaries on the outside.

'The one thing which struck me about Bates was his need to have even someone like me as a friend. He demonstrated a curious loyalty towards me by warning me that there was a plot to kill me by several Loyalist prisoners on our block. He told me: "I've warned them that they will have to go through me to get to you."

'His own kind, however, knew that he was a guy with a short fuse and they were fond of winding him up. Also on our block was Joseph Mains, a homosexual who was convicted of buggering young boys who were in care in the infamous Kincora Boys' Home in Belfast. Some of the Loyalists kept suggesting to "Basher" that he should "kill that sonofabitch Mains" who was "nothing but a pervert".

'A knife was smuggled out of the prison kitchens and Bates agreed to kill Mains. Luckily, I saw "Basher" walking from his cell and heading in the direction of Mains's cell with the knife in his hand and I followed him and persuaded him not to allow himself to be used. Murphy was also in the H Blocks at that time but he kept a low profile. He was always frightened that we would bump him off but quite honestly we were too busy planning to escape and we had men on the Blanket and Dirty Protest at that time. You must remember it was prior to the big Hunger Strike and we had no wish to sidetrack ourselves. We knew we would get him eventually. I remember being told that the people in the place who really frightened Murphy were the guys on the Blanket Protest. I was informed that Murphy was convinced that once they came off the Protest they would murder him. That was the rumour which reached him. He saw them as the really extreme guys. In prison the priorities are not to kill other prisoners. That can always be arranged later.'

In contrast to Bates, Moore was a realist. He accepted life in prison and was content to adopt a lower profile and become a model prisoner, rejecting the evangelical proselytizing which had captured Bates for a short time. In some respects this was in keeping with the pattern of Moore's earlier life until the moment Murphy unlocked the mechanism which revealed him as a mass murderer.

Many people have said of Moore that his demeanour and general attitude to life never suggested he was capable of mass murder until he met Murphy. Unfortunately, there is the other view that the potential was always there and that the apparently insignificant Moore had, lurking in his psyche, a potential for killing which was waiting to be exploited. Moore's mother acknowledged the hidden potential of her son but only after his deeds were revealed in court. The night after Moore was sentenced she telephoned Nesbitt and thanked him for putting her son in prison.

A former Maze Prison officer, who met Moore and Bates after they arrived in the Maze in autumn 1979, recalls that Bates was in trouble almost immediately but that Moore tried to restrain his former accomplice: 'I was on security watch during an afternoon when a football match was in progress. The teams were made up of both Republican and Loyalist paramilitaries. Bates was a defender and at one stage he was the subject of a rough tackle by a chap who was from one of the Republican organizations. Bates did not retaliate but reserved his venom for later that day. I was on duty when the prisoners were having dinner in the canteen. Bates approached a table with a newspaper rolled in his right hand and without warning beat this other prisoner over the head until others dragged him away. The prisoner was the chap who tackled him during the match. Inside the newspaper I found a metal bed-leg. Moore, or "Willie" as we called him, was always quiet and obedient as though he was hiding something. Somehow, I always had the feeling that underneath his calm exterior was something sinister but it was never manifested in action for me or my colleagues. Now Murphy, he was different. He was one dangerous little bastard but he was careful because he was serving his time; biding his time to get out and he was not going to upset the apple-cart.'

Gerard McLaverty will not forget the year 1979. It was the year that the men who tried to kill him were brought to trial; but a further experience not revealed at the time was that Gerard McLaverty was close to death some three weeks before the trial. He was walking out of a Belfast city centre pub when a man produced a gun and began firing indiscriminately, one bullet missing McLaverty by inches. Only the quick thinking of a bodyguard, assigned to McLaverty by Nesbitt, saved his life; the bodyguard threw McLaverty to the ground. The gunman turned out to be a member of the Security Forces who was suffering severe mental stress at the time and who fired his weapon aimlessly, probably oblivious to the danger he was causing.

Simultaneously McLaverty was dealt another cruel blow when he was offered a paltry £700 in compensation for his various injuries. Gerry Fitt, MP, now Lord Fitt, reacted angrily to this news and accused the Secretary of State for Northern Ireland, Roy Mason, of ignoring the contribution which had been made by McLaverty. Speaking in the House of Commons, Fitt described the offer as insulting and called for an urgent review of Government policy with regard to compensation for those whose actions led to the conviction of terrorists. In reply Roy Mason suggested Fitt was 'exploiting' McLaverty and Fitt responded: 'What does Mr Mason want me to do . . . ignore it?' The Northern Ireland office pointed out that the offer was made before the Butchers were jailed and that it represented McLaverty's loss of earnings during his recuperation, his family's dependency and the extent of his injuries and their psychological effect. Gerry Fitt was unquestionably correct in challenging the compensation offer and in leading a campaign to have it increased. The offer of £700 was, in the circumstances, not just derisory but also immoral, given the nature of the Butcher case and what McLaverty had actually suffered. The offer was also lacking in political judgement since it served to discourage those who might be inclined to follow the example of McLaverty in testifying against sectarian murderers.

Finally, Gerry Fitt's efforts, together with those of McLaverty's lawyer, Pascal O'Hare, resulted in a renewed offer of compensation in the region of £5,000 to £7,000.

15
'Mr X.' is Back

While Lenny Murphy was in prison the UVF in West Belfast was restructured. The leadership was glad to be rid of Moore and his associates and relations with the UDA were placed on a more secure footing. West Belfast was carved up between the two organizations, with each one recognizing that their activities, whether military or in terms of extortion and racketeering, required careful delineation. Greater control was also exercised over units, unlike the Murphy period when the Brown Bear team had been able to conduct its own operations and have its own weapons without authorization from the Brigade Staff. There remained in the ranks men who looked upon Murphy as a hero, but senior figures in the Brigade Staff were determined that on his release he would not enjoy his earlier authority or freedom of action.

C Division had also changed, with the murder squad now under the direction of John Fitzsimmons who had assisted Nesbitt so ably in the mid- to late 1970s. Nesbitt retained his interest in Murphy at a distance and says: 'We knew what to expect, but people do not understand the problem we faced with Murphy's release. It was impossible to have constant surveillance in that area at the time. There was not the technology we have today, and an unmarked car would have been detected and the information conveyed to the paramilitaries. All we could hope to do was inform every member of the personnel in C Division to watch out for Murphy, who he associated with, and any suspicious activity. Remember, we had learned a great deal from our previous experience with Murphy,

Moore and the others and we knew that it was important to recognize the unpredictable as much as the predictable.'

Lenny Murphy walked out of prison on the evening of 16 July 1982, some three years after his gang had been jailed, and made his way to Brookmount Street. He was released from Crumlin Road Prison, since it is usual for convicted criminals to be transferred, prior to their release, from the Maze to Crumlin Road, where they undergo a readjustment programme. Murphy knew that certain things had changed. His wife and nine-year-old daughter were no longer a part of his life but that did not matter to him. While he had been in prison, his wife had spent a holiday in Spain with one of the men involved in the Cliftonville Road shooting of Mary Murray. Nesbitt claims that Murphy learned of his wife's affair shortly after her return from Spain: 'Mr A. visited him and told him about his wife going off with Mr D. and asked if Lenny wanted the guy hit but Lenny said he would sort the guy out on his release from prison.' Murphy's wife was no longer part of his thinking; he was more concerned with re-establishing himself as a figure of power in the Shankill district.

Twenty-four hours after gaining his freedom he was celebrating in the company of Mr A. and Mr B. in the Rumford Street Loyalist Club at a party in his honour. Before midnight a stranger, six feet tall and sporting a beard, entered the club. The stranger, whose appearance and facial expression might have suggested that he was mentally retarded, was thirty-three-year-old Norman Alexander Maxwell, shabbily dressed and of no fixed abode. Maxwell, a Protestant, had ventured into the club in the way he often entered other premises in the Shankill area. Such money as he had would be spent on alcohol, and he lived for the main part in Salvation Army Hostels. Murphy regarded Maxwell's entrance as an intrusion and he enquired whether his drinking companions knew the identity of the stranger. When they told him that Maxwell was unknown to them Murphy decided that he should be taken to the yard at the rear of the club and questioned. Maxwell went willingly to the yard with Murphy and another man, who has never been identified but whom I believe was Mr A. treated Maxwell roughly and, according to George Sheridan who witnessed the episode, Maxwell became 'bolshie'. Sheridan, who was later given four years' imprisonment for withholding information about this incident, told police that 'he had no stomach' for the proceedings and left the yard. But before he left he saw the beginnings of the attack on Maxwell by Murphy which culminated in a severe beating. As Maxwell fell to the ground, Murphy and his accomplice continued to kick their victim about the head and face. Murphy left Maxwell bleeding and moaning on the ground and walked back into the club where he asked for the keys of a car parked nearby. He then proceeded to drive the car over Maxwell and repeated this act several times. When he was satisfied that Maxwell was truly dead he loaded his body into the boot of the car and drove to Alliance Parade off the Old-park Road, where he dumped the corpse. Murphy did not need to travel this distance merely to find some waste ground but, once again, his criminal mind was in operation. When the body was discovered and identified police assumed, because of Maxwell's religion and the place where the body was found, that a sectarian murder had been carried out by the IRA. Murphy was back on his killing ground and doing what came naturally to him. His behaviour established for all those in the club that he intended to carry on as before. A police inspector told the inquest jury that if the man who killed Maxwell had known his victim's true identity and circumstances he would not have killed him. This inspector was obviously not familiar with the history of Lenny Murphy. In the words of the Coroner, the attack on Maxwell was 'the most barbaric and brutal assault one could imagine.'

After Maxwell's murder, Murphy set about rebuilding

his unit, searching out young men who would give him unquestioning loyalty. Life in prison had deprived him of certain luxuries – a woman in his life and a car of his own. A car was essential if he was to impress any women he happened to meet, but for this he needed money. The only way Murphy knew to acquire money was to steal it. It was suggested to him that an easier means would be to extort money from businessmen, so he revisited an Oldpark Road shopkeeper from whom he had extorted money in 1976 and told him that his six years in prison gave him the right to demand a substantial payment. The shopkeeper rejected the demand and stated that times had changed and he was no longer obliged to pay up. Murphy left, threatening that he would find a means to make the man pay. The story which unfolded after this visit is best described by an informant who knew both Murphy and the shopkeeper: 'Lenny was back on the Shankill Road and he needed to show to everybody that he was back with a vengeance and that he was top dog. That meant that he needed flashy clothes and a car to help his image. When Lenny got out things had changed and there had been a lull in the violence and some paramilitaries were living off the fat of the land from building site fraud and extortion or protection money from business people. The guy Lenny approached on the Oldpark had another partner and Lenny knew that. They were not wealthy people but the brother kept two horses in a field on the mountainside off the Hightown Road. Lenny made enquiries about the horses and he went up there and shot the animals. When I heard about it, I thought that Lenny had been watching the film *The Godfather* on his release. He was a bit like some of the characters in that film.'

Another source told me that Murphy had cut off the horses' heads.

Murphy tried to muscle in on another racket in the Shankill area, which involved placing gambling machines in bars and clubs, but his attempts to do so were not appreciated by certain members of the UDA who were themselves already controlling this activity. When Murphy arrived at one pub he was attacked by the owner, a well-built man and a former leading member of the UVF. So affronted was Murphy that he later had the man pistol-whipped.

Within six weeks of his release from prison Murphy had pieced together a new unit and had enough money to make a down payment on a large, second-hand Rover car. The car was purchased from a showroom in Bangor run by thirty-year-old Brian Smyth who, until 1978, had been a member of the West Belfast UVF. Murphy told Smyth that he would pay the remainder of the debt within one month.

On the Shankill Road Murphy became a familiar sight as he drove around in his large Rover, appearing to all as a flashy and well-heeled terrorist. He found himself a girlfriend who lived in the Glencairn Housing Estate but he continued to maintain a home at 65 Brookmount Street while his previous house at number 74 was being refurbished by the Northern Ireland Housing Executive, who were carrying out the rehabilitation of housing in the area. Murphy's parents and his brother William were still living at 12 Brookmount Street, but his brother John resided elsewhere in the Shankill area. Murphy began spending a lot of time with his new girlfriend, Hilary Thompson, who was in her late twenties and well aware of Lenny's reputation. Hilary Thompson has since gone to live in Larnarkshire in Scotland with an ex-member of the UDR, who left Northern Ireland because he feared his life was in danger.

Murphy did not restrict his social life to the Shankill Road but would make frequent visits to pubs in the centre of Belfast and would also be seen at other pubs and discos around town. Jim Cusack, an experienced investigative journalist with the *Irish Times*, recalls seeing Murphy in a bar and says that he was always well dressed and behaved like a man about town. According to Cusack, Murphy was known to many young people who were unaware of his violent history, and while in bars the Butcher would frequently joke with other customers. His lavish lifestyle did not, however, go unnoticed in paramilitary circles, where it was resented because of its brash, public display. The Brigade Staff became concerned by the fact that Murphy was adopting an image which was not in keeping with a member of the UVF in a working-class neighbourhood such as the Shankill.

As far as his car was concerned, Murphy decided not to fulfil his promise to pay Smyth the remainder of the money due, and as a result Smyth telephoned Murphy on 9 August and indicated that he would visit him to collect the sum owing to him. Murphy was affronted and embarrassed at the prospect of Smyth accosting him publicly about the debt but he reluctantly agreed to meet the car dealer in the Rumford Street Social Club to discuss the matter. Smyth travelled by car to the club one evening, accompanied by two friends, one of whom was Samuel Carroll. The meeting with Murphy degenerated quickly into an abusive exchange between Murphy and Smyth, with Murphy stressing that it was unwise to demand money, but that the debt would be paid in several days. As if to seal this agreement, Murphy handed Smyth a drink but after a few sips Smyth became violently ill and was ushered into the toilets at the rear of the Club. When he emerged, Murphy was no longer on the premises. Smyth told Carroll that he was convinced Murphy had tried to poison him and that he was fortunate not to have taken more than a few sips of the drink. At 10P.M. Smyth asked his companions to drive him to the Mater Hospital. He still felt ill and wished to be examined because he was convinced that there was poison remaining in his body. As the three men drove down the Shankill Road towards the hospital, Smyth remarked to Carroll that a motorcycle was following their car. As Carroll turned the car into Crimea Street, the motorcycle pulled alongside and the pillion passenger signalled to Carroll to stop which he did. Carroll gave this version of the events which followed to police: 'There had been bother that evening and we thought someone wanted to pursue the matter. Brian and myself got out of the car and our friend was asleep on the back seat. I saw the silhouette of a man and there were shots.'

In fact there were eight shots fired directly into Smyth, killing him instantly. Carroll later told a Coroner's Court that the RUC held him for three days after the shooting and suggested that he lured Smyth to Belfast to be shot. Carroll said he firmly denied this. He told police that Murphy had given him an assurance that he (Murphy) had not been involved in the killing. The Coroner, James Elliott, said it was a peculiar case and newspaper reports attributed the killing to an internal feud between Loyalist paramilitaries. C Division of the RUC quickly clarified the matter, suggesting that the killing was not the result of a feud but rather a personal dispute between members of the UVF. There is little doubt that the murder squad in Tennent Street harboured suspicions that Murphy was implicated and so did the UVF Brigade Staff. The Brigade Staff carried out an internal inquiry but were unable to establish the motive or identity of the murderer. Those within the UVF who suspected Murphy were worried that he was again showing that he was beyond their control, and was creating problems for them at a time when they considered morale was high within their organization. Murphy, in their view, was also bringing what one inform-ant described to me as 'heat' into the Shankill, meaning the presence of additional police making enquiries and interviewing suspects. The man who shot Smyth was, in fact, Murphy and the killing had all the hallmarks of the motorcycle murder of Pavis ten years earlier.

293

On the morning of 22 October, fifty-four-year-old
Tommy Cochrane bade goodbye to his wife, Lily, and
their twenty-six-year-old son, Glen, and drove from his
home in the Glenanne area of County Armagh towards
the linen factory, where he had been employed since leaving school. Tommy Cochrane was known to friends and
neighbours as a quiet, inoffensive man who spent much
of his spare time patrolling the Border areas as a part-
time soldier in the Ulster Defence Regiment. His wife
was a district nurse and the couple were regular churchgo-
ers who were respected for their community work. After
joining the UDR in 1970 Cochrane quickly reached the
rank of sergeant. The area in which he lived, like many
rural parts of Northern Ireland which span the border
with the Irish Republic, has been a killing ground where
the IRA has murdered hundreds of UDR men as well as
Protestants not involved in the Regiment. The remoteness
of the area, coupled with the fact that many people who
are potential targets for the IRA live in isolated hamlets,
has made County Armagh one of the most violent areas
of Northern Ireland. In recognition of this problem facing
his community Tommy Cochrane joined the UDR and
thus came to the attention of the Provisional IRA, since
much of his work involved not just patrolling the border
but also manning roadblocks and searching vehicles and
pedestrians. On 22 October, he never reached his place
of work but was abducted by the IRA, who issued a statement to the media claiming that they were holding him 'for
interrogation because of his crimes against the Nationalist
community'. Over the next twenty-four hours appeals for
his release were made by politicians and churchmen to
the IRA and its political wing Sinn Fein. Lily and Glenn
Cochrane were held in tragic suspense because there was
no response from the IRA and no way of knowing what
terror Tommy might be suffering at the hands of his
captors. The IRA's use of the word 'interrogation' carried
its own terrible implications. The Cochrane family had

known the meaning of grief when ten of Tommy Cochrane's Protestant workmates were murdered by the IRA in the Kingsmill massacre. Tommy was fortunate not to have been travelling with them in the minibus on the day they were shot.

On Saturday evening, 23 October Lenny Murphy was again drinking in the Rumford Street Club. His conversation switched to the kidnapping of Cochrane, who was still held captive. With Murphy were men who had recently become associated with him: William Mahood, Noel Large, William 'Wingnut' Cowan, and another man who, for legal reasons, will henceforth be referred to as Mr M. and who until this period had had no connection with any of the crimes described in this book. Mahood and Cowan were members of the UVF, while the twenty-five-year-old Noel Large, like Murphy himself, had joined the UVF in his teens to become a ruthless terrorist with a long history of crime. Large was married with a baby girl and lived in East Belfast and, although not strictly under Murphy's control, he was willing to operate alongside him. Murphy walked away from his companions and was seen talking to other members of the UVF from the Shankill area. He proposed to them that they should kidnap a Catholic and hold him to ransom against the release of Cochrane. Murphy could not find any agreement to his suggestion and a heated debate ensued which resulted in him storming out of the club and motioning to his companions to follow his example. Outside, he held an impromptu meeting which was attended by the UVF men with whom he had discussed the proposal a few minutes earlier. Murphy explained once more that if they were to hijack a taxi and pick up a *Taig* they could hold him hostage on the basis that they would release him in return for the IRA releasing the UDR sergeant. A further argument ensued and it was pointed out to Murphy that the IRA might already have killed Cochrane and, even if not, the UVF would permit no such deal. Murphy walked away, signalling to Cowan to follow him. Mahood remained in the club while Large went in search of some takeaway food.

Murphy's plan was more daring than the one he described. He intended to hijack a black taxi on the Shankill Road and drive it to the Falls Road, where he would abduct a Catholic. Black taxis plied their trade on the Falls Road in much the same way as on the Shankill and potential passengers would simply wave them down. In this way Murphy believed he could pose as a bona fide taxi driver. The Falls Taxi Association, like the corresponding Association on the Shankill, operated on the basis of its members purchasing London-type cabs and picking up passengers at random on the street. Yet there was nothing to indicate that a particular taxi belonged to the Falls Association, and those who hailed taxis on either road would assume that they were being driven by members of the Association which operated in that district. Murphy decided, however, that Cowan should drive the taxi while he remained in the rear seat, as he had done on other occasions when he had killed people. It would be Murphy's task to deal with the 'passenger' as soon as the taxi was requested to stop.

At midnight, with two female passengers on board, Oliver Stephen Patrick drove his taxi down the Shankill Road. Patrick had hired the taxi several months previously from the North Belfast Mutual Association. As the taxi passed Rumford Street, Patrick was waved down by two men who got into the vehicle alongside the two women. After a short distance the two women got out of the vehicle, whereupon the two male passengers threatened Patrick and ordered him to drive to the Rumford Street Club. Outside the club, Patrick was ordered to get out of the taxi and walk away but not to report the theft until the following day. Patrick walked to his brother-in-law's house and was driven home. As instructed, he did not report the theft of his taxi until 8.30A.M. the following day. This failure was later described in an internal police document as follows: 'You may feel that he did not act in the role of a good citizen and his actions may well have come within the meaning of Section 5 (I) Criminal Law Act (Northern Ireland) 1967.' No charges were brought against Patrick. Everyone who lives in Northern Ireland is conscious of the fear which terrorists can engender. In Patrick's case, he may well have been concerned about the risk not only to himself but to his family if he disobeyed Murphy's orders. Driving on the Shankill, as Patrick did every day, it is likely that he knew of Murphy's reputation and was too frightened to play the role of the good citizen.

Cowan drove Murphy along the Falls Road from the direction of Millfield as arranged. On this occasion Murphy was not armed nor was he carrying the customary wheel brace.

Earlier that evening forty-eight-year-old Joseph Donegan, an unemployed joiner with seven children, was at home talking with his wife. Donegan, a Catholic born in the Lower Falls area into a family of thirteen children, had married his wife, Eileen, in 1955 and the first years of their marriage were spent in lodgings on the Falls Road. When their first child was due, Joseph and Eileen Donegan had acquired a small two-bedroomed house in Balkan Street in the Lower Falls, where all their seven children were born. In 1972, an IRA bomb intended for an Army patrol exploded three doors away from their home and Joseph Donegan decided to move his family to the Ballymurphy housing estate in West Belfast. But he remained fond of the Lower Falls area and during five years of unemployment between 1977 and 1982 he paid weekly visits to pubs and clubs in the Lower Falls.

At 8.30P.M. on 23 October Joseph Donegan received a phone call from his friend, James Quinn, inviting him for a drink in the Pound Loney Club in Cullingtree Road in the Lower Falls. Quinn remembers Donegan entering the club at 9.00P.M.: 'He was in good form and didn't appear to have taken drink. We talked, had a game of pool and a few drinks. Frank Gillan came into the club and joined us. We left the club at ten, went to a music hall nearby and had some more drink. I was drinking pints of lager and Joe was drinking bottles of Guinness. Until he left at 12.10A.M. Joe would have had one pint of Guinness and twelve bottles of it. He didn't have any more to drink than normal that night and he wasn't drunk. He left on his own while I was in the toilet. When he normally left the club, Joe walked up Albert Street onto the Falls Road, where he would look for a taxi or walk along the Falls until one came along.'

Joseph Donegan rarely talked about events in Northern Ireland. He was not involved politically and rarely voted. But he was aware of the dangers which existed and often pointed out to his children that many people had been killed simply because they were in the wrong place at the wrong time. His daughter Anne, a journalist with the *Irish News*, confirms that her father was not politically minded and all he enjoyed was 'a game of pool, a drink and a smoke'.

As he walked along the Falls Road, Joseph Donegan must have been unaware that there was any danger of his being abducted. He waved to an oncoming taxi which happened to be the one with Murphy riding in the back seat. Murphy did not get out but waited until Donegan stepped into the taxi and closed the door. As Cowan swung the taxi towards Millfield and the Shankill Road, Murphy launched his attack. Donegan put up a fierce struggle, and by the time the taxi reached Brookmount Street its rear windows were covered with blood. Murphy went berserk, beating Donegan into submission and forcing him onto the floor of the taxi, where he kicked him repeatedly.

The taxi stopped outside Murphy's former residence at 65 Brookmount Street which was now vacant. Cowan dragged Donegan from the vehicle while Murphy held open the door. They took the injured man into the kitchen area of the house and Murphy told Cowan to 'hold the

Taig' while he walked across the street to his new home and returned with a spade and a pair of pliers. Donegan was still resisting but was savagely beaten again by both men. Cowan was then told to drive to the Rumford Street Club and to fetch Mr M. When Cowan returned, both he and Mr M. watched as Murphy continued to beat and torture Donegan. Murphy used the pliers to pull many of Donegan's teeth from their roots. Finally he dragged Donegan, who was still alive, onto the concrete floor in the yard at the rear of the house. He handed the spade to Mr M. and told him to 'finish off the *Taig'* but to wait until he had regained consciousness and then ask him who he was. In his frenzy, Murphy had forgotten to find out his victim's name, which he needed if he was to make phone calls to bargain for Cochrane's release. He had no intention of keeping Donegan alive, and at no stage, I believe, would he have prevented himself beating and torturing his victim. However, he was prepared to maintain a pretence that his hostage was alive.

By 12.30A.M. the police were searching for Donegan after his nineteen-year-old daughter, Briege, reported her father's disappearance. Meanwhile Murphy and Cowan left Mr M. with Donegan and made their way in the taxi to Rumford Street so that Murphy could make his proposed telephone calls. Before the taxi reached the club, Cowan saw Large walking along the pavement and stopped the vehicle. What follows is a record of a conversation Large later had with police which describes the moment he met Murphy and Cowan. This account is taken from police interview notes:

> The defendant Large stated that as he left a chippy, a black taxi stopped and Lenny called him over. The defendant was asked where Lenny was in the taxi and he stated that he was in the back. The defendant was asked who was driving and he hesitated and then said, 'Wingnut'. The defendant stated that he then got into the back of the taxi beside Lenny and the rear windows had blood on

them and he asked Lenny where it came from and was informed that they had got a *Taig* on the Falls Road and he was in Lenny's house. The defendant was asked where the house was and he said he did not know but it was somewhere off the Shankill. The defendant went on to say that Lenny sent him into the house to find out the man's name and age. Wingnut and Lenny headed off in the taxi. In reply to further questions the defendant stated that Lenny had given him a key and he used it to open the front door. The defendant went on to say that he went to the backyard, which was covered in, but there were no lights. He saw the figure of a man standing in the backyard and he went over to speak to him and tripped over something. The defendant said he asked the man where the *Taig* was and the man replied: 'You have just walked over him.' The defendant then stated that he looked down and could see what he thought was the figure of a man on the ground. The defendant said he could hear the man breathing heavily and groaning and from the smell he knew the man had shit himself. When further questioned, the defendant stated that he told the other man to ask the man his name and age. The man did not answer. The other man told the defendant that the *Taig* had put up a fight when being taken into the house and got a beating. At one stage they thought he had taken a heart attack. The other man then told the defendant that he did not think the man could hear him when he asked for his name and age. The defendant then said that when the man on the ground did not answer, the other man started to beat him with the spade. He was asked where the Catholic was being hit and he said it was 'round the head'. The defendant said that during the time the man was being beaten, the spade broke. The defendant was asked who was doing the beating and he replied. . . . [Large gave detectives at this point a surname bastardized by the addition of the letters 'ie']. The defendant was then asked for the proper name and stated that he did not know but he came from the Balysillan area. The defendant said he told Mr M. to stop beating the Catholic when the shaft broke because he, the defendant, thought the Catholic was dead at that stage. The defendant was asked where the shaft broke and he lifted a pen and paper that he had been doodling on and drew a diagram resembling a spade with a wavy line at the top of the shaft, close to the handle and stated that that was where the shaft broke. The defendant went on to say that when the shaft broke, he told Mr M. that he thought the Catholic was dead. The defendant said that if he was to make a statement he could not name names because he would 'be done in prison'. He was asked what he did after Donegan died and he said they waited in the yard for ten minutes.

Large's testimony confirms that the killers did not learn the name of their victim. Murphy entered the house some minutes after Mr M. had finally killed Donegan and told Large and Mr M. to leave the premises and board the taxi, which was parked outside with Cowan in the driving seat. Large observed Murphy emerge from the house five minutes later and walk to a Cortina which was parked behind the taxi. Murphy climbed into the front passenger seat. Large's testimony did not reveal that the Cortina also contained a driver, Mr A.

Cowan, acting on Murphy's orders, drove away from Brookmount Street and proceeded to Glencairn Way in the Glencairn Estate where he stopped the taxi. Murphy and Mr A. arrived a short time later and, while Mr A. remained in the Cortina, Murphy approached the taxi and ordered Cowan and the others to leave the vehicle. At this point Murphy returned to the Cortina and, from the boot of the car, produced a can of petrol and the broken spade which was used to kill Donegan. He placed the spade in the taxi, sprinkled the vehicle with petrol and set it alight. Mr A. drove Murphy and his accomplices to the Shankill Road. By setting fire to the taxi, Murphy was destroying crucial evidence, though there was still the matter of disposing of Donegan's body. As for making phone calls, Murphy knew he would be obliged to wait for the name of his victim to be relayed on the radio news the following morning.

When the killers reached the Shankill, Large left the car and went to spend the night at Cowan's house. Murphy returned to his home in Brookmount Street knowing that Donegan's body was in a house opposite. The Cortina driven by Mr A. was the property of a convicted prisoner, James Irvine, who was in custody but had placed the vehicle in the care of a man whom I will refer to as Mr N. Police notes regarding this vehicle read as follows:

> On the night of October 23 Mr N. had consumed a lot of drink. At 12.15A.M. on October 24 he reported to police that his white Cortina car, registration TO19395, had been stolen from outside his house. On the afternoon of this date it was located at Highdene Crescent, close to where Mr N. resides. This vehicle was then returned to – Mr N.'s home. Mr N. then went to various Loyalist clubs on the Shankill, during which time he met and talked to members of paramilitary groups and was instructed to leave the Cortina at his house and leave the keys with a member of the family. He did in fact leave the car outside his home, giving his eighteen-year-old daughter, – , custody of the keys before continuing on a drinking spree, finally returning home at 7.00P.M. whereupon he discovered that the Cortina was not parked outside his house. On enquiring from his daughter as to the whereabouts of his car, he was told that two men had called during his absence, collected the keys and drove off. He then went to bed but was awakened at 3.00 A.M. by his daughter saying the police had found the car. He was arrested and questioned but released without charge. It is believed that Mr N. is connected with the UVF who use the Cortina as a staff car. He is a drunk who performs the role of messenger for the price of an occasional drink.

The fact that the car was taken by Murphy early that evening confirms that he had a killing in mind. A police document suggests that Mr N. could have been considered to be in breach of the 1967 Criminal Law Act because of his involvement. I cannot explain why he was not charged but I would speculate that the police intended to use him as a witness in return for not pressing charges.

With the disappearance of Sergeant Cochrane and Joseph Donegan, the two families who were sharing a similar agony conveyed sympathy to each other. Demands were made by churchmen and politicians on both sides for the release of the two men. Provisional Sinn Fein reacted with predictable duplicity: 'While we sympathize with the Cochrane family we must point out that Sergeant Cochrane is a serving British Army Officer who is well aware of the risk. Joe Donegan is an innocent man kidnapped by Loyalists simply because he is a Catholic.'

Once again the Provisionals had callously demonstrated that they were neither interested in listening to pleas for clemency nor concerned about how they might be viewed by the Protestant community.

Joe Donegan's death did not prevent Murphy attempting to hoodwink the public into believing that Donegan would be released safe and well in return for Sergeant Cochrane. On Sunday at 1.40P.M. Murphy made a phone call to Cormac Boomer, a member of the Social and Democratic Labour Party, who recalls:

I returned to my home to find my wife, Alice, speaking on the phone. She signalled to me to take the receiver from her and I could tell by her expression that she was frightened. I took the receiver, identified myself, enquired who was calling and asked if I could be of assistance. From that point the following conversation took place:

– Are you Cormac Boomer?
– Yes.
– Can you get in touch with the Workers' Party?
– I probably can but why do you ask and who are you?
– Listen. We have Donegan and we want you to tell Mary McMahon of the Workers' Party to go on television

303

and radio and make an appeal to the Provos to release
Cochrane. Do you understand?

– Yes. But why the Workers' Party and why Mary
McMahon?

– Mary McMahon is the only one these people will
listen to. She has contacts and they respect her.

– What do you mean she has contacts? Have you tried
to contact her or the Workers' Party direct?

Cormac Boomer recalls that at this point in the conversation the pitch of the caller's voice intensified and the
caller said: 'Listen you, this conversation has went on long
enough and is being terminated. You have your instructions. Contact Mary McMahon. We have Donegan and if
the Provos do not release Cochrane by midnight we will
put a bullet in his head. Do you understand?'

Before the caller went off the line, Cormac Boomer
courageously expressed his disgust: 'There is not much to
choose between you and the Provos. You are all bloody
heroes.'

The conversation was not hurried at any point and,
according to Boomer, the male caller's voice appeared
distorted. Boomer was convinced that the call was made
from a private line. In fact, it was made by Murphy from
the club in Rumford Street. Two similar calls were made
by him to the home of Father Desmond Wilson who lived
beside the Donegan family. Father Wilson was on holiday
but a friend answered the calls and during each of them
Murphy claimed to be speaking on behalf of the UVF,
which suggests that he was acting with the knowledge of
the leadership. The UVF leaders did know about the
abduction of Donegan from media reports but were not
told at that stage that he was dead. In these latter calls,
Murphy demanded that the Roman Catholic Cardinal,
Thomas O'Fiaich, should be contacted to beg for the
release of Cochrane. Murphy ended the first call with the
words 'A dead UDR man is a dead Donegan,' and in the
second call he threatened that if matters were not resolved

to his satisfaction he would dump the body of Joseph Donegan on the doorstep of the Donegan family home.

On Sunday lunchtime Large heard from Murphy that he was required to assist with the removal of Donegan's body from 65 Brookmount Street and was to proceed there immediately to receive further orders. Large later told police that when he arrived at the house, he found himself in the presence of a man unknown to him; like many of Murphy's previous accomplices, he was lying. He knew that Mr A. was the 'unknown man'. Mr A. told Large to return to the house at 7P.M., when the body would be removed via an alleyway at the rear of the house to a waiting car. While he was talking to Mr A., Large saw Donegan's body, which was at this time wrapped in a blanket with the feet protruding and was still on the floor of the yard.

When he returned at 7P.M. Mr A. was present, and the two of them carried the corpse into the alleyway where they expected Cowan to be waiting in a car with the boot already open. As they stood in the alleyway holding the corpse they observed Cowan experiencing difficulty in reversing the car. Suddenly a young couple walked past the entrance to the alleyway and Cowan, fearing they had seen the body, drove off. Large and Mr A. simply abandoned the corpse and ran off. Murphy was angered by this bungled operation but realized his accomplices could not return to his house for fear the police had been informed.

The following morning, several shipyard workers making their way to work discovered the body. One, who thought he had passed a bundle of discarded clothes, retraced his steps to see a pair of feet protruding from a blanket.

When police arrived on the scene they found Murphy's back door lying open and they proceeded to search the premises. Blood was spattered over the ceiling, walls and floor of the kitchen and teeth with the roots attached were lying on the floor. In a small room leading to the yard, they found more blood and teeth.

When I was shown the photographs which were taken at the time I was horrified and sickened by the evidence of bestiality. One of the photographs depicted a teddy bear lying on a bedroom floor, and this symbol of innocence juxtaposed against the surrounding images of indescribable evil was both macabre and chilling.

By 9.00A.M. that day television cameras arrived to record the scenes at Brookmount Street, where people were staring down the alleyway. One of the detectives from C Division told me that, while he was watching news film of the murder scene on television that evening, he identified Lenny Murphy as one of the spectators. Police officers at the scene of the crime also recognized Murphy, and he was arrested at 9.30A.M.

The Pathologist's report found that there were twenty lacerations to Donegan's head and body, and bruising and abrasions to most of his limbs. The pathologist concluded that the multiple injuries to the limbs would not have caused death but the combined effects of the severe injuries to the head, face and neck could have been the cause of death. He would have lost consciousness from severe internal bleeding and died during a period of coma, though there is no way of knowing whether he was dead when Large and Mr M. left him in the early hours of Sunday. The post-mortem found that there were only three teeth left in his mouth, numerous fractures of facial bones, ribs, skull and thyroid cartilage. The pathologist deduced that blows, probably from a fist, were delivered to the neck and throat and would have caused temporary respiratory difficulties.

On the Monday morning the Donegan family, like the Cochranes, were sitting at home anxiously awaiting news of their loved one. Anne Donegan has said that when news reached them of a body having been found in the Shankill area, they suspected it was their father. She told a *Belfast Telegraph* reporter: 'We have come to accept that this body is our Daddy. We only hope now that Mr Cochrane is still alive and they will release him.' The same reporter asked Gerry Adams of Sinn Fein for a statement about Sergeant Cochrane and was told: 'We have been trying since Friday to get clarification of the condition of Sergeant Cochrane and of the IRA's intentions towards him. Our failure to get clarification arises directly from the heavy presence of British Army and RUC in the area. As soon as we get clarification we will ask the IRA to issue a statement.'

Seamus Mallon of the SDLP reacted to this statement with anger and dismay: 'Those who abducted Mr Cochrane are as responsible for the death of Mr Donegan as surely as if they themselves had battered the poor man to death. For the Sinn Fein to try to tell us they cannot contact the IRA is a blatant lie.'

RUC Headquarters issued a statement echoing some of the points made by Seamus Mallon: 'It is impossible for anyone in Northern Ireland, and that includes the IRA, not to be aware of what is happening at present.'

In a leading editorial the *Irish News* called for the release of Thomas Cochrane and added that the IRA's 'inhumane crime had caused enough grief already'.

When Glenn Cochrane heard the news of the death of Joseph Donegan he phoned the Donegan home and expressed sorrow on behalf of himself and his mother, who was too griefstricken to speak on the phone. He also contacted three major newspapers in Northern Ireland and placed insertions in sympathy for the Donegan family.

Anne Donegan made another appeal to the IRA and she commented to Anne Purdy of the *Newsletter*: 'We do not want Mrs Cochrane to go through what my mother is going through now. I plead with them to let him go to his family. Mrs Cochrane is still hoping and waiting. Our time of waiting is over. My Daddy was a good man who did not belong to any organization. I believe both sides of our community are wrong. We have allowed this situation to go on for too long. The blame is on both sides. How could they do it to my Daddy?'

When police arrived at the Donegan home to inform the family officially of the death, there was a further poignant moment for Mrs Donegan and her children. The policemen produced a wrist watch, which the family had bought Joseph Donegan for his birthday in 1981, and a bracelet. These were used for identification purposes. Given that Joseph Donegan's face was unrecognizable, this was a compassionate decision. A family friend, Edward O'Kane, courageously offered to identify the body formally.

Because Donegan's body had been found at the rear of Murphy's former home and blood inside had proved to be that of the dead man, one would assume that the police now had Murphy directly connected with the crime. That, however, was not the case. Though Murphy was not actually living in the house at the time, any fingerprints of his found there could be easily explained. Detective Inspector John Fitzsimmons ordered Murphy to be taken for interview and fingerprinting at Castlereagh Holding Centre. While being fingerprinted the following conversation took place:

Murphy: What do you think of my new car, Fitzy?
Fitzsimmons: I haven't thought about it.
Murphy: C'mon, what do you think I paid for it?
Fitzsimmons: I don't know.
Murphy: (Laughs)   C'mon Fitzy, what do you think?
Fitzsimmons: You certainly didn't pay for it. You were inside, so where would you have got the money?

Murphy laughed again and Fitzsimmons says that this was just another example of Murphy getting kicks by playing games with the police. Fitzsimmons put it to Murphy that he had been involved in the Donegan killing but Murphy just laughed and told him to prove it. The police couldn't, and Murphy was released.

The murder of Donegan was, in the words of a leading member of the UVF, 'the final nail in Murphy's coffin'. Another UVF man put it this way at the time: 'If Murphy had simply shot the guy, it would have been another killing but to batter him to death, our own people don't like that. We ended up carrying the can for the cut-throat jobs and the publicity did not help our image. Now Murphy is at it again and he'll have to be stopped.'

The IRA were no less callous than Murphy, and the Cochrane family was obliged to wait for almost a week before Tommy Cochrane's body was dumped on the border. He had been beaten and shot. His injuries were not as extensive as those of Donegan but the two crimes were equally dastardly and cruel.

Noel Large was finally brought to justice following a series of eighteen interrogation sessions conducted by Detective Sergeant Wilbert McClenaghan of Mountpottinger Station in East Belfast, assisted by Detective Constable Stirling and guided by Detective Chief Superintendent Hylands. In the opening interrogation session Large expressed the fear that if he made a statement he was likely to receive a stipulated sentence, and this he wished to avoid. He referred to someone he would only name as 'Doc' who would poison him in prison if he named anyone. Detective Sergeant McClenaghan's interview notes show that Large admitted to a series of robberies and then talked about the first murder he had committed. In reading these notes I recognized immediately certain traits in Large's character which Murphy must also have detected:

> 'I shot Eugene Mulholland dead in 1981.' The defendant was asked to relate the circumstances surrounding this murder. He asked for a drink of water which Detective Constable Stirling got for him. He drank the water and then said: 'I shot him with a .357 Magnum.' The defend-

ant stated that he and another man went to Delhi Street off the Ormeau Road. They were to shoot an IRA man. The defendant was asked which car he used and he replied that it was a red Ford Cortina. The idea was to lie in a garden and wait for the man coming from a pub and when he came down the garden to let him have it. He said the UVF had intelligence that the man was in the IRA and he went out every Friday night and it was a Friday night that they went out to get him. The defendant said there were too many police about so they drove down the Ormeau Road to see if they could get any other *Taigs*. Somewhere around the Hatfield Bar they saw a fellow walking along the pavement and they called him over. He walked towards them and then ran off. The defendant did not feel that he could hit him so he did not fire and they drove on towards the Markets. They saw a man walking up the Ormeau Road on the left and the defendant got out of the car in a side street and walked up behind the man and shot him in the back. Detective Constable Stirling asked the defendant how he was attracted to this man's attention and the defendant stated: 'He took off into the air like a fucking angel.' The defendant laughed. He was asked what happened then and he said that the man landed on the pavement on his stomach with his head turned to one side and that he (the defendant) walked over and stood at the man's head and looked into his face and he bent to do this. He then went on to say that he looked straight at the man and took a deep breath and then he (the defendant) let him have it on the side of the head and there was a dark red hole where the bullet went in. He went on to say that to make sure he was dead he put another bullet in the top of his head. The defendant was asked how he could have looked the victim in the eyes when he was standing vertically above him. The defendant got up from his chair and walked away from the table, clasped his two hands in front of him with his arms outstretched as if he was holding a gun. He then flexed his knees, arched his back, bringing his hands to within a foot of the floor and stated that the man's head was just below the gun. The defendant then pretended to fire the gun

and he demonstrated the recoil of the gun as he fired it.
He then sat down and said: 'That's it.'

The remainder of Large's confession, which was made in
February 1983, was littered with the comments of a young
man without remorse for his actions. The Magnum used
to shoot Mulholland was also used in the killing of an
eighty-year-old woman in the Markets area of Belfast, and
Large was one of her murderers.

Large's statement shows similarities to the methods
used by the Butchers, though his operations were mainly
carried out in the Markets and Ormeau Road areas of
Belfast. The perceived wisdom was, however, exactly the
same. He had enjoyed killing Mulholland, and Murphy
recognized this trait.

The killing of Donegan demonstrated that Murphy was
capable of forming another unit, and it could be surmised
that he was intent on designating Large to perform the
role once played by William Moore.

According to Murphy's family, Lenny began to receive
death threats after he had been arrested for the Donegan
murder. His movements became erratic and unpredictable, which would seem to support this claim, and he
was no longer seen regularly on the Shankill Road. His
girlfriend saw him only at times of his choosing and without advance warning. He became concerned about the
UVF leadership's attitude towards him and indicated to
friends that, should anything happen to him, certain members of the Brigade Staff were to be informed that they
were not welcome to mourn at his funeral. The UDA also
had no affection for Murphy and believed him to be a
psychopath and a menace to their operations in West
Belfast. They viewed his actions as inviting too much
police scrutiny and activity and the Donegan killing confirmed this view. After such killings the RUC swamped
an area for days with increased security which was not
welcomed by the different paramilitary organizations. The

murder of Donegan and the fact that his body had been left outside Murphy's home suggested to many that Murphy was careless, if not crazy. There were others who wished Murphy dead and, from the moment of his release from prison, were preparing to assassinate him. These people were members of the Provisional IRA and the Irish National Liberation Army. Both groupings set up special hit squads with orders to be at the ready to kill Murphy at any time, day or night. They knew from media coverage that Murphy was Mr X. though I suspect that, like most terrorist groupings, they did not rely solely for information on what appeared in print.

Murphy was aware of the newspaper stories and became more concerned about his personal safety. When he was arrested after the Donegan killing, he gave his address as 92 Forthriver Park, the home of his girlfriend. He used this tactic throughout his terrorist career, and police files contain numerous addresses supplied by him with the Percy Street address always prominent among them. Following the Donegan murder he spent most nights at the home of his girlfriend. His routine was to drive there in his mustard-coloured Rover car and park at the rear of the house, entering the premises through a back door.

At 6.40P.M. on 16 November, Murphy drove to the Glencairn Housing Estate and made his way to Forthriver Park, oblivious of the fact that a blue Morris Marina van was trailing him, keeping a safe distance and travelling at a steady speed. As Murphy parked at the rear of Hilary Thompson's house and turned off the engine the blue van turned slightly, with its rear facing the Rover. Suddenly the back doors of the van were thrown open and two gunmen emerged, one armed with a .9mm sub-machine gun and the other with a .38 Special revolver. They opened fire on Murphy who, unaware of their presence, was about to open the door of his car. He was hit by twenty-six bullets in the head and body and died instantly. That night no grouping admitted responsibility for the killing but the following day the Provisional IRA said they were responsible and, as if to prove their claim, they gave journalists specific details of the calibre of the weapons used in the murder. Their delay in issuing a statement was, they said, to allow their unit to escape after the killing. They claimed this had been made easy by the fact that Murphy was known to be involved in internal feuding within the UVF and so when he was shot the police concentrated their efforts in quite the wrong direction.

The circumstances surrounding Lenny Murphy's death have been the source of much speculation with some people saying that it was not the IRA who killed him but Loyalist paramilitaries. Noel Large, who was sentenced to life imprisonment for the murder of Donegan six months after Murphy's death, had this to say about the Murphy killing when being interviewed by Detective Sergeant McClenaghan:

> Large was informed that he had no reason to distrust us and he said he was between the devil and the deep blue sea, as it was either a question of doing time or finishing up like Lenny. The defendant was asked if he meant Lenny Murphy and he stated that he did. He was asked what he knew about Murphy's death and he stated that he did not know who done it, but that he believed it was his own kind. The defendant was then asked what bearing Murphy's death had on him and he replied: 'When I told you I was stood down, I did not tell you that I was to be kneecapped and that hasn't happened yet. Who knows, it might be a nutting job.' He was asked if he was saying that some members of the UVF might shoot him dead and he shrugged his shoulders and replied, 'You don't get to be a military commander without making a few enemies.'

This transcript, like others in this book, has never been in the public domain and its contents demand examination. Large was, in fact, admitting to police that he had been 'stood down' by the UVF, meaning that he was no longer

active and was waiting a decision about his fate. My
enquiries revealed that because of his involvement in the
Donegan murder Large was to be court-martialled, and
that could have resulted in a kneecapping or, as he put it,
'a nutting job' (meaning that he would be shot through the
head). The UVF leadership viewed the Donegan killing as
a serious breach of discipline and knew that Murphy had
been advised against abducting a Catholic by senior members of the organization during the heated debates in the
Rumford Street Social Club. The Brigade Staff knew they
could easily deal with Large and the other accomplices
but the question of punishing Murphy for his actions
presented serious difficulties, some of which I have already
outlined in this book. There was also the fact that Murphy
was a prominent member of the organization and was held
in high esteem by many young men in Loyalist paramilitary
circles. The basic problems facing the leadership were
that, firstly, if they decided to court-martial Murphy and
kneecap him he would always present a threat to them;
secondly, if they chose the more severe penalty of
execution and Murphy found out in advance, he would be
likely to exact revenge; finally, the execution of such a
prominent member would bring the organization into disrepute in Loyalist circles and please the IRA. The public
humiliation which would have arisen from the UVF
executing one of its most infamous figures was not a course
of action the leadership was prepared to undertake. So
who did kill Murphy?

To answer that question, one has to look at the contacts
which have been formed between the paramilitaries on
both sides of the political divide. In the seventies racketeering and building site fraud were on the increase and the
paramilitaries carved up areas of Belfast so that they could
each equally benefit from criminal activities of this kind.
They reached agreements for mutual benefit even though
bitter enemies. Without such cooperation, each of the
paramilitary groupings could swiftly prevent the other from

sharing in well-organized scams, so the killings could continue but in one area of life there would be tacit agreement that there should be no interference from either side. As a result, many strange arrangements have been made which allow frequent contact between terrorists.

The Provisionals claim that they killed Murphy, but Nesbitt proved from his investigations that it was impossible to mount constant surveillance on suspects in Loyalist areas of West Belfast and I have quoted him as saying that when Murphy was released in 1982 C Division could not monitor his movements. How could the IRA achieve what the RUC found impractical – the tracking of Murphy in his own territory? They could not have done so without collusion with Loyalist paramilitaries. According to my sources the IRA were told that there was one constant factor in Murphy's routine: his daily visit to Hilary Thompson, and that on a specific day a tip-off would be given to confirm that Murphy was heading from Brookmount Street or a Shankill Road club to Forthriver Park.

The IRA, I was told, kept an assassination unit on standby in the Ligoniel area and another in the Ardoyne, in readiness for the all-important telephone call. Another factor which supports the collusion theory was presented to me by an RUC detective who had access to the file on Murphy's death. The file contains an outline of the circumstances surrounding the murder, which ends with the conclusion that it was 'possibly a killing in which a Loyalist or Loyalists were involved'.

The blue van used by the 'hit squad' was hired weeks earlier in the Braniel area of predominantly Protestant East Belfast. When the killers fled, the van was found burning at Forthriver and Harmony Hill, strategically placed to block anyone pursuing the gunmen. A car, which was used to spirit away the gunmen from Forthriver into the Nationalist enclave of Ligoniel, was also found the same day. It had been hijacked the previous day in the Andersonstown district of Catholic West Belfast.

Most of these elements would support strongly the IRA claim that their men shot Murphy but there is one detail, missing from newspaper reports but in the Murphy file in Tennent Street, which might lead one to suppose otherwise. The missing detail concerns items found near the scene. Close to Murphy's girlfriend's house was a gap in a hedge leading to a field, a shortcut known only to locals. Through the gap in the hedge, police found masks and gloves which they believe were used by the gunmen who shot Lenny Murphy. One is obliged to ask why two IRA men, who had a van at their disposal and a car waiting at the point where the van was to be abandoned, should decide to make off on foot through the Protestant Glencairn estate?

The *Irish News* carried what it described as an 'exclusive' in December 1982 claiming that Murphy had been killed by Loyalists with guns provided by the IRA. The author of the 'exclusive' said that Republican sources confirmed that 'Murphy was killed in a unique, joint operation by the IRA and Loyalists to eliminate a "mutual problem".'

It is possible that the gunmen discarded the gloves, masks and, possibly, the guns before making off in the van, though eye-witness evidence does not indicate that there would have been sufficient time to engage in this type of manoeuvre. On the other hand, the items found by the police could well have belonged to any of the Loyalist paramilitary organizations who, as I have shown, used Glencairn as a base. The Provisionals may well have killed Murphy but I would contend that they could not have done so without the assistance of a person or persons from within one of the Loyalist paramilitary groups.

A man who lived near the scene of the shooting ran from his house on hearing the gunfire and found Murphy slumped over the steering wheel of the Rover. He lifted the dead man out of the car, wrapped him in a blanket and placed him on the roadway. This man's wife saw the

blue van being driven slowly past her home and says that
it arrived in the vicinity of Murphy's car a short time after
he had brought his vehicle to a halt. She saw the rear
doors of the van being flung open and seconds later
observed blue flashes. She made no mention in her statement to police of seeing the gunmen making off on foot,
but saw the van drive away.

On 20 November six masked gunmen fired a volley of
shots over the coffin containing Lenny Murphy, outside
his mother's home in Brookmount Street. The coffin was
draped in an orange and purple flag and police were kept
from the scene by a phalanx of black taxis which sealed
off the street from the Shankill and allowed the masked
gunmen to escape. Traffic was prevented from using the
Shankill Road by about thirty taxis which blocked the main
road and many of the side streets. As the cortège moved
slowly down the Shankill Road, a lone piper played 'Abide
with Me'. The coffin was flanked by men in battledress.
Journalists and television cameramen were warned not to
take pictures of the mourners, and some journalists were
threatened and told to leave the area. Prominent among
the mourners were leading members of the UDA and
UVF, though certain high-ranking members of the UVF,
who had been informed of Lenny's comments before his
death that certain people would not be welcome at his
funeral, did not attend.

The cortège proceeded from the Shankill to Carnmoney
Cemetery on the outskirts of the city, where there was a
heavy security presence in attendance. The lone piper led
the mourners to the grave, where a brief religious service
took place. As the mourners left, two solitary gravediggers
began their task of filling the grave.

The *Belfast Telegraph* carried eighty-seven death notices,
including ones from Moore and Bates. Ironically there
was a notice of sympathy from Dessie Balmer, whom
Murphy had ordered to be shot on the day Shaw was
murdered. Other notices read:

From old friends, Dinks, Harper, Hacksaw, Fox, Dick, Basher, Noel, Head-Monkey, Artie and Stewartie, all written from their current home address, B Wing, H-Block, the Maze prison.

At the going down of the Sun we will remember Him.

His Aunt Agnes penned the following tribute to Lenny: 'Nothing could be more beautiful than the memories we have of you; to us you were very special and God must have thought so too.'

Lenny Murphy's mother reacted to his death by saying that he had been planning to leave Northern Ireland because of police harassment. She echoed the view of her family and friends that the police had killed Lenny, or were responsible for 'setting him up', and she told Noel Adams of the *Belfast Newsletter*: 'Lenny was a man who spoke his mind . . . he believed in his country . . . he was so outspoken he was a target for propaganda. I don't know if he was a member of the UVF.'

Residents of Glencairn interviewed by Noel Adams after the funeral said they had seen the van used in the killing at least half an hour before the shooting and one of them claimed that a call was made to Tennent Street Station to say that the vehicle had been acting suspiciously. There is no note on the police file that any such call was ever made.

The Murphy family alleged that there had been a twenty-four-hour guard on Murphy and this had been withdrawn twenty-four hours before his death. The police have dismissed this allegation as 'absurd'. Mrs Joyce Murphy also said that a detective had told Lenny that he would not be alive by Christmas and it was because of the sinister nature of this warning that he had been planning to leave Northern Ireland. 'The police never left him alone from the day he got out of prison,' added Mrs Murphy.

She told other reporters that her son had never led the 'Shankill Butchers', but Peter McKenna writing in the *Irish Independent*, quoted a UDA leader as saying: 'Lenny was a typical psychopath.'

A comment from Joyce Murphy which captured the attention of many journalists who interviewed her was: 'My Lenny would not have hurt a fly.'

It is unlikely that Joyce Murphy and the other mourners at the funeral on 19 November were aware that there was someone else of significance buried in Carnmoney Cemetery; a young man who once travelled down Belfast Lough and pointed to the graveyard; a young man who enjoyed writing songs; Stephen McCann.

We may never know the identity of the killers of Lenny Murphy. Many people in paramilitary organizations, both Republican and Loyalist, are willing to admit that the Provisionals carried out the actual killing but with assistance from Loyalists. One source within the Loyalist paramilitary world told me that there were many within the ranks of both the UDA and UVF who were of the opinion that Murphy had to be 'wiped out' because he could not be controlled and was about to start a sectarian war which would generate too much police 'heat' on Loyalist areas of West Belfast and jeopardize other operations, including racketeering. This source was of the opinion that the Provisionals provided weapons as payment for information leading to the murder of Murphy. When I asked about the presence of the gloves and balaclavas in Glencairn after the shooting, I was told that the guns were also left behind but were spirited away since they were part of the deal.

The Provisionals have always contended that they shot Murphy as a result of information supplied by their own intelligence officers. I do not doubt that they shot him but would they be willing to admit that they had had assistance from Loyalists? And would Loyalists ever admit that they helped the IRA kill a man who received a hero's funeral and whose headstone reads: 'Here Lies A Soldier'?

In the years following Lenny Murphy's death two other leading members of the UVF from West Belfast were assassinated by the Provisional IRA. The first was John Bingham who was regarded by many as Murphy's successor though this was not strictly accurate in that Bingham was not involved in grisly murders. He was believed, however, to have been implicated in the murder of several innocent Catholics. Bingham's death was followed by the gunning down of William 'Frenchie' Marchant as he walked along the Shankill Road. The UVF carried out an internal enquiry to establish whether anyone in the UVF ranks had supplied information to the IRA which led to the deaths of the three. The enquiry concluded that no one in the organization was responsible but that the similarities in the killing of the three UVF men indicated that someone in Loyalist circles had provided information to the IRA on the whereabouts of the three a short time prior to their deaths. Murphy's killing initially aroused suspicion that the Provos were supplied with vital intelligence because of the obvious difficulty of mounting a concerted surveillance of their target in a predominantly Protestant neighbourhood.

The murder of Bingham reinforced this suspicion. He was shot in his home in the staunchly Protestant district of Ballysillan in North Belfast. Bingham, like Murphy, was security conscious and shortly before his death was living in the tiny, remote village of Millisle on the County Down coastline. On the night of his death he was attending a pigeon-fanciers' get-to-together and returned home earlier than expected by his wife. He had specially-secured doors in his home but did not have time to lock them. He no sooner entered his house when an IRA murder squad arrived and shot him dead.

Marchant was shot within a short distance of premises

used by a political grouping affiliated to the UVF. His day-to-day movements were erratic which suggested that on the day of his death the Provos received a phone call indicating his presence on the Shankill Road. The Provos when planning a killing of this nature have an assassination squad on standby in an area close to where their intended target is believed to be.

The UVF enquiry did produce one piece of information which linked Murphy, Bingham and Marchant. Each of them had quarrelled at different times with James Pratt Craig, the UDA leader in West Belfast. The UVF Brigade Staff concluded that this was merely a tenuous link and insufficient to permit them to act against Craig who was a leading figure in a powerful organization. Craig was a stocky man in his early forties who led a flamboyant life-style evidenced by his choice of expensive clothes and jewellery and his retinue of admirers. He ran protection rackets on building sites in the west of the city and extorted money from other businesses such as shops, clubs and pubs. His police file was packed with details about his activities and the many suspicions about him, but the RUC found it impossible to persuade people to give evidence against him. He was frequently seen drinking in Loyalist clubs in the Shankill area, dispensing largesse from the profits of his criminal activities. He was not intelligent but was cunning, boastful and ruthless, and believed he could display his new-found wealth with impunity. He was an ex-boxer who used his physical talents to bad effect and at the outset of the present conflict was in prison for criminal offences. However, in prison he joined the UDA and became the self-styled commander of an increasing number of UDA offenders in the Maze Prison.

David McKittrick, now Ireland Correspondent of the *Independent*, recalls being told by an IRA leader that Craig explained his method of maintaining discipline amongst UDA prisoners in these words: 'I've got this big fucking hammer and I've told them that if anybody gives me trouble, I'll break their fucking fingers.'

Craig was present at the anti-sectarian assassination conference in the Maze which is referred to in the introduction to this book and it was Craig who, at the same conference, told his companion, Sammy Smyth, to keep his views to himself, views which eventually led to the Provos killing Smyth.

Craig was willing to communicate with the Provisionals within the prison and established contacts which were put on a more formal basis when he was released. He formed a working relationship with the Provos when racketeering led to the paramilitaries carving out areas of the city for their exclusive use. This arrangement ensured that, while sectarian killings continued, they did not interfere with the working relations between the racketeers. It also guaranteed that Craig was never at the top of an IRA hit list.

The RUC believe Craig was involved in several murders but there are only two which I know can be firmly attributed to him. The first was the shooting of an innocent man in a UDA club in the Shankill area. A UDA member entered the club and told Craig he had a pistol which was 'jamming'. He handed the weapon to Craig who casually levelled it at shoulder height, his hand outstretched, and pulled the trigger. The gun fired and a bullet struck the head of a man playing pool, killing him instantly. Craig had the body removed from the premises and dumped in a nearby alleyway.

The second murder was of a fellow member of the UDA, William 'Bucky' McCullough. McCullough discovered that Craig was taking large sums of money for his personal use from UDA funds acquired from the extortion rackets. Craig was worried about the accusation and decided that McCullough had to die. Craig sought a meeting with the INLA, the organization which murdered Airey Neave, and this was held in a bar in Belfast city centre.

Craig told the INLA man present that McCullough was involved in sectarian murders and provided additional information which led to McCullough being shot at his home.

Craig also faced a serious problem in 1982 when Lenny Murphy was released from prison. Murphy was not fully aware of the extent to which Craig was in control of racketeering in West Belfast with the result that within a short time Murphy was at loggerheads with Craig who issued threats to Murphy through intermediaries. The message to Murphy was a simple one: 'Don't encroach on my territory.' Murphy, as we know, was not easily intimidated. Craig recognized this and maintained a tight form of security while Murphy was around.

If Murphy had lived would he have acted against Craig, or was he intending to do so before he died? In 1987, five years after Murphy's demise and following the murders of Bingham and Marchant, the UDA for its part felt obliged to examine Craig's activities and lifestyle. His behaviour, particularly in relation to criminal pursuits such as extortion, was causing acute embarrassment to the UDA leadership and, in particular, its political spokesman, John McMichael.

I met McMichael on several occasions in 1987 and he voiced suspicions that Craig was out of control and was believed to be providing the IRA with information on Loyalist paramilitaries. McMichael was an impressive figure who was developing a political strategy for the UDA and the Protestant working class and his efforts were praised by leading political figures in the Nationalist community. He believed he needed to change the image of the UDA and to present a political alternative to chaos. He perceived Craig's activities as anathema to a policy which required the UDA to possess a clean image if its political thesis of shared-responsibility Government was to achieve cross-community consensus.

McMichael demanded that the UDA's ruling body, the

Inner Council, force Craig to stop racketeering and interrogate him in relation to the deaths of McCullough and the three members of the UVF. McMichael's concerns were further heightened by the broadcast of an Independent Television documentary presented by the investigative journalist, Roger Cooke. The programme exposed Craig as a leading criminal and the public reaction to the broadcast, leading to demands for the UDA to be proscribed, galvanized McMichael into action and he set up his own enquiry into Craig and those who surrounded him. McMichael discovered that Craig was spending money on lavish continental holidays at least twice a year and was generally living a 'champagne lifestyle'.

The investigation was in its infancy when a bomb exploded under McMichael's car at his home, killing him. The Provisional IRA admitted responsibility for the murder but there was little doubt within the UDA and UVF that, once again, the Provisionals were kept informed about their target's movements on the day of his death. The evidence, circumstantial though it was, pointed to Craig as the man with the motive.

Younger elements in the UDA who supported John McMichael decided after his death in December 1987 that they would not allow the matter to rest and they continued the enquiry on a furtive basis. They discovered, by means which I am not in a position to reveal, that the RUC's anti-racketeering squad, CI3, videotaped a meeting between Craig and a member of the IRA's Northern Command.

On the evening of 15 October 1988 Craig was lured to the Castle Inn in East Belfast for a meeting with other members of the UDA. He travelled to the bar in the belief that he was secure and that the death of McMichael was part of the past. As he sat drinking, two men in overalls, wearing ski masks and armed with automatic weapons, burst into the premises and sprayed the public bar reserving aimed shots for Craig who died instantly.

The UDA's military wing, the Ulster Freedom Fighters, admitted responsibility for killing Craig and apologized for killing an elderly man who was in the bar at the time of the shooting. They said they knew Craig had provided the information which led to the Provos killing McMichael. Privately, they confirmed a belief that Craig also acted in concert with the IRA and the INLA in the killings of Murphy, Bingham, Marchant and McCullough.

Maybe Craig did set up Murphy; the evidence is circumstantial, the type of evidence which enabled Murphy to survive for so long. While writing this book I was told that on the night Murphy died, a leading member of the UDA was sitting in a house in the nationalist district of West Belfast with members of the INLA waiting for news about Murphy's fate. The description of the man fits with Craig's. It begs the question of whether his contact, as in the case of McCullough's death, always remained the INLA from that moment onwards and whether it was that organization which provided the Provisionals with the information they required. He may also have channelled information through them to the Provisionals in respect of the McMichael killing because it came at a time when the INLA was busy sorting out internal rifts caused by a feud. The answer to it all lies with two men who are dead.

Conclusion

Many people are referred to in this book by letters of the alphabet. This is necessary for legal reasons but I also feel that it is not my role to seek to identify people who have not been brought to justice; that is a task for the authorities.

I never saw it as my responsibility to go beyond the existing evidence, or to indulge in fantasy or speculation, or to jeopardize the lives of others, irrespective of their political allegiance or the evidence implicating them in crimes.

One of the primary lessons I learned from writing this book is that the public expects the police to bring all terrorists to justice yet they do not take into account the rules governing police behaviour and the laws of evidence. There are those who conveniently blame the RUC for not proceeding against known offenders but I hope I have shown that in some instances the RUC recommends a course of action which lawyers representing the Director of Public Prosecutions then rule to be legally unwise or untenable. When the public calls for action against terrorists there is a general assumption that the means are available to effect prosecutions. That is not so. Terrorists are schooled in evasion and they learn anti-interrogation techniques. When police manage to acquire accomplice evidence, there is always the risk that this kind of evidence is not the best means of proceeding with a prosecution. Northern Ireland has experienced the 'supergrass' system but it was rejected by many Nationalists and Unionists, who demand nonetheless that the police resolve the terrorist problem using judicial means. Despite police successes, which C Division certainly had, it is my contention that the present system is inadequate.

The story of Lenny Murphy and his gang supports my thesis that no matter how determined the police may be the system is easily exploited by terrorists on both sides of the community. I do not know the solution to this problem and I do not feel it is my responsibility to provide one for Northern Ireland society, but I believe that Murphy and his gang exemplified the problem facing the law enforcers.

The policemen, both uniformed and CID personnel, whom I interviewed, impressed me as dedicated men doing a difficult job and applying themselves to their responsibilities better than many other professionals I have met. They made mistakes, some serious, but they exploited their opportunities when it proved essential. Throughout the writing of this book I was aware that I possessed the advantage of hindsight, and I constantly sought to test my findings against the overwhelming problems associated with policing in Northern Ireland. Some of the lessons I learned from this exercise have been accepted by the RUC. I had access throughout my research to confidential files and notebooks and to police personnel, and at no time did the RUC seek to hinder my work. There was never any question of the manuscript being vetted by the RUC and, at the time of publication it has not been viewed by the police force.

On many occasions I asked myself why I decided to write this book. Perhaps the genesis lay in my co-writing *Political Murder in Northern Ireland* which was published in 1973 and dealt with the nature of sectarian murder and mass murder in my society. That book revealed for the first time the hidden depths of depravity which existed and the grisly dimension to the tribal conflict between the two communities. Thereafter I always believed there was a work to be written which would explain in greater detail the precise nature of mass murder and the personalities

327

drawn to it. The impetus for pursuing that course of action may well have been my feelings when I was shown post-mortem photographs of Stephen McCann in 1979. During the years that followed, I wrote about other matters but my thoughts constantly returned to the murder of McCann and subsequently the Butcher killings. I had a desire to discover why it all happened. Who could possibly commit such crimes and what was it in my own society that engendered such brutality? I hope this book, if it has not provided all of the answers, will at least have created the basis for debate about the nature of prejudice.

One of the episodes in the book which contrasted starkly with the brutality was the Christian love and sorrow expressed between the Cochrane and Donegan families. This occurred on a larger scale after the bombing at Enniskillen too, and yet the killing goes on. Nonetheless, the Cochrane and Donegan murders illustrate one salient dimension to the situation: terrorists are impervious to expressions of morality even when such expressions are part of a public disavowal of violence. I began the book by stating that prejudice can lead to ridicule or extermination, and unfortunately the events in this book prove that where the paramilitaries are concerned it is more likely to be the latter.

There is a question which many readers will ask: how long will the Butchers spend in prison? The answer is that I do not know. A number of terrorists who were found guilty of murder and who were not given stipulated sentences by the courts have been released in recent times. The decision about the release of the Butchers remains with the executive arm of the Government. Life imprisonment, as we know it, is an indeterminate sentence, in that the length of it is not determined by the Courts. Training school orders and the old borstal training schools are similarly indeterminate. In the case of an indeterminate sentence, decisions about release on 'licence' are made by the executive (in the case of Northern Ireland by the Secretary of State) and not by the judiciary.

In some countries, especially the USA, there are partially indeterminate sentences where the Court specifies a maximum and minimum amount of time to be served, leaving the specific release date to the executive to decide, which in practical terms means the recommendation of the Prison Governor. The argument for this practice is that it provides an incentive for good behaviour in prison. With the exception of 'life', training schools and the old borstals, the British system has not favoured indeterminate sentences; they are regarded as an unfortunate attack on the independence of the judiciary. Current trends, even where juvenile offenders are concerned, favour fixed and determinate lengths of custody (e.g. youth custody in Britain and parallel recommendations in the Black Report on Juvenile Justice in Northern Ireland). Murder is the one crime where the punishment has always breached the independence of the judiciary. In the days of hanging, the executive (the Home Secretary in Great Britain) could always reprieve. Similarly, the executive decides on the length of a life sentence, even though the normal practice is for the Home Secretary/Secretary of State to accept the advice of the Life Sentence Review Committee which includes representation from the judiciary and, where possible, the sentencing judge. So-called stipulated life sentences where the judge has stipulated a minimum number of years, or in the case of Moore and Bates, 'natural life, meaning life', will be borne in mind by the executive when they are considering whether Moore and Bates will be released, but they are not legally binding.

Indeterminate sentences do not attract remission. Other sentences in Northern Ireland, and this applies to several members of the Butcher gang, attract fifty per cent remission. This means that if a prisoner has not committed a disciplinary offence (which could be punished by an 'Order of Forfeiture of Remission'), he must be released when he has served half his determinate sentence. This does not apply to 'lifers'.

Earlier I mentioned that Bates was denied privileges because of his behaviour and, for the benefit of the reader, I shall explain the procedure. Disciplinary offences in prison are listed in the Prison Rules. Minor offences, as specified in the rules, are dealt with by the Governor, who can caution, restrict privileges for short periods, order 'cellular confinement' (i.e. in a punishment block) for a short period, or order forfeiture of remission subject to a low maximum. Serious offences by persistent offenders are referred by the Government to the Secretary of State who will, in most instances, delegate his authority to the prison board of visitors. This is what happened with Bates. The board of visitors has the same powers as the Governor but its awards are greater in length (e.g. for any one offence the board can order fifty-six days of 'cellular confinement', restriction of privileges until release, even for a 'lifer', or loss of remission for 180 days). Board of visitors adjudications are subject to appeal to the Secretary of State or judicial review in the High Court; legal assistance (in certain cases) can entitle a prisoner to be legally represented at a sitting of the board.

Because 'lifers' are not entitled to remission, the board cannot award forfeiture of remission in their case. It tends to rely on the use of 'cellular confinement' and substantial doses of loss of privilege, as it did with Bates. It does not mean that 'lifers' such as Bates and Moore have less to lose, as Bates pointed out when he was brought before the board. On the other hand, an adjudication by the board is noted on the prisoner's record and could possibly influence the Life Sentence Review Committee's decision about recommending a release date. It can be argued that the uncertainty about a date for release and the attendant anxiety that that creates provides a strong incentive for an offender not to offend in prison. A 'lifer' who has not been released can be recalled to prison to continue his sentence; he does not need to commit another offence to be recalled.

The views of the Butcher trial judge, Turlough O'Donnell, will carry considerable weight when the Life Sentence Committee reviews those cases, as it must. Some of the gang will be due for release within the coming decade. Already, McIlwaine, the former member of the UDR who was involved in the McLaverty assault and abduction, has been released from prison. I was told that on his release his marriage collapsed, he was unemployed and was drinking heavily. A short time before his arrest in 1977 he was dismissed from the Ulster Defence Regiment. Nationalist politicians later exploited his membership of the UDR to make further demands for the disbandment of the Regiment. I feel there are aspects of this which need to be clarified. McIlwaine attended weekly meetings of the Windsor Bar unit of the UDR at Dunmore Park in Belfast for a few months after he joined in 1974. In subsequent years his attendance was erratic. Taking this into account, one is obliged to ask why he was not dismissed until a short time before his arrest. I believe that once the RUC began searching for him after they obtained Moore's statements they informed the military authorities that a member of the UDR was on a wanted list.

The RUC deny this and yet all the evidence points to the fact that McIlwaine was permitted his membership for years and nothing was done about his attendance until a period when he was being sought by the police in relation to serious crime. The Regiment should not have had McIlwaine in its ranks. Here we have a man associated with the Butcher murders and with known members of a terrorist organization. Like Fletcher, the UDR sergeant whose gun was used to kill McQuaid, McIlwaine spent much of his time in terrorist haunts. He was a part-time soldier with access to weapons, ammunition and possibly files containing information on people in the other community who were suspected of involvement, or sympathetic involvement, with the IRA. The McIlwaine and Fletcher cases illustrate the need for careful vetting within the UDR and regular security checks on its members.

There were several other people dealt with by the Court whom I have previously mentioned: John Alexander Murphy and Potts were each given two years' imprisonment for the attack on Underwood. Noel Large was found guilty of being implicated in five murders and was given life. For their involvement in the Donegan killing, William Mahood was given a three-year suspended sentence for impeding the arrest of others and 'Wingnut' Cowan was found guilty of manslaughter and sentenced to fifteen years.

I do not suppose that the murder of Lenny Murphy and the complex nature of it will be unravelled, because his killing, as one journalist commented, was like the plot for a Frederick Forsyth novel. One of the words used to describe Murphy is 'psychopath'. Strictly, the word refers to a pattern of behaviour – for example a weak conscience, an inability to profit from experience or to form warm relationships – rather than to the cause of the behaviour. The questions of diagnosable mental illness is clearly related to criminal responsibility. Strong medical evidence could lead a court to determine a defendant 'unfit to plead', in which case he is committed to a secure mental institution. At the end of a normal trial, where the defendant is assumed to have criminal responsibility, it is still possible for the defendant, after proper medical evidence, to be committed to a mental hospital rather than a prison. This was something Judge O'Donnell must have considered when he was presented with the Butcher crimes but, as it turned out, the defendants were declared by a psychiatrist to be sane and not suffering from a diagnosable mental illness. I suspect the same analysis would have applied to Murphy had he ever been so tested.

Informed criminological opinion regards psychopathy as a behaviour syndrome with multiple and interacting causes. Part of the cause is social, e.g. the cultural climate in which the psychopathic behaviour is manifested; part may indicate deep underlying causes dating back to childhood. The critical question concerns whether the social climate is sufficient cause or whether it is merely a precipitating cause, i.e. the context in which a pre-existent condition manifests itself. That represents the difference between the offender in Northern Ireland who, had it not been for the terrorist war, would have stayed out of trouble, and offenders who were on a collision course anyway and would have offended even had there been no civil unrest. Murphy, I believe, and some of the other gang members too, would fit perfectly into the latter definition.

Much of this book was devoted to the victims but, as Nesbitt often reminded me, the victims with whom he had to deal were the living. I will understand if the friends and relatives of those killed do not read this book because they are still living with the tragedy but I think other people should know about the brutality, if only to know what it is and understand why it is expressed. This book should not be seen as, nor should it be used for, condemnation of the Protestant population of Northern Ireland. Unfortunately there are those within Ireland who seek to justify their own actions, legitimize violence or condemn a whole community because of the actions of some within that community. If this book had been an examination of the IRA I would similarly have made the point that the Catholic population cannot be held responsible for the actions of those within its midst. This book is an attempt to understand how and why terrible crimes have been committed and not an exercise in apportioning blame or expressing support for any of the protagonists in the conflict.

Index

336

Index